THE CULTURAL
CONTEXT OF
LEARNING
AND THINKING

THE CULTURAL CONTEXT OF LEARNING AND THINKING

An Exploration in
Experimental Anthropology

by Michael Cole
John Gay
Joseph A. Glick
Donald W. Sharp

IN ASSOCIATION WITH
THOMAS CIBOROWSKI, FREDERICK FRANKEL,
JOHN KELLEMU, AND DAVID F. LANCY

Basic Books, Inc., Publishers
NEW YORK

© 1971 by Basic Books, Inc.
Library of Congress Catalog Card Number: 73–158446
SBN: 465–01498–4
Manufactured in the United States of America

TO THE KPELLE CHILDREN OF LIBERIA

We have spent time in Liberia and some of us live there. Americans are the uninvited guests of people who are worse off for our coming and who suffer us because they do not have the power to do otherwise. We believe that there is no undoing the harm that Americans as a group have brought to our hosts.

It has been traditional in the past for individuals who feel as we do to "try to help." Such warm feelings, while necessary, are not sufficient as an agent of change. The analytic approach taken in our work represents our best guess at how to make "progress" in the human sciences. It is offered apologetically to the people of Bong Country of Liberia, as our small token of thanks.

Foreword

GEORGE A. MILLER
The Institute for Advanced Study

Every culture has its myths. One of our most persistent is that nonliterate people in less developed countries possess something we like to call a "primitive mentality" that is both different from and inferior to our own. This myth has it that the "primitive mind" is highly concrete, whereas the "Western mind" is highly abstract; the "primitive mind" connects its concrete ideas by rote association, whereas the "Western mind" connects its abstract ideas by general relations; the "primitive mind" is illogical and insensitive to contradictions, whereas the "Western mind" is logical and strives to attain consistency; the "primitive mind" is childish and emotional, whereas the "Western mind" is mature and rational; and so on and on. In its most frightening form, this myth includes the claim that these differences are genetically based and derives from this fact that other people are just not as intelligent as Caucasians.

The dangers inherent in this hodgepodge of half-truths do not derive solely from the blunders they inspire in our relations with the Third World. The same stereotype is likely to be applied to ethnic minorities living in the West. Foreign and domestic policies based on such beliefs are paternalistic at best, and at worst can degenerate into frank repression and exploitation. It is of practical importance, therefore, to establish the true facts of the matter.

It is also of theoretical importance. If such opinions were true, the theory and practice of psychology and anthropology would be very different from what they would be if such opinions were false. Because the issue is so important, many anthropologists and some psychologists have attempted to test the myth. The present volume is a valuable contribution to this tradition of research.

No one would care to deny that differences exist. Any denial would be tantamount to saying that differences in experience that result from living in widely different cultures and technologies have no important psychological consequences. Rather, the argument concerns the nature of those differences, and their sources. Must the differences be attributed to innate differences in ability? Or can they be attributed largely to cultural differences in training and experience? In the course of this book the reader will grow increasingly skeptical of the need for genetic explanations. Evolution has not created two different human minds—one for Westerners, another for everybody else. It is culture that develops certain potentials of the human mind here and others there.

But how should the difference be characterized? Are we really abstract, and they concrete? It is difficult to believe that anyone capable of mastering a human language with all of its codified abstractions and conceptual relations could be totally incompetent to cope with abstract concepts. The difference must be more subtle than that. Yet many psychologists, working from a conception of intelligence developed in their study of children growing up in the industrialized countries, have resorted to such terms in their efforts to characterize the performances they have found in more static societies.

All too often psychologists have taken some test of measurement developed in a Western context and applied it directly to children and adults in a very different cultural context. The "primitive people" usually score rather poorly, so poorly that it is difficult not to conclude that they are hopelessly inferior to their Western counterparts. Moreover, since it is widely believed that intelligence is genetically determined, the differences in test scores have too frequently been interpreted as demonstrating genetic inferiorities. In this way psychological research has often strengthened popular belief in our ethnocentric myth of Western superiority.

But such tests were designed to produce an overall score, or figure of merit. They were not designed to explore the cognitive processes by which the score is achieved. One cannot conclude from low test scores that a person "has" or "doesn't have" certain psychological abilities or potentialities. All one can conclude is that, whatever the person "has," he probably wasn't using the same cognitive strategies that a Westerner automatically adopts. The following pages provide convincing examples of this difference.

What learning experiences influence a person's acquisition of a particular cognitive strategy, or his decision that it is appropriate in a particular situation? This reformulated question is crucial for the psychologist's understanding of thought and cognition, and it cannot be answered adequately without careful consideration of the culture in which a person lives and the environment in which his previous learning experiences occurred.

One advantage of reformulating the question this way is that it opens up for the psychologist lines of communication with social anthropologists who have also been interested in the cognitive processes of the people they study. Psychometric evidence that has suggested the inferiority of native thinking, and that has often been interpreted as indicating the absence of certain cognitive abilities in the genetic endowment of such people, has stood as a barrier between psychologists and anthropologists and has frustrated the kind of valuable collaboration that this book represents.

Unfortunately, most psychologists are poorly prepared by education or acculturation to understand the mental processes of people living in relatively static, traditional cultures or to grasp the full implications of the fact such people's experiences have not required them to develop and use many of the cognitive strategies that our Western experience has instilled in us. But suppose we test such people on things for which their experience *has* prepared them. Suppose we send them to school and give them an opportunity to learn our Western way of thinking. Suppose we probe behind their apparent failure in order to discover how they have interpreted an unfamiliar task. Would we then be so confident that they are inferior and not merely different?

These are the difficult but enormously important questions with which this book grapples. And it is greatly to their credit that the authors have asked the right questions, have struggled vigorously and often successfully to bridge the cultural gap between themselves and their subjects, and have successfully demonstrated that psychological and ethnological methods can be integrated in a fruitful search for the answers.

Preface

Our interest in the relation between culture and thinking grew out of a specific practical problem: Liberian tribal children experience a great deal of difficulty with Western-style mathematics. The difficulties experienced by Kpelle children in north-central Liberia led us to ask the question: if we knew more about the kinds of mathematical knowledge that these children bring to school, might we not be in a better position to teach these children the kind of mathematics that we wanted to teach them?

In pursuing this line of inquiry, we began with a set of fairly straightforward, pragmatic questions. What kinds of things do tribal people count and measure? What kinds of geometrical knowledge is exhibited in such activities as building a house? How does mathematics enter into everyday activities like rice farming, going to market, dividing food among members of a family?

When we looked into these matters, we found that there were certain tasks that the Kpelle people performed considerably better than Americans whom we asked to perform similar tasks. For example, the tribal people were exceptionally good at estimating various amounts of rice. Other tasks that at first seemed to be closely related gave the Kpelle great difficulty. For example, when measuring lengths, the tribal people were both inaccurate and inconsistent. In looking for the source of the differences between the two kinds of estimating tasks, we discovered that rice farming is central to the tribal culture and involves a network of related activities. On the other hand, for the Kpelle, length measurement is a very specific activity that depends on the thing being measured, so that, for example, the metric for cloth is not the same as the metric for sticks.

These observations fit quite well with what our common sense and many anthropologists have suggested. People will be good at doing the things that are important to them and that they have occasion to do often. The generalization implicit in this theory of cognition is that primitive cultures tend to make different sorts of intellectual demands than technologically advanced cultures. It is often inferred as a consequence that primitive peoples will be less advanced intellectually except in special areas of experience. People who hold this view usually make the additional assumption that when the cultural conditions change, so do the skills of the people.

This notion of culture-specific skills can be contrasted with what might be termed an ability theory, which is especially prevalent among psychologists. The general thrust of the ability theory is that for a variety of reasons different groups or individuals develop "better," "more," or "more powerful" generalized intellectual abilities than others. This view is most obvious in the work of psychologists who use IQ tests to assess intellectual performance. Their basic assumption is that different subtests call forth different kinds of abilities, and that a high score on a particular subtest means a high ability in that area.

There have been a great many arguments in recent years about "culture-free" IQ tests, racial differences in IQ, and the like. We do not propose to enter that argument directly, but raise it here because the basic underlying assumption is very widely shared. It reoccurs, for example, in a great many theories of cognitive development (Piaget, Werner, Bruner) where development is seen as the acquisition of more powerful, higher-order structures: more development means more powerful structures. Moreover, the structures are seen as hierarchically organized so that missing early points in the sequence precludes later development. In the view of J. S. Bruner and his colleagues (for example, Greenfield and Bruner, 1966), some cultures "push" cognitive development further than others. If you have not been pushed far, you lack the more powerful cognitive structures. A presently popular application of this principle is the current psychological approach to "culturally disadvantaged" children.

It is important to recognize these two orientations at the outset because they distinctly color the nature of research on culture and cognition. One important assumption of the aptitude approach is that a given task (whether it be a question on an IQ test or a Piagetian problem) evokes the same kind of behavior regardless of who performs the task. The logic of the task itself and the cognitive processes it taps are comparable, even though content may be subject to cultural variation. Clearly, if the same task evokes widely different behaviors in subjects from different cultural backgrounds, the aptitude approach is going to lead us astray. If we think we are assessing the amount of aptitude X when in fact a subject is engaged in behavior Y, our conclusions are likely to mean little.

We believe, on the other hand, that one *cannot* assume that psychological tasks, be they derived from theories of cognitive development or the structure of intelligence, evoke the same kinds of behaviors in subjects from different cultures. When we present a task to a subject and he appears to respond randomly or stupidly, the first question we must ask is "what is the subject doing?" Behavior is *never* random, although it may seem random to an observer with a particular orientation. Only after it is determined that subjects from two groups are engaged in the same activity (applying the same processes), can one ask questions about their relative abilities.

We have found it strategically useful to pursue such research in a culture that varies drastically from the middle-class, urban culture in which most of the readers of this book live. The very fact of great cultural differences will make it harder for us to assume that our subjects see the problem as we do. By maximizing the chances that our subjects will do things differently, we may be able to determine the conditions that evoke different ways of learning and problem solving. We wish to identify the behavior evoked by different kinds of intellectual tasks and to seek in the cultural environment explanations of the fact that different groups manifest different intellectual behaviors.

This exposition will not follow the oftentimes confused course that our own research has taken over the last half dozen years. Rather, we shall present our findings according to our present understanding of the problems we have been studying. In certain places this presentation may appear to be incomplete, incoherent, or incorrect. We know that we have only begun to find ways to understand the relation between culture and cognition.

Much of our dissatisfaction with the work that has preceded ours derives from two sources. First, little empirical evidence is available concerning the relationship between culture and cognition. Second, where evidence exists, it is too often seriously accorded the status of "fact," before the many problems involved in cross-cultural inference and investigation have been explored.

Our narrative begins with an analysis of the terms *culture* and *cognition* in Chapter 1. A major stumbling block to analysis of the relation between culture and cognition is that these basic terms are used in various ways by different writers, each of whom presumes that he is writing about the same topic as his predecessors. This problem is particularly acute when we consider that philosophers, logicians, anthropologists, sociologists, and psychologists understand the term *thinking* in vastly different ways. In particular, we will ask how it could be that intelligent and scholarly individuals came to believe that Western man is the intellectual superior of his non-Western brethren. This idea, moreover, has led some to think that so-called primitive adults think in the same way as children in Western society.

In Chapter 2 and 3, we will introduce the cultural setting in which most of our work was carried out. Concentrating on the Kpelle of Liberia (and assuming knowledge of our own culture), we have tried to gather evidence relevant to the cultural sources of learning and thinking. Some, but by no means all, data were gathered in a very orthodox fashion. Careful analysis of the Kpelle language and formal elicitations of the structure of various semantic domains will be presented side by side with excerpts from essays written by high-school students and other shreds of evidence collected by a variety of people connected with our project in recent years. This presentation will, of course, depend heavily on more orthodox data with which our anthropological colleagues, particularly James L. Gibbs and William E. Welmers, have provided us.

Using this ethnographic material as background, we will turn to experimental investigations of three major classes of learning phenomena. We will consider the role of classification in memory and learning, the process by which attributes are combined to form concepts, and the way in which various problems are solved.

Study of these questions using Kpelle subjects is of particular theoretical interest. In addition to significant differences in general cultural features, the Kpelle language is structurally quite different from English, permitting study of longstanding questions about the relation between language, culture, and thought. Second, education in the American style is new to Kpelleland. Its relative rarity and the fact that school attendance in the lower grades is more or less determined by the whimsy of outside agents, allows us, in theory, to separate the influence of experience and maturation on the development of cognitive skills. The fact that virtually all normal children in Western Europe and the United States between the ages of five and seven years begin to attend school where they learn to read and write, is a major theoretical problem for contemporary psychological theory: Are developmental changes in cognitive skills the result of aging or the special experiences of the classroom?

Chapter 4 on classification in learning concentrates on the way in which material is organized by the learner and the teachers. A wide variety of learning conditions and subject populations is included in our studies of this problem as we investigate such questions as the relation between literacy and memory, and the effect of introducing varying degrees of structure into the materials and the procedures for learning them.

Chapter 5 also is concerned with the influence of social factors on concept formation, but emphasis shifts to an analysis of stimulus-specific versus generalized learning.

The chapter on problem solving (Chapter 6) studies tasks that vary in their complexity and in the importance of verbal formulations for their solution. At one end of the scale are experiments using discrimination learning techniques and very simple physical stimuli. At the other end of the scale are a series of riddles, verbal logical problems, a traditional game, and a court case.

Throughout the book we have attempted to relate the experimental tasks to naturally occurring problems and modes of problem solution and to depend on Kpelle formulations of these problems. But in this regard our reach has far outstripped our grasp.

In Chapter 7 we return once again to the general questions that we raised in this preface. With the added perspective of our success and failures behind us, we attempt to evaluate what we have learned about the relations between culture and cognition and try to point out the implications of these findings both for future research and for immediate application, particularly the problems posed by the poor educational performance of America's minority groups.

In order to solve the problem of writing for interested laymen as well as specialists in different disciplines, we have tried to keep highly technical material out of the body of the text. Where we believe that more detail will be of special interest to a significant proportion of the readership, we have included appendices that may be found at the end of the book.

We have also avoided detailed discussion of the many methodological problems which attend the actual conduct of cross-cultural research, restricting our attention to problems of principle which we view as crucial to the cross-cultural, interdisciplinary enterprise that we have undertaken. However, much of our message resides in questions of method, so some discussion of such matters will be found scattered throughout the text.

If there is a general principle to be gleaned from the method upon which our work is based, it derives from our belief that the people we are working with always behave reasonably. When their behavior appears unreasonable, it is to ourselves, our procedures, and our experimental tasks that we turn for an explanation.

Acknowledgments

The research on which this book is based would not have been possible without the support of many institutions and individuals.

The basic financial support was provided by a grant from the National Science Foundation (GS-1221). Data analysis was greatly facilitated by a grant of free time by the computing facility at the University of California, Irvine, where Michael Cole was a faculty member during the years in which this work was done. Individual fellowships to Donald Sharp (from the National Defense Education Act) and Thomas Ciborowski (from the U.S. Public Health Service) have made their participation in this work possible. Additionally, a research grant to Joseph Glick from the National Institute of Child Health and Development (HD 03947) supported portions of the analyses of data and writing of this book.

We owe a great debt to the many people in Liberia who assisted us materially and intellectually. Dr. Christian Baker and his colleagues at Cuttington College provided us with an invaluable base of operations. The people of the town of Sinyee have continued to put up with our incursions and have shared with us their time and facilities. We are particularly in debt to Johnnie Kwiipɔɔ, Mrs. Rose Sambola, and Zephaniah Ukatu for their assistance in gaining access to subjects and informants. In addition, many school administrators and town chiefs provided facilities without which this work could not have been carried out.

We need also to acknowledge the assistance of many people who worked for us at various times in the capacity of informants or experimenters: Moses Buno, Joseph Campbell, Yakpalo Doŋ, Michael Dinobi, Franklin Dunbar, Francis Dunbar, Joseph Keller, Akki Kulah, Arthur Kulah, Richard MacFarland, Paul Mulbah, Paul Ricks, John Wealar, Charles Wellington, Albert Wungko, Sulɔŋtɛ Gbɛmɛlɛŋ, John Kellemu, Michael Mbaebie, and Albert Wolokolie.

In the United States, we owe our thanks to the teachers and administrators in the Laguna Beach and Newport-Mesa school districts in California who opened their classrooms to our research. We were assisted in this work by Barbara Hanson.

A great intellectual debt is owed to our colleagues in the School of

Social Sciences at the University of California, Irvine. The atmosphere of the school influenced a great deal of the research described in this book. We particularly want to acknowledge the help of Jean Lave and Duane Metzger whose careful and critical reading of early drafts of this work greatly improved its quality.

The work of William Welmers and James Gibbs, referred to at several points, has been supplemented frequently by their advice on many matters pertaining to the Kpelle and Liberia.

Finally, we wish to acknowledge the support of the Rockefeller University for providing a haven in which this book could be written and the aid of Kay and William Estes whose material and intellectual support have greatly influenced what we present here.

Contents

Contents

Illustrations following page 36.

THE CULTURAL
CONTEXT OF
LEARNING
AND THINKING

ONE : Culture and Thinking

"What kind of a bird are you if you can't fly"? chirped the bird. "What kind of a bird are you if you can't swim"? replied the duck.

S. PROKOFIEV,
Peter and the Wolf

The Problem of Many Disciplines

This book is concerned with a recurrent problem in man's inquiry into his own nature: how do people's thought processes relate to the culture in which they are raised and in which they live?

From the large body of scholarship bearing on the general issue of culture and cognition, several very general approaches which are influential among some groups of social scientists can be identified. A major line of argument concerns the implications of differing belief and classification systems: one school of thought maintains that salient differences in beliefs and category systems represent no more than differing conventions with little impact on thought processes; the opposing school holds that *either* a difference in beliefs *or* a difference in classification systems is sufficient evidence for differing thought processes. A completely different line of argument maintains that all evidence from group phenomena such as beliefs and language categories is irrelevant to understanding processes that are properties of individuals; only a study of the individual as a member of his group can lead to reliable information about culture and cognition.

So tangled are these theoretical approaches and so different are the data that adherents of the various approaches bring to bear on the issues, that choice among viewpoints is all too often an accident of one's own disciplinary training—the implicit acceptance of a disciplinary definition of what constitutes good evidence about thought processes.

In this introductory chapter we will review the development of the

3

presently rather confused state of theory concerning culture and cognition. It is our intent to make clear the source of present disagreements, especially as they derive from implicitly different ideas of what the major phenomena are that need explaining and the data relevant to such explanations. Without some understanding of the source of these disagreements, future theoretical progress is likely to be limited, and research such as that which we will present in later chapters will be doomed to exist in isolation from intellectual currents of which it should be a part.

Anthropology

Anthropology developed as the study of human diversity. However, during its early history the specific question of the relation between culture and cognitive processes arose only as a byproduct of other concerns. During the latter half of the nineteenth century, anthropologists asked broad questions: What gave rise to the diversity of human cultures? Were there multiple sources or a single source of the human race? How can one explain the presence of similar customs and inventions in widely separated parts of the world?

E. B. Tylor suggests in his classic work, *Primitive Culture* (1874, p. 1), that "the condition of culture among the various societies of mankind, in so far as it is capable of being investigated on general principles, is a subject apt for the study of laws of human thought and action." Thus, considered in one very broad sense, the study of culture is the study of human thought.

Following this approach, some anthropologists asserted a cause-and-effect relation between similarity of cognitive processes and similarity of cultural institutions. But it was a debatable point which was cause and which was effect. The argument that cultural differences "explain" cognitive differences was used by the founding fathers of anthropological theory, Herbert Spencer, E. B. Tylor, and L. H. Morgan. They believed that human society evolves in a continuum from primitive to civilized society. This argument, bolstered by the biological theories of Darwin and Huxley, assumed that the evolution of intellect can be inferred from the assumed evolution of culture.

Two further assumptions beyond the basic premise that cultural differences imply cognitive differences were widely shared in the nineteenth century. First was the universal belief that society is evolving and simultaneously progressing toward a literate, technological state like that of the West. Second was the biological notion that young organisms "recapitulate" the anatomical history of their species during embryological development, an idea that buttressed the evolutionary argument. This doctrine became popular in both psychology and anthropology, and is usually summed up in Ernst Haeckle's aphorism, "Ontogeny recapitulates phylogeny." To some anthropologists interested in evolutionary sequences, these two assumptions suggested that primitive adults represent an early form of the adults of advanced societies. The European child also represents an early form of the European adult. Hence, according to this argument, the primitive adult is equivalent to the civilized child.

To many at the present time this line of reasoning and the assumptions on which it rests appear farfetched. However, to post-Darwinian, nineteenth-century social scientists steeped in the theory of evolution, they seemed almost self-evident.

The publication of *The Mind of Primitive Man* by Franz Boas in 1911 is in several ways an important and highly influential landmark in anthropological thinking about thinking. Boas was critical of the logic of both racial and evolutionary theories as well as the data upon which both were based. He rejected the basic assumption that similarity in thought implies similarity in culture as well as the formally equivalent argument that differences in culture imply differences in thought.

After looking closely at the historical antecedents, racial composition, and distinctive cultural features of modern societies, Boas comes to the conclusion still accepted by the overwhelming majority of anthropologists: that we can prove neither the equation of race and culture nor the existence of cultural evolution. Further, he asserts that whereas "the existence of a mind absolutely independent of conditions of life is unthinkable" (p. 133), nonetheless, "the functions of the human mind are common to the whole of humanity" (p. 135).

Particularly important is Boas' attack on the proposition that observed differences in culture and belief are evidence of fundamental differences in thought processes. First, he challenges the reliability of many of the reports on which such theories are based. Second, he challenges the belief that one can draw inferences about thought processes from traditional beliefs and customs of a people. He suggests that it would prove equally misleading to use traditional American beliefs about nature and society as evidence about American logical processes.

Boas did not intend to deny the existence of intellectual differences among human groups. In fact, at certain points in his argument against racial determinism, he confirms his belief, mentioned above, that mind and experience are intimately related. However, he introduced a new issue into the discussion by his suggestion that these intellectual differences among groups are *not* fundamental. Although there is some ambiguity in his use of the term *intellectual,* the thrust of Boas's argument seems to be that previous observers failed to understand the people they were describing and then mistook their own lack of understanding as evidence of their informants' stupidity.

Primitive Mind

In spite of Boas's trenchant arguments, interest in the implications of belief systems for understanding individual thought processes has continued to appear from time to time in anthropological literature.

One of Boas's major targets was the French sociologist Lucien Levy-Bruhl. Relying exclusively on the published reports of missionaries, travelers, and early anthropological observers, Levy-Bruhl began, in 1910, to publish a series of monographs on the thought processes of primitive peoples. The first of these books (translated as *How Natives Think*) met with strong and continuing disapproval from American anthropologists, of whom Boas was a leading spokesman. In the tradition of French sociology at the turn of the century, Levy-Bruhl held that every culture is characterized by a set of general beliefs, which he called "collective representations." Whereas the collective representations of the average European are exclusively intellectual and distinct from the motor and emotional realms, in the primitive person these basic beliefs are fused with emotional components. In discussing primitive mentality, Levy-Bruhl coined the unfortunate term *prelogical,* to characterize the rules by which basic ideas are combined. In addition, Levy-Bruhl assumed, contrary to Boas, that primitivity of material and religious culture is sufficient evidence to prove the existence of primitive mental processes.

One can readily see why Levy-Bruhl's position upsets anthropologists. Not only do they question his sources and his tendency to speak of primitives in general without recognizing differences among various non-Western, nonliterate groups, but also they challenge his basic assumption that primitive culture implies primitive thought.

The major point made by most critics was that

the facts about many cultures demonstrate that all peoples *at times* think in terms of objectively probable causation, just as *at times,* they indulge in explanations that relate a fact to an *apparent* cause. What the comparative study of culture, based on first-hand contact with many peoples, has taught is that all peoples think in terms of certain premises that are taken for granted. Granted the premises, the logic is inescapable. [Herskovitz, 1962, p. 361]

A modern attempt to account for the phenomena described by Levy-Bruhl is presented in the brilliant discussion of traditional belief systems and their relation to the logic of Western scientific thought by Robin Horton (1967*a,b*). Horton contends that there is considerably more similarity between the thought patterns of African and Western peoples than Levy-Bruhl realized. Horton's basic premise is that all peoples try to understand their world by developing explanatory theories. He proposes compelling analogies between the theories that underlie traditional African belief systems on the one hand, and Western so-called scientific beliefs on the other. For example, basic to both African and Western theory is the quest for unity underlying apparent diversity. In this context the African cosmology can be viewed as a way to reduce the diversity of everyday experience to the workings of a limited number of opposing forces. Moreover, both theories place events in a causal context wider than that provided by common sense. For example, the African diviner relates disease to antisocial and malevolent feelings among people, a practice that may have real adaptive significance in the African context. Western thinkers likewise look beyond common sense to germs and genes. A third parallel is that in both kinds of societies, common sense and theory play complementary roles. For instance, common sense is used to cure minor ailments and only when common sense fails is more high-powered theory brought to bear on the problem.

Horton explores the differences between traditional and scientific thought in terms of the fundamental difference between "open" and "closed" belief systems. Characteristics of primitive belief systems emphasized by Levy-Bruhl, such as "mystical" thinking, the concrete nature of collective representations, and belief in divination coupled with a rejection of chance, are shown to be misinterpretations of assertions based on a closed belief system, in which there is little "awareness of alternatives to the established body of theoretical tenets." In the open situation of "scientifically oriented cultures, such an awareness is highly developed" (Horton, 1967*b,* p. 155). In fact, the logic of the closed system does not differ from that of its open counterpart. On the contrary,

7

different premises give rise to differences that then systematically mislead outsiders into basing their theories on the obviously alien and exotic phenomena they observe.

A quite different approach to the phenomena labeled "primitive mind" is taken by Claude Lévi-Strauss (1966), who emphasizes differences in the kinds of categorizations produced by different peoples. In so doing, Lévi-Strauss uses differences in beliefs to infer both differences and similarities in underlying thought processes. However, he maintains that the thought processes he identifies in primitive cultures are not at some lower stage in the development of the human mind. Rather, he suggests, they represent different strategies by which men make nature accessible to rational inquiry. Both Western and non-Western strategies seek objective knowledge of the universe; both proceed by ordering, classifying, and systematizing information; both create coherent systems. These and other similarities have led Lévi-Strauss to conclude that the two types of thought systems are based on "the same sort of mental observations."

What then are the differences among primitive and civilized thought processes, according to Lévi-Strauss? The basic difference seems to involve the kinds of attributes that are used in forming classes. Primitive classification systems are based on qualities that are readily seen and experienced, whereas modern science relies more on properties that are inferred from necessary relations in the structure of the objects classified. For example, fruits and vegetables are classified by the average shopper in ways quite different from those of the botanist. Primitive classification systems generalize from overt properties of the members of the system and are thus limited by the concrete experience of the community.

One might ask next how classification systems enter into such areas of thought as problem solving. Lévi-Strauss suggests an answer when he distinguishes between two types of scientific endeavor. He characterizes non-Western, primitive science as exemplified by the jack-of-all-trades, who has a bag of things that he uses to make other things. The tools are never specifically designed for the task at hand, but rather constitute a collection of things preserved "because they might come in handy"; thus their function depends upon the particular occasions in which they are used. The jack-of-all-trades is contrasted with the engineer, whose inventory of tools is not a fixed set, originally adapted to other purposes, but is variable, depending on the task at hand. In contrast, the engineer has a fixed and stable structure of making and using tools, whereas in the primitive's system a particular object is likely to have a rather amorphous and shifting status because of the nature of his classification system. In this way, Lévi-Strauss asserts, there is an intimate relation between modes of classifying objects and ways of solving problems.

The New Ethnography

Lévi-Strauss' concern with the implication of differing kinds of category systems is shared in somewhat different form by a movement in modern anthropology variously called ethnoscience or linguistic anthropology.

The major thrusts of the movement are neatly encapsulated in a definition of culture offered by Frake (1963, in Manners and Kaplan, 1968, p. 513): ". . . culture: how people organize their experience conceptually so that it can be transmitted as knowledge from person to person." Two major assumptions are contained in this definition: (1) that the underlying organization of experience is reflected in communicative (linguistic) behavior, and (2) that category systems differ widely from culture to culture.

In keeping with these basic notions, the ethnoscientists have adopted, as their major methodological goal, the development of linguistically based formal techniques which

provide the ethnographer with public, nonintuitive procedures for ordering his presentation of observed and elicited events according to principles of classification of the people he is studying. To order ethnographic descriptions solely according to an investigator's preconceived categories obscures the real content of culture. [Frake, 1963, in Manners and Kaplan, 1968, p. 513]

To the extent that his description of category systems is accepted as a reflection of basic thought processes, the ethnoscientist sides with those who maintain that cultural differences in thought processes are reducible to differences in classification. However, the relationship between formally elicited category systems and the "contents of men's minds" has been a point of enduring controversy.

Some authors maintain that successful formal analysis reflects the cognitive processes of the informant and other members of his culture. An example of such an approach is the componential analysis introduced by W. Goodenough (1956), which seeks to determine the "dimensions of contrast" that allow the informant to group items into sets. A. F. C. Wal-

9

lace (1962, p. 351), among others, claims that such procedures form "a calculus which describes cognitive processes." To use another term employed by Wallace (Wallace and Atkins, 1960), the ethnographic description reflects "psychological reality."

Opponents of this viewpoint within anthropology (see Burling, 1964; Hammer, 1966) argue that it is useless to argue over the psychological reality of an elicited category system. Not only are such claims unverifiable, but there can be multiple descriptions of any finite set of terms as well. There is no way to determine, *within the method,* which is more real. While the basic theoretical position is still a very controversial subject within anthropology (see, in addition, Romney and D'Andrade, 1964; Tyler, 1969), the *methodological advances* of the ethnoscientist have won general acceptance.

Linguistics

Although exceptions can be found (Jesperson, 1921, Book 1), professional linguists have for the most part shared the anthropologists' belief in the "psychic unity of man," although this conclusion has been reached via quite different routes by different schools of linguists. The first such route asserts the doctrine of linguistic relativity and the closely related idea that language shapes thought.

Linguistic Relativity and Linguistic Determinism

Although their ideas are anticipated by Karl Wilhelm von Humboldt in the nineteenth century, the twentieth-century linguists Edward Sapir and Benjamin Whorf are the best-known proponents of a theory of linguistic relativity. The deterministic aspect of their position is well expressed by Whorf:

It was found that the background linguistic system (in other words, the grammar) of each language is not merely a reproducing instrument for voicing ideas but rather is itself the shaper of ideas, the program and guide for the individual's mental activity, for his analysis of impressions, for his synthesis of his mental stock and trade.

Formulation of ideas is not an independent process, strictly rational in the old sense, but is part of a particular grammar, and differs, from slightly to greatly, between different grammars. We dissect nature along lines laid down by our native languages. The categories and types that we isolate in the world of phenomena we do not find there because they stare every observer in the face; on the contrary, the world is presented in a kaleidoscopic flux by our minds—and this means largely by the linguistic system in our minds. We cut nature up, organize it into concepts, and describe significances as we do, largely because we are party to an agreement to organize it in this way—an agreement which holds in the pattern of our language. The agreement is, of course, an implicit and unstated one, *but its terms are absolutely obligatory;* we can not talk at all except by subscribing to the organization and classification of data which the agreement decrees. [Whorf, 1956, p. 212]

Thus it is concluded that the structure of language determines the structure of thought.

Whorf builds on this and other arguments to demonstrate the relativity of language. For example, in a posthumously published paper, "The Linguistic Consideration of Thinking in Primitive Communities" (in Whorf, 1956, pp. 65 ff.), Whorf makes a vigorous assertion of the overall functional equality of all languages. He includes as evidence statements that in certain domains American Indian languages are superior to standard European languages:

It takes but little real scientific study of preliterate languages, especially those of America, to show how much more precise and finely elaborated is the system of relationships in many such tongues than ours. By comparison with many American languages, the formal systematic organization of ideas in English, German, French, or Italian is poor and jejune. Why for instance, do we not, like the Hopi, use a different way of expressing the relation of channel of sensation (seeing) to result in consciousness, as between "I see that it is red" and "I see that it is new"? We fuse the two different types of relationships into a vague sort of connection expressed by "that" whereas the Hopi indicates that in the first case seeing presents unspecified evidence from which is drawn the inference of newness. . . . Does the Hopi language show here a higher plane of thinking, a more rational analysis of situations, than our vaunted English? Of course it does. In this field and in others, English compared to Hopi is like a bludgeon compared to a rapier. [Whorf, 1956, pp. 84–85]

The claim is often made that a certain language is poor in abstraction because of rich detail of terminology for some aspect of their environment without a corresponding general term. Examples which are often quoted are the variety of Eskimo words for snow or Arabic words for horse. Whorf would reverse the argument and say that, rather than implying a poverty of language, these examples indicate greater differentiation and much more subtle appreciation of the particular domain in question.

It is not our purpose here to review the literature concerning the linguistic-relativity hypothesis (see Miller and McNeil, 1968, and Fishman, 1960 for summary discussions). Important for our purpose is the assertion, arrived at using different evidence from that offered by the social anthropologist, that thought processes of all peoples are functionally equivalent and that they can be inferred from linguistic behavior.

The Generative Tradition

A rather different strain of inquiry has developed following the tradition that Noam Chomsky (1966) calls "Cartesian Linguistics." The Cartesian school elevated language to a central role in differentiating human and animal behaviors, and saw in language a manifestation of the distinctive features of human cognition. According to this view, possession of language is sufficient evidence for a type of mental functioning, unexplainable solely by those mechanical principles sufficient to account for animal activity. At present this viewpoint is championed by the so-called transformational linguists.

The transformational analysis has emphasized that all human speakers must be highly structured. No theory of cognition that fails to take linguistic competence into account can be considered adequate. Differences in knowledge are readily accepted, but differences in capacity or the "deep structure" of language are denied.

These assertions combine to form a point of view which de-emphasizes cognitive differences between different linguistic (cultural) groups. This view is more fully developed by the modern transformational grammarians who have added new insights into the relationship between culture (here embodied in language) and cognition. They have sought to advance linguistics beyond purely descriptive analysis to a broader attempt to provide a generative theory of grammatical understanding. An important insight of this school is that any given language can generate an infinite set of sentences, only a few of which have been experienced by any speaker of the language. In order for a speaker to generate sentences he has never before heard, he must use a complex rule system to create the new, but rule-governed, sequences called sentences. It is clear that human speakers, competent in their own language, store and use productive rules in a complex and nonmechanical fashion.

Psychology

The Impact of Darwin

When Darwin's work first appeared, psychology was just beginning to establish itself as a discipline separate from philosophy. Under the impact of evolutionary theory, an early preoccupation with introspection and the laws of sensation and consciousness gave way to the comparative study of animals, children, and adults. The problem of psychology became the problem of how various organisms, particularly man, adapt to their environments. Two natural offshoots of this interest were a more intensive study of children and their development and a study of human adaptation to different cultural and natural environments.

Developmental Psychology in the Evolutionary Mode

Within psychology the idea that the development of the child recapitulates the history of the race enjoyed even more widespread popularity than in anthropology; it was embraced by one of the founders of American developmental psychology, G. Stanley Hall. Hall's student, A. F. Chamberlain, summarizes what he believed to be the relevant literature in *The Child: A Study in the Evolution of Man* (1901). Although more cautious than many of his fellows, Chamberlain draws what he considers to be significant parallels:

The mind of the child and the mind of the savage, when differences due to the presence of manhood and womanhood in the latter, diversity of environment, influence of higher culture, prolonged infancy, social environment, etc., have been taken into consideration, present many interesting parallels of a general sort. *Naivete* that touches upon genius, suggestibility of great extent and sometimes of a very high order, resemblances in mental association, modes of thought and of thought expression, dream-life, mind-content. It must be remembered, however, that it is now the savage, now the child, who in one of these things touches the highest genius or sinks into the deepest ignorance—the capacity for mental progress and development rarely finding equal expression in both everywhere and at all times. In comparison with the child, the savage, who so often anticipates higher culture, higher morals, higher arts, suffers because we seem inevitably to rate ourselves higher and him lower than each really is. [P. 456]

One of Chamberlain's points concerns the so-called phenomenon of arrested development, which was discussed repeatedly in the early anthropological literature. N. Miller (1928) gives a typical treatment of this topic, citing a variety of reports that children raised in various tribal groups are initially precocious but concluding that "the perspicacity of the primitive child comes to a dead halt, however, at puberty" (p. 125). This arrested development is attributed to such factors as sexual excess and alcoholism; a conclusion which obviously reflects Western folklore rather than non-Western reality.

Chamberlain offers an explanation of this "fact" that has a very modern ring. He hypothesized that the "arrest of mental development" was not found in civilized people because of ". . . the greater number of learnable things which the environment of civilized peoples provides, and the care and trouble which the community takes to make the acquisition of these things possible. Not the mind so much as the schools of the two stages of human evolution differ" (p. 456). He asserted, moreover, that this "arrest" is known and is clearly reversible among Western children after the age of puberty.

Chamberlain's argument, although couched in theoretical terms long out of fashion, is reminiscent of contemporary arguments that severe environmental differences dramatically affect individual development. However, psychologists of his time failed to follow up these early speculative efforts with experimentally verifiable theories of culture and cognitive development.

A Hiatus: 1910–1950

When the initial flush of enthusiasm for evolutionary schemes began to fade, psychologists' interest in cross-cultural research into mental development seemed to fade with it. Instead they turned to the study of culture and personality and to standardized intelligence testing.

Hypotheses growing out of Freudian psychoanalytic theory provided the original impetus for research into the relation between culture and personality by such anthropologists as Bronislaw Malinowski, Clyde Kluckholn, and Margaret Mead. Some anthropologists tested the way in which such institutions as the family gave rise, for example, to the Oedipus complex (Malinowski, 1922). Others, reversing the causality, sought to determine how various personality characteristics might shape cultural institutions (Kardiner, 1939).

The use of standardized intelligence tests among differing cultural and racial groups has generated considerable controversy in recent years. The major points at issue have been: what can be inferred from differences in test performance? Do they measure some underlying "capacity" of the individual, or are they simply useful devices for predicting school performance? This latter question is difficult enough to answer for the white middle-class American population on which the tests were standardized. It is virtually impossible to answer for groups differing simultaneously in culture and racial composition from the standard group (for reviews of the voluminous literature, see Klineberg, 1963; Vernon, 1969; Jensen, 1969; Deutsch, 1969).

Data from these tests are of extremely limited value for our purposes because there is so little agreement about what kinds of cognitive processes were being tested. To be sure, subsections of such tests may claim to measure abstraction or relational thinking, but, in fact, items in these sections (as in the entire tests) were chosen because they were effective in predicting school performance. For this reason, in many cultures, such tests predict successful performance in Western-style schools (see Vernon, 1969), but what such predictions say about elementary learning processes is unknown. (See the excellent discussion of these issues by LeVine, 1970.)

Contemporary Psychological Approaches to the Study of Culture and Cognition

In recent years psychologists have shown a renewed interest in the cultural context of human development. In this more recent work, moreover, they approach the problem with a richer store of theoretical and experimental tools than they possessed at the turn of the century. Between 1910 and 1950 only a very few psychologists used variations in culture as indicators of cognitive processes. A few of these efforts took place in the 1930s. F. C. Bartlett (1932) performed experiments on the relation between culture and memory which we will describe later. There were scattered attempts to use intelligence tests as a starting point, rather than a measuring stick, for an analysis of culturally influenced cognitive skills (Nissen, Kinder, and Machover, 1935). And, anticipating things to come, Margaret Mead set out for New Guinea to test the generality of the sequences of cognitive development posited by Jean Piaget (Mead, 1932). However, only in the postwar era did psychologists become broadly interested in the study of culture and thinking. At least two different concerns are represented in this resurgence, namely, the use of cultural variations to test the generality of theories developed

15

in a Western setting, and the study of the relation between thought and language.

An early effort to test Western theories with non-Western data was Heinz Werner's use of anthropological data to support his theory of cognitive development (Werner, 1948). Werner's general thesis was that development implies qualitative changes in both the structure and dynamic properties of behavior. Structurally, the developing organism shows greater differentiation through the elaboration of hierarchies. Dynamic behavior is said to become more flexible, stable, and articulated. For Werner, "primitive" states are earlier on the developmental continuum and appear frequently in children, tribal peoples, and mental patients. Not unexpectedly, Werner's views (see also Werner and Kaplan, 1956) aroused strong resistance from anthropologists who accused him of committing a nineteenth-century error by equating primitive adults and "civilized" children.

Werner's writing has not always been criticized on adequate grounds. His position was not intended to be a strong claim about either genetic endowment or possibilities for developmental change. His major goal was to provide a general structural parallel (not material identity) between child and primitive, which would allow one to seek and order information about other societies in terms that coordinate with an organization of knowledge about individuals within our own society. A deeper criticism of his work would center around the heuristic potentialities of using one category system to describe another system. The ethnoscientists would claim that this is in itself a direct violation of anthropological method.

A theoretical problem of particular interest was the relation between language and thought. During the 1950s this interest of American psychologists in language behavior led to an awareness of the implications of linguistic differences for differences in thinking. Psychologists and anthropologists met together to discuss problems of language and culture (Osgood and Sebeok, 1954; Hoijer, 1954) and helped to develop the new discipline of psycholinguistics. The writings of Whorf were published in 1956 with a long introduction by a psychologist, John Carroll, and at about the same time scholars began to make experimental studies of the linguistic relativity hypothesis (Brown and Lenneberg, 1954; Carroll and Casagrande, 1958).

During the 1960s the relations between, on the one hand, language, thought, and culture and, on the other, culture and cognitive development dominated cross-cultural psychological research. Moreover, research on child development reflected a more integrated concern with the influence of language, culture, and cognitive skills. The single most widely used theoretical context for cross-cultural research in recent years has been Piaget's theory of cognitive growth. Frequently, however, as J. S. Bruner, R. Olver, and P. Greenfield (1966) pointed out, the study of Piaget's theory has been confined to quantitative specifications of the age lag of some specified "foreign" children behind European children as they move from one developmental stage to another.

The strategy followed in the work of Bruner and his colleagues, as well as that of J. J. Goodnow (1969) and D. Price-Williams, W. Gordon, and M. Ramirez (1969), has been to try to identify the way in which some cultures "push" cognitive development earlier, longer, and better than others. A universal finding of this research is that attendance at Western-style schools enormously speeds up the development of problem-solving skills.

According to Bruner, Olver, and Greenfield (1966), two factors dominate in producing this result. First, children in school must learn to solve problems involving objects and events not present at the time. Second, schoolchildren learn to read and write. Price-Williams and his colleagues (1969) have shown that analogous acceleration is obtained when children are already very familiar with a particular aspect of their environment. For example, potters' children are very adept at a Piagetian problem involving estimates of quantities and types of clay.

A corollary to this kind of theorizing is that just as some cultural conditions accelerate the rate of development, the lack of certain critical experiences may delay or preclude development. Bruner, Olver, and Greenfield cite, as analogous to the so-called early arrest of cognitive functioning, their finding that tribal Wolof adults do not seem to understand that when liquid is poured from one container to another, the amount is conserved.

Another popular line of developmental research seeks to document the relation between cultural-environmental factors and "psychological differentiation" (see Witkin, 1967; Dawson, 1967). Research based on H. A. Witkin's understanding of psychological differentiation moves beyond Werner's generalization to demonstrate on the basis of experiments in perception that certain sociocultural traits (such as strict, directive upbringing) will lead to "less differentiated" (less analyzed and articulated) cognitive functioning.

These studies have attempted to specify the cultural variables that account for particular aspects of cognition. Although the enterprise is still in its infancy, it is potentially far more fruitful than searches for any population difference that gives rise to a difference in test scores, with no accompanying effort to specify the source of the diversity (for a recent review of cross-cultural psychological research, see Cole, 1972).

Toward an Experimental Anthropology

Considering the long traditions that have generated the anthropological, linguistic, and psychological approaches to the study of culture and cognition, it would be excessively foolhardy of us to pretend to a grand synthesis removing all the barriers to interdisciplinary understanding. Our more modest goal is to create a research strategy that is consistent with the major methodological requirements that each discipline brings to this problem. The remaining chapters of this book are a summary description of our efforts. But before describing the research itself, we want to explain the considerations that motivated our choices of strategy.

It should be emphasized that when we began this line of research several years ago (Gay and Cole, 1967), we had no coherent overview of our goals and the proper methods to achieve them; we were faced with what we considered a concrete problem in "applied anthropology" in trying to understand African difficulties in learning Western mathematics. By bits and pieces, as we tried to make sense of what we were doing and to plan rationally how next to proceed, we began to develop a set of principles for guiding our inquiry, which led to a more explicit theoretical awareness. We still lack a complete and consistent "meta-theory" of cross-cultural research, but we will attempt to make explicit our current understanding of the enterprise. To this end we can abstract from the preceding discussions a set of very basic concerns of anthropology, psychology, and linguistics in the study of culture and cognition.

Anthropologists emphasize that cognition cannot be studied as an activity isolated from its cultural context. To study cognition is to study cognitive behavior in a particular situation and the relation of this behavior to other aspects of the culture. A second primary concern is that the investigator not impose his views and categories of experience on the phenomenon being studied, but rather that he make his behavior patterns fit those of the people he studies. Since the anthropologist is likely to reject evidence from belief systems as irrelevant to understanding individual thought processes, no general theory of thinking has arisen in anthropology, although a beginning has been made by the ethnoscientists.

The psychologist is primarily interested in the study of various cultures in order to test the generality of hypothetical cognitive processes. His primary concern is with the *process* of cognition, although he is willing to consider *content* where it can be shown to influence process. In his search for evidence about cognitive processes, the psychologist leans heavily on the experimental method, although this was not always the case. In the period around the turn of the century, many unverifiable statements about "what the subject is thinking" were to be met in the psychological literature, in which the data were often of an anecdotal or observational nature. This practice of using naturally occurring behavior sequences as direct indicators of underlying thought processes was severely criticized by C. Lloyd Morgan (1891, pp. 327 ff.), who pointed out the difficulty of identifying a correct prediction of a single event as an example of true reasoning. Morgan distinguished two kinds of inference, "perceptual" and "conceptual." A perceptual inference is one taken from direct experience, in which the connection might be remembered. For example, the expectation of rain when thunder clouds appear is a perceptual inference. A conceptual inference is also based upon experience, but is reached through the exercise of the reasoning faculties. It is based upon the process of isolation and analysis and predicts occurrences that have never before been experienced. The major ambiguity in the analysis of single, naturally occurring events is that it is difficult to know if the conclusion is reasoned or remembered.

Considerations like these, combined with the reliance on observable behaviors as the basic data of psychology, led psychologists to define thinking in terms of new combinations of past experiences. The new combinations are made to obtain a goal or solve a problem. For example,

Thinking . . . may be provisionally defined as what occurs in experience when an organism, human or animal, meets, recognizes and solves a problem. . . . The process of thinking involves an active combination of features which as part of the problem situation were originally discrete. [Humphrey, 1951, p. 311]

The term *cognition,* now common in psychology, once was roughly synonymous to *thinking.* However, it is now used to refer to the range of phenomena that the nonpsychologist speaks of as "thought processes." For example, Bruner (1957), in a well-known article, says that cognition is present whenever the subject "goes beyond the information given." Examples of elementary cognitive capacities discussed by Bruner are the formation of equivalence classes, the learning of redundancy, the learning of coding systems, and theory building (which involves the combination of the three former capacities to account for new phenomena). Similarly, U. Neisser (1968, p. 10) says that cognition is involved in an activity that displays formation and construction. A consequence of the psychologists' emphasis on new behavior or transformations of old behavior has been the study of situations that involve learning new things, or at least reorganizing old things. The question then becomes: is it necessary to hypothesize something more than simple association or rote recall, to account for these activities?

The linguist has two concerns. First, he wishes to test the fundamental proposition that the cognitive capacities of the individual are reflected in his language. Followers of Chomsky and Whorf may draw different inferences from this linguistic principle, but both are concerned with the role of language factors in cognitive performance. Second, the linguist wishes to refine and make generally available techniques for pursuing the ethnographic interests of the anthropologist.

Although it is doubtful that linguists in general agree on a definition of cognition, Chomsky and his fellow transformational linguists take a view of cognition roughly consistent with that proposed by Bruner and Neisser. They assert that the cognitive processes of the speaker must in some sense be as complex as the language he speaks. The central message of contemporary linguistics is that simple associations cannot in principle explain a person's infinite capacity for producing new utterances. By reasonable extrapolation, theories that do not assume such generative powers in the thinker cannot be expected to explain thinking.

Our own "synthesis" of these concerns can be characterized in two ways. First, we wish to study the relation between a person's home culture and the kinds of cognitive skills he develops. Our data concerning culture as well as the individual activities within that culture require that cognition not be isolated from other activities of life. Quite the contrary—as we indicated in the preface to this volume, common, everyday activities provide the basic materials for the discovery of significant cultural variations that may be related to cognitive variations. If, as we hypothesize, cognitive skills are closely related to the activities that engage those skills, we have to be able to specify the kinds of tasks that people in different cultures routinely encounter. We also want to be able to characterize the nature of the differences in activities that are implied by cultural changes such as those introduced by Western-style schooling or literacy. In addition, we believe that the study of cognitive processes cannot ignore content, particularly the basic categories of experience that are relevant to the processes under scrutiny. Finally, ethnographic analysis sets a kind of endpoint of any analysis of cognition; it provides a picture of the intelligent, adaptive behaviors that people engage in every day. Whenever our analysis suggests lack of competence, we must always look to our basic ethnographic observations to see if that same lack of competence is manifested in routine activities. If not, it is more likely that our analysis, rather than our subjects, is incompetent.

Second, we believe that the experimental method is an important tool for understanding cognition. Our work starts with certain Western notions of cognitive process as embodied in various experimental tests. Hopefully, we will reach at the end a bidirectional, comparative analysis both of our own culture and of other cultures.

Cross-cultural experimentation, even embedded in a culturally appropriate context and carefully qualified by sound anthropological, psychological, and linguistic canons, is not inherently a trouble-free tool. Much of our thought and energy has been devoted to developing methods for designing experiments that would neutralize two major objections to cross-cultural experimental research—one from the anthropologist, the other from the psychologist.

The anthropologist makes the fundamental criticism that *in principle,* the experimental method is not applicable in nonliterate cultures. No matter what measures a psychologist may take to make his experimental procedures clearly understood, his materials familiar, and his procedures straightforward, the very fact that he asks a member of a nonliterate community to answer a set of questions or to seek the solution to a hypothetical problem violates cultural norms. The anthropologist concludes that the behavior displayed in this way cannot be considered a reflection of normal cognitive functioning.

We can accept the proposition that there are real and important problems in using the experimental method in cross-cultural research. But we reject the conclusion that cross-cultural experimental research is useless. The problems involved are not unique to this particular domain of inquiry, nor do they compel us to retire to the role of participant observers, simply because we recognize that our means of obtaining data influence the data we obtain.

The situation is not unlike that which obtains today in the study of animal behavior. For many years experimental psychologists have used the Norway rat and the Carneaux pigeon to study the laws relating the conditions of reinforcement to the frequency and patterning of simple behaviors (lever pressing, key pecking) in animals. In recent years a group of scientists interested in animal behavior, but calling themselves ethologists, have challenged the research strategy of the psychologist, pointing out that an animal's behavior is specific to his species and is related closely to specific aspects of his physical and social environment. The ethological strategy calls for the study of the organism in his natural environment as a means to understanding his capacities and the functional relations between his behavior and various environmental events. Extremists among both psychologists and ethologists claim that *nothing* useful can be learned from following the opposite strategy. But the general consensus is to seek functional laws where they can be found—the problem comes from overgeneralizing one's results to domains where they do not apply.

All controlled observations, including experiments, affect the data one obtains. Just as an experiment is never a normal part of a subject's everyday life, so an observer can never become a normal part of a social group's everyday experience. The strategy in both cases is to seek to *minimize and evaluate* the extent of the distortion that observation introduces into the natural situation. Exactly the same problem arises in making inferences from experiments with Western children and adults, and one often hears complaints that it is difficult to know how to extrapolate laboratory findings to "real life." Our intuition tells us that the problem of extrapolation may be even more difficult in nonliterate societies, but this is a cause for careful study, not despair. If our data support theories that have predictive power, the result, although not perfect for all purposes, can be considered useful. The proof of that pudding we defer to later chapters.

The second objection to cross-cultural experimentation comes from the psychologist who is concerned with the logic of experimental design and inference. This objection can be expressed best through an example from our previous work. We asked persons to view small dots on a card for time intervals between one-tenth and one-hundredth of a second and to tell how many objects are present (see Cole, Gay, and Glick, 1968, pp. 184 ff. for details). American adults are consistently accurate at this task so long as six or fewer dots are presented, but with more dots become markedly less accurate. The hypothesis has been proposed from these and other data that humans have a limited but definite "information-processing capacity" (Miller, 1956). A natural question to ask is whether normal adults in a radically different culture show the same behavior. When we tried this experiment with a group of American college students and Liberian tribal people, we found the Liberian performance both different and significantly poorer than that of the college students.

The experiment as described above can be criticized by both psychologist and anthropologist since it is not clear how to interpret the results. We do not know what inferences about cultural differences, either general or specific, are warranted. We could explain these results in many ways, some cultural and some methodological. How do we narrow the range of acceptable inferences? Furthermore, how can we make inferences that have general import, rather than relevance to this problem only?

We suggest that there are two ways out of our difficulties which can be used separately or together in psychological-cultural research. First, as Donald Campbell suggests:

We who are interested in using such (cross-cultural) comparisons for delineating process rather than exhaustively describing single instances must accept this rule: *No comparison of a single pair of natural objects is interpretable.* . . . However, if there are multiple indicators which vary in their irrelevant attributes, and of these all agree as to the direction of the difference on the theoretically intended aspects, then the number of tenable rival explanations becomes greatly reduced and the confirmation of theory more nearly certain. [Campbell, 1961, pp. 344–345]

Second, as we have pointed out elsewhere, whenever possible, inferences about differences between cultures with respect to a given cognitive process should depend on the pattern of performances within the cultures being compared.

These two principles require us systematically to vary the content and context of the experiment, while maintaining the central principle. However, such a program of experimentation may be exceedingly costly and time-consuming. It is necessary, therefore, to determine what inferences we can draw even under limited conditions.

The strategy of focusing on cross-cultural comparison of patterns of performance makes possible certain permissible inferences, even for a single experiment. In the case of the tachistoscopic dot-recognition experiment, we can draw permissible cross-cultural inferences from the following facts:

1. American subjects are more accurate in their reports of the number of dots; as already reported, American accuracy begins to fall only when more than six dots are presented, while the Liberian accuracy falls from the outset (three dots).

2. There is little or no difference in performance between the two cultural groups when three dots are presented.

3. If the dots are presented in a patterned, instead of a random array (.·. or ⠒ ⠒, for example), American performance is improved relatively more than Liberian performance. Moreover, the American subjects make "patterned" errors, (saying ten instead of eight when shown four pairs of dots), while the Liberians do not.

These and other findings in the complete experiment effectively reduce the number of hypotheses that can account for the pattern of performance of our two cultural groups. For example, such hypotheses as poor eyesight, fear of the experimenter, and the strangeness of the estimation task for the Liberian subjects are not consistent with the facts that there are essentially no cultural differences using three dots and that the patterning helps only the Americans.

In short, by designing our experiment to assess *patterns* of performance between groups and across cultures, we can greatly reduce the dangers of irrelevant explanations and time-consuming experimental variations. Moreover, in so doing we have narrowed the range of variables that need concern us.

In the chapters that follow, we will describe the results of several years of research during the course of which these ideas were developed. It will be apparent that the aspirations we describe in this section exceed our grasp. Wherever possible we have followed the strategy of multiple experiments emphasizing patterning of results. We have, in addition, tried to locate the experiments within cultural contexts that were themselves the objects of study. Finally, we have proceeded on the belief that we are always dealing with normal human beings whose behavior is organized and meaningful within its natural context. When we encounter behavior that appears inappropriate, disorganized, or meaningless, we have tried to make such observations a starting point for inquiry, rather than proof of inferiority. We hope that the resultant characterization of the relation between culture and cognitive activity will reflect the richness and variety of human thinking, whatever its cultural context.

24

TWO : An Unorthodox Ethnography

> An anthropologist's description of a cul-
> ture is like a myth in that it "is a narra-
> tive that organizes data for some
> purpose."
>
> P. BOHANNON

Introduction

The rather abstract prescriptions for doing cross-cultural experimental research with which we concluded Chapter 1 tell us that in order to enrich our understanding of the relation between culture and cognition, we have to do something more than transport our experimental devices to an alien culture to "see how the natives do." We begin the task of specifying the nature of this "something more" by providing background data on the people who have been the focus of our study, the Kpelle of Liberia. Because our special concern is to understand the relation between features of Kpelle culture and the learning and problem-solving process of individuals, we need to consider issues not ordinarily a part of ethnographic descriptions as well as standard ethnographic data.

To begin with, we will introduce the major cultural variables that we think important for understanding variations in cognitive processes. Beginning with these guesses about significant variations among groups, we will turn to a rather general description of Kpelle life and the national context in which it exists. This general discussion leans heavily on the prior ethnographic work of scholars such as J. Gibbs (1965) and J. L. Sibley and D. H. Westermann (1928). We will discover that there is considerable heterogeneity in contemporary Kpelle culture. In tracing a little of the history and the social forces that have shaped Kpelle culture, we hope to provide some understanding of how the situation we describe arose. We also hope to give the general reader some feel for global aspects of Kpelle life so that he can approach our experimental work with at least a small part of the intuitive familiarity he has when our subjects are schoolchildren from suburban southern California.

Although this traditional ethnographic material will be useful in obtaining a general introduction to the groups on whom the experimental work will focus, it gives us very little insight into the detailed nature of the activities that members of the various groups engage in or the way in which they learn and solve problems. Consequently, we will provide additional data which are not to be found in previous ethnographies and which, unfortunately, are of a rather fragmentary and unsystematic nature. From recordings of conversations, court cases, school essays, and a variety of miscellaneous sources, we will piece together what we know of the mundane activities of Kpelle people that engage them intellectually. We hope that this material will serve two purposes. First, it should provide clues about the sources of performance differences among groups when they are encountered with our experimental tasks. Second, it should provide us with a picture of everyday Kpelle intellectual activities against which to measure the impressions gained from experimentation.

We begin by describing the major variables of concern to us as we undertook this "unorthodox ethnography."

The Overall Design of the Research

We cannot claim to understand fully either Kpelle life or cognition. We claim only an interest in such important examples of cognition as learning, problem solving, classification, and memory, coupled with some hunches about the cultural variables that influence them. In later chapters we will develop these intuitions into particular hypotheses leading to experimental studies. For the present we will outline the major cultural and subcultural variables that might be generally related to cognitive variation and describe informally the resulting subject populations used in most of our studies.

The major contrast that we have employed in our studies is between the traditional Kpelle and the Kpelle who have attained some degree of Westernization. However, this comparison is by no means straightforward.

Schooling represents the single most powerful institution for producing nontraditional, acculturated people, not only in Liberia, but throughout sub-Saharan Africa. L. Doob (1960) has, for instance, used formal education in Western schools as his index of acculturation for Africans. He asserts that it produces more significant differences than other variables he has worked with, and that it is positively related to such other indices of acculturation as occupation, knowledge of English, and place of residence.

Schooling in particular is related to literacy, another variable that many authors believe to be very important in determining the way in which people learn and think. Although the schoolchild becomes literate and Westernized at the same time, it is possible, at least in theory, to separate these two factors. One way, suggested by G. Jahoda (1961), is to develop an "index of acculturation" based on the kinds of artifacts —for example, thatched roofs or corrugated iron roofs—used by people in their ordinary lives. It makes good sense to believe that a car mechanic, even though illiterate, will function intellectually in ways that differ from a rice farmer. A second way to separate schooling and literacy is to take advantage of special situations in which literacy is attained without formal schooling. Two such situations suggest themselves in the Liberian setting, although we have made little use of them: the use of Arabic by Mandingos, and the use by the Vai of the syllabic form of writing invented by a member of their tribe in the 1820s (Dalby, 1967).

Schooling and literacy are both thought to be related to a whole series of cognitive changes, one general characteristic of which is greater flexibility. For example, in Horton's (1967a, b) discussion of the difference between open and closed belief systems, literacy is said to be of great importance. Traditionally oriented peoples are said to be less able to see alternative solutions to problems because of their belief in "the one correct way." Doob, writing as a psychologist, sums up these observations and ascribes to acculturated peoples less dogmatism, greater proficiency in novel situations, a facility for abstract thinking, and greater ease in the use of language to describe one's feelings and reactions to the environment (Doob, 1961, pp. 325 ff.). In this connection J. Goody and I. Watt (1962) go so far as to say that:

It is probably that it is only the analytic process that writing itself entails, the written formalization of sounds and syntax, which make possible the habitual separating out into formally distinct units of the various cultural elements whose indivisible wholeness is the essential basis of the "mystical participation" which Levy-Bruhl regards as characteristic of the thinking of non-literate peoples. [P. 345]

Bruner et al. (1966) also suggest that education affects intellectual development; they contend that formal education is required for the development of certain cognitive skills. Both European and American developmental research are limited by the fact that in these two areas of the world all normal children begin to attend school between the ages of five and seven years. This is the same age at which certain crucially important increases in children's intellectual capacities have been repeatedly noted (cf. Piaget, 1955; Bruner, Olver, and Greenfield, 1966; Kendler and Kendler, 1968; Luria, 1960). For this reason it is impossible to say whether these changes come by the mere fact that the maturing organism interacts with its environment, or come because of special environmental features, such as those provided by the school.

One of our primary aims will be to specify adequately by experimental analysis the domains in which acculturated and traditional people differ in their ways of thinking and to separate, where possible, the effects of literacy and acculturation.

Cross-cultural developmental research can also test the oft-repeated claims of anthropological and psychological observers that primitive peoples manifest precocity of mental development, followed by an early arrest (Miller, 1928; Werner, 1948). We can compare developmental trends in those who have and have not been Westernized at various ages through adulthood.

In addition to schooling and age we are concerned with language. Although knowledge of English is one of the measures of acculturation and is highly correlated with school attendance, we can separate these variables and investigate certain questions of the relation between language and learning of major importance to the question of cultural differences in thought processes.

Although other variables could have been investigated, our own interests and skills, combined with conditions in the area in which we worked, lead us to study the influence on cognition principally of age and education, and secondarily of language and degree of acculturation.

Both great opportunities and great difficulties arise from choosing the Liberian hinterland as a place to do cross-cultural research on cognitive processes. The opportunities arise from the great degree of cultural diversity within a single ethnic group, while major difficulties stem from the fact that several of the most important variables clearly covary. For instance, in studying the contrast between traditional and acculturated Kpelle people, we have to consider changes in vocation, number of languages spoken, literacy, school attendance, and travel, to mention but a few of the most obvious factors. Some of these changes are closely linked (literacy and education), whereas others are only partially correlated (number of languages and travel).

A major virtue of Kpelleland for developmental research lies in the fact that whether or not a particular child attends school is more a matter of chance than is true in Western society. Schools were built along the roads, which reach only a small number of the towns. Moreover, only some of the children in even these road towns actually attend school. As we remarked earlier, a major difficulty with present important developmental theories is their reliance on studies of children who begin school at exactly the same period when many important changes are said to occur in the child's cognitive capacities. Although comparisons of educated and noneducated Americans would be possible, the noneducated Americans would differ greatly from the cultural norm, whereas in Liberia the schoolchildren, if anything, are the ones who differ from the cultural norm.

Age would seem to be a straightforward variable to measure, but, in fact, few Kpelle know their age in years. As a consequence, estimates were often based on information supplied by parents, older siblings, or town elders, who were familiar with Western measures of age. Because of the unreliability of such estimates, we resorted to the use of age-ranges rather than specific ages to define our groups. The particular age ranges we used were chosen to facilitate comparisons with experiments conducted by others in the United States and to permit evaluation of various theoretical statements about the relation between age and performance. Although we used younger (four to six years) or older (sixteen to eighteen years) children in certain special experiments, normally we used six to eight, ten to fourteen, and eighteen to fifty year olds as our basic age-defined groups.

Further complicating cross-cultural comparisons of the effects of age and education on cognition is the fact that Kpelle children start school at widely varying ages. Although there has been a strong effort by the government to restrict first-grade admission to six-year-old children in recent years, the average age of children in the second grade is probably near twelve years, while first graders' average age is probably closer to eight or nine. Often children remain in the first grade until their English is deemed adequate to move ahead, a process that may take several years. This situation makes simultaneous cross-cultural equation of age and education virtually impossible; it is also one of the many reasons that we have come to emphasize the relations among variables within a culture (as in our example of the perception of random and patterned visual displays in Chapter 1) rather than direct cross-cultural comparisons.

The education variable, by itself, would seem to depend solely on the child's grade level. However, even grade is not an absolute because the achievements of Liberian children at a given grade level are not comparable to those of American children at the same grade. In many studies, for a number of reasons, we treated the first two grades as equivalent and representative of a rather low level of achievement. The higher grades (fourth through sixth) were chosen as representative of a higher level of achievement, assumed to include literacy and a relatively good command of English. High-school groups were also included in certain of the experiments, although the number of students attending high schools in Kpelleland is extremely small.

The degree of acculturation presents the most serious problems of measurement because of the vagueness of this much-used concept. Our solution, easier to justify on pragmatic than on theoretical grounds, was to select as "tribal adults" nonliterate rice farmers in the eighteen- to fifty-year-old age range who spoke no more than a few words of marketplace English. In this case also the judgment of our assistants was an important factor in deciding who belonged to this group. We chose Westernized subjects, called by the Kpelle *kwii,* from persons engaged in some semitechnical work who spoke enough English to communicate with members of other linguistic groups.

We must mention finally that perhaps 70 percent of our subjects, except in the case of the youngest children, were male. Females in general lead a more sheltered life and are not expected to participate, except within their own secret society, in worldly matters. This is a potential variable of interest that we have not systematically investigated.

Having sketched some of the major variables determining the choice of subject groups, we turn now to an informal description of the lives and abilities of the groups defined by these variables. In so doing, we emphasize those facts and features of Kpelle life that appear relevant to our experimental concerns.

While this description has the surface appearance of an ethnography, we intend it to serve two different but related functions. First, and most generally, we seek a natural context for the artificial realities of our experiments and elicitations. Second, we wish to highlight the cultural and cognitive achievements of the Kpelle because they provide important clues to the level of sophistication of cognitive processes involved in the technology and social life of the people.

Our description begins with a general treatment of the Liberian context and of the place of the Kpelle within that context. We then turn to a more detailed look at the two groups at the polar opposites on the dimensions of education and Westernization, namely the nonliterate tribal adult and the schoolchild.

The Kpelle Background: Natural and Political

The Kpelle tribe consists of some 250,000 persons living in central Liberia and perhaps an equal number in southern Guinea, where they are called the Guerze. Our work was confined to the Liberian side of the border. The Kpelle share linguistic and cultural features with a large group of forest and savanna tribes extending from Senegal in the northwest to Ivory Coast on the southeast. The general features of these peoples are described by Murdock (1962).

The Kpelle live in tropical rain forest, most of which, following several hundred years of cultivation, is secondary growth rather than virgin forest. Kpelle country consists of low forested hills interlaced with swamps, small streams, and an occasional river. Superimposed are the upland rice farms, paths, and villages of the Kpelle tradition, as well as the plantations, motor roads, and Westernized towns of *kwii* Liberia. The rainfall varies from 200 inches on the coast to 80 inches in the interior and is concentrated mainly from April to November. As a result the vegetation is heavy and lush. The soil is poor and lateritic, yielding restricted opportunities for diversified agriculture.

Today's Kpelle are a part of the Republic of Liberia. However, contacts between Kpelle tribal people and Westernized, urbanized representatives of the national government are not as old as the republic itself, now a nation of 43,000 square miles and slightly more than one million persons. Liberia was founded in 1821 as a haven for freed American slaves. In the four decades prior to the American Civil War, approximately 19,000 ex-slaves were sent from the United States or taken off slave ships in transit to the United States and settled in Liberia. They were aided by a handful of missionaries, agents of the colonization societies, and traders to form a government on the American model. The new nation of Liberia, independent in 1847, consisted at first only of a few settlements on the seacoast and on the short navigable portions of several major rivers, even though it claimed a large interior area. The best overall summary on Liberia is contained in the U.S. Army Handbook (1964). For a critical survey of current economic conditions, see Clower et al. (1966); for an account of political development, see Liebenow, (1969).

Contacts between settlements of those who came to be called Americo-Liberians and the interior tribes were limited at first to labor on farms and trade in agricultural goods. The Americo-Liberians were drawn originally from tribes extending all the way from Senegal to Angola and had little or nothing in common with the tribes of the Guinea coast. Many of those who returned from the Americas spoke English, which became the official language of the new nation. Many were Christians who considered it their duty to rule and civilize the natives. Their model was the ante-bellum American South, and their aim was to build a prosperous Christian republic with the help of tribal lands and labor.

Contact with the Kpelle tribe was very limited at first. Missionaries reached Kpelle towns toward the middle of the nineteenth century, and in the 1860s the Liberian explorer Benjamin Anderson passed through the northern portions of Kpelleland. By the 1870s Kpelle laborers were found on settlement farms, and regular trading points were established at the upper edges of Liberian settlements where Kpelle farmers brought their produce in exchange for Western goods.

Until 1910, the various groups of Kpelle dealt with the Americo-Liberians as one tribe with another. But in 1910, in response to British and French encroachments on lands claimed by the Liberian Department of the Interior, central authority was imposed on the people of the interior. The American-based system of government applied directly only to those who had become "civilized," but provided the ultimate authority for all others. In 1965 this dual system was abolished, and the interior tribes were brought within the same political framework as the rest of the country, under the unification policy of President W. V. S. Tubman.

Until 1945 the Liberian presence in Kpelle country was limited to taxation, recruitment of labor for rubber plantations, the administration of justice, and the maintenance of border posts. There were also foreigners, mostly missionaries and Lebanese traders, but these were few in numbers and weak in influence. During the years before 1945, the number of Kpelle men who had worked for Firestone Rubber on its plantation at the southwest edge of Kpelleland increased, and so did the appetite of Kpelle people for the goods and ideas that could be obtained from the new world outside.

Since World War II there has been vastly increased contact between Kpelle society and the Western cultures represented not only by the Americo-Liberians, but also by the many Americans and Europeans who came to Kpelleland on missions of mercy and money. In 1946 the all-weather road, which had previously reached only peripheral Kpelle towns, was pushed to the Guinea border right through the center of Kpelle country, following a traditional Kpelle path. Branches of this road now lead also to Sierra Leone and Ivory Coast. The first branch of the road represents a rapidly growing focus for Westernization. On the junction of this road and the branch to Sierra Leone, what had formerly been a temporary war camp now became the administrative and trading town of Gbarnga; there foreigners and members of every Liberian tribe live together in a community of perhaps 5,000 persons. Near Gbarnga are an agricultural research station, Cuttington College (which was the base of much of our research), two hospitals, several mission schools, and a number of farms owned by educated Liberians.

The road has clearly been the greatest instrument of change in Kpelle country. Towns that had been extremely isolated because a government official, missionary, or trader could reach them only after a five- or six-day walk through tropical rain forest were now exposed to the outside world. Today a rough index of the extent to which a town maintains Kpelle traditions is its distance from the main road, even though every town has to some extent felt the influence of the rapidly encroaching, Afro-urban culture of the coastal region.

A few years after the road was completed, the American government, through the Agency for International Development (AID) began an extensive program of building schools in the interior. Prior to that time, only missionaries or an occasional literate Liberian had provided Western education in Kpelle country. But today most principal towns along the road have elementary schools, which begin instruction with the teaching of English in a pre-first-grade preparatory class and terminate at the sixth grade. Of those children who begin school, only a small percentage complete the sixth grade.

Participation in the money economy is likewise increasing at the present. There are Lebanese stores in almost every road town, and money with which to buy goods is available from a variety of sources. Most

Kpelle men either sell farm produce or work for a plantation, iron mine, or other foreign enterprise for some period in their lives. In one recent year every householder had to pay approximately fifty dollars in taxes of one kind of another, requiring at least a minimal participation in the national economy. Except for people living in the most remote areas, the traditional life as it once existed is impossible, although many persons deviate from the past as little as they can and often with the greatest reluctance.

The interaction between traditional and modern life is particularly evident in a typical road town. A close look at Sinyee, an average-sized (approximately 125 huts) town 115 miles from the capital city of Monrovia, located on a small feeder road off the main highway, suggests that it is a transitional town, subject to a great deal of Western influence. The Western anthropologist or educator entering the town for the first time will see the road leading to the town, the government school on his left, and many square houses with corrugated iron (called zinc in Liberia) roofs. Two rather substantial shops serve as general stores; in addition, there are many smaller shops. Many of the people wear Western-style clothes, and virtually all of the cloth worn by the people, even when not sewn into Western-style clothing, is commercially printed. Many of the townsmen work for nearby Cuttington College; many have worked at some time for the Firestone Rubber Company plantation eighty miles to the southwest or one of the other large economic concessions. All pay yearly taxes to the government and all are ultimately subject to the national legal system. Approximately 300 children between the ages of five and eighteen attend the government school. The Western anthropologist or educator might be tempted to ask if there are *any* traditional Kpelle people in the town, or anywhere nearby.

In fact, much of the ethnographic material on the Kpelle was gathered in this and similar transition towns, which contain many traditional elements. Although more traditional Kpelle towns could be found, especially towns that are far from the nearest motor road, virtually every town in Kpelleland has been touched to some extent by Western culture; at the same time virtually every town has retained important elements of the tradition. We will attempt to describe both the important aspects of this tradition and the changes that have taken place.

We have adopted different stances toward the question of what constitutes a Westernized (*kwii*) Kpelle, depending on the task at hand. In accord with the argument outlined above, we have as a rule used school attendance as the major contrast with traditional Kpelle culture.

Since Western material goods can be found in so many country stores in the Liberian hinterland, access to shotguns, lanterns, canned goods, and radios would not seem to differentiate *kwii* and traditional Kpelle. Yet not all partake of commerical conveniences in equal measure—to acquire zinc for one's roof, one must earn money. To earn money, one must either grow an excess of rice, grow a cash crop, or work for wages. The people we have characterized as traditional tend to do these things to a lesser degree than the *kwii* people; when they do them, they tend to share the profits with their relatives. Involvement in the money economy (working for Firestone Rubber, an iron mine, Cuttington College, or some other Western institution) brings one in contact with English speakers, for in this multitribal country, English is the lingua franca. In order to reach areas where wages are offered, it is often necessary to leave Kpelle country. The person who does so can no longer depend on his tribe and family, but must turn to new forms of nontraditional, perhaps multitribal, organizations (Little, 1958). When the traveler returns home, he finds the traditional authority considerably less imposing; after all, he has experienced alternative social organizations and belief systems which are more powerful and rewarding in terms of the new currency. He keeps more for his own immediate family and beings to seek ways to escape the zero-sum economy of the extended family. Even though such a person is not educated, he is well on his way to becoming *kwii* rather than traditional.

Yet many people remain close to the traditional ways: the town chief, the leaders of the men's and women's secret societies, and many families who engage in traditional agricultural activities with a minimum of involvement in the money economy. It is to this traditional, relatively less *kwii,* group that we now turn our attention.

The Traditional Kpelle

Farming is the major skill mastered by all adult Kpelle. As J. Gibbs points out (1965, p. 200), there is a Kpelle term that may be translated either *farm* or *work*. The major crop, upland rice, is so important that a Kpelle proverb states that a man has not eaten if he has not eaten rice.

The Kpelle distinguish more than twenty varieties of rice and the basis for classification are many: color (white, red, and black), length of germination, yield, place of growth (upland or swamp), and size of grains. Our informants indicate that which rice is planted depends, among other things, on the type of seed available, the type of land to be farmed, whether the rice is to be sold or used for one's family, the time of year, and the reserves of rice from last year's crop.

Although, like farmers everywhere, the Kpelle must know his crop and his land and must work hard, the actual technology of Kpelle rice farming is simple, by American standards. The farming cycle begins in February or March, toward the end of the dry season. A plot of land that has lain fallow for at least seven years is cleared of brush by the men, usually working in one of several types of cooperative work groups called *kuu*. Trees such as the citrus and palm, which are economically useful, and certain cottonwood trees, which are thought to have supernatural powers, as well as stumps of other trees are left standing. After the cut foliage dries, the entire area is burned, then cleared and burned again, and left to stand until the rains arrive to soak the ashes into the soil and loosen the soil for planting.

At this point the women take over and plant the seed rice, scratching the surface of the soil with short-handled hoes and planting the seeds in the furrows. From the time the rice is planted until the harvest, some four to five months later, the family spends a good deal of time on the farm. The men build a small lean-to ("kitchen"), which serves first as a home away from home for the family when work demands that they sleep at the farm, and later as a storage shed for the crop. A fence of sticks held together by vines is built around the farm to help keep out small foraging animals, and traps are made to catch those animals that bypass the fence. Children, who participate in earlier portions of the work according to their strength, have primary responsibility for protecting the ripening crop from the ubiquitous rice birds. Sticks and slingshots are the main weapons in the child's arsenal. In November and December the whole family harvests, dries, and stores the rice.

The Kpelle have what we would consider a very elaborate system for measuring rice in its harvested and processed form. Cut rice is measured by bundles, which are bound together into stacks and then stored in sheds. When the people need the rice, which has been stored on the farm, the women thresh it and beat it. The rice so prepared is measured by the cup, bucket, tin, and bag. Rice is normally sold for ten cents a cup, which is the size of two English measuring cups or one pint dry

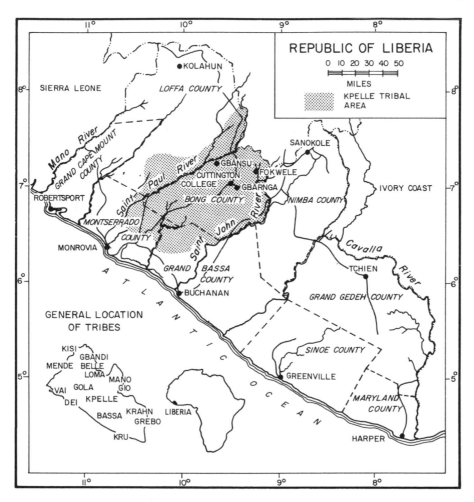

Map of Liberia and Adjacent Areas, Showing Kpelle Land.

The Traditional Town of Gbansu as Seen from the Air (Cole)

Houses in a Traditional Town (Cole)

The Kwii Quarter of the Transition Town of Sinyee (Cole)

Rice for Sale in Sinyee (Gay)

Housing in Sinyee (Gay)

The Major Western-Style Store in Sinyee (Cole)

The Contents of a Lebanese Store on the Road from Monrovia (Cole)

A Rice Farm with a Rice Kitchen in the Foreground (Love)

Graduation from the Sande Bush School in Gbanway, 1967 (Gay)

(Love)

(Cole)

Children of Sinyee

measure. However, the price varies according to the season and the availability of rice. The largest measure for harvested rice is the bag. There are nearly 100 cups of rice in the typical bag in which rice is imported or sold from one part of Liberia to another. This fact is known to the Kpelle, who value a bag of rice at 100 times the going rate per cup.

In addition to rice, other crops are grown on the rice farm such as cassava (also called manioc in other areas) and green vegetables. Still other foods such as palm and kola nuts are gathered in the forest. Even among the traditional farmers some cash cropping can now be found, and to the extent that sugar cane (for rum) and coffee require new farming techniques, the traditional farming technology is undergoing modification.

Building a House

Rice farming is by far the most time-consuming work of the traditional Kpelle, but there are other skills that everyone learns. For example, all members of the community help in the building of a house.

The traditional Kpelle house is usually round and windowless, with a cone-shaped thatch roof. It consists of a simple room in which people cook, eat, and sleep. The fire is built in the center of the house, and over the fire a meat drier is hung from the rafters. Around the edge of the hut are raised mud shelves which serve as beds. The house is cool, dark, and relatively free from insects because the fire sends smoke into the thatched roof.

The hut itself is constructed of a framework of light poles, interwoven with thin branches and lashed together with vines. The walls are then finished by applying wet earth mixed with mud from a termite hill, and the roof is thatched with the broad leaves of a palm tree. The construction of the house exhibits at least implicit knowledge of what may be termed geometric axioms and engineering rules. The placement of uprights in the walls is determined by attaching a string to a center pole and etching a line in the earth in a circle around the center stick. The roof sticks are longer than necessary to join the center pole to the wall, providing both an overhang to protect against rain and firmer support at the center.

Since the advent of Westerners into Kpelleland, many of the houses are built in a rectangular form with corrugated iron roofs. Here, too, an understanding of a basic geometric axiom is manifested; in order to assure a rectangular house, two straight sticks of equal length are crossed at their middle and the corners of the house staked out. The modern house has rooms and windows, and the cooking is usually done in a detached kitchen behind the house.

Specialists: The Blacksmith and the Medicine Man

In addition to activities engaged in by all or most of the community, there are tasks performed only by specialists. These include blacksmithing, weaving, bonesetting, and traditional medicine. Many of these specialties have rituals and taboos, restricting its practice to members of particular groups or secret societies. For instance, bonesetting can be learned only by a direct patrilineal descendant, but any man can become a blacksmith.

Partly because he is an important figure in the secret society and partly because he produces the tools for housemaking and farming, the blacksmith has high status among the Kpelle. All blacksmiths can make cutlasses, knives, hammers, and other tools from scrap iron (in former days, from iron smelted in Kpelleland). In addition, skilled blacksmiths can make needles and guns.

A low-protein diet, the ubiquity of parasites, and the increased number of diseases due to Western contact has made health a major concern for the Kpelle. Until recently, perhaps 75 percent of all children died at an early age, and the Kpelle considered a person old before the age of fifty. The Kpelle defense against disease and death is summed up under the term translated "medicine," although it has a much wider range of meaning than the apparently equivalent English term. Medicine includes not only herbs, but also the use of various objects, beliefs, and institutions. The medical practitioner (*zoo*) is a specialist in one or more of these areas and is also a skilled observer of the social context of disease. (See Harley, 1941; Welmers, 1948; Orr, 1968 for discussions of Kpelle and related medical practice; see also Horton (1967*a,b*) for a discussion of the larger context of medicine in Africa.)

Language and Traditional and Technological Activities

Such additional specialized activities as the making of bird and animal traps or the preparing of dyes do not materially alter the overall picture of a society with a relatively uncomplicated technology and attendant lack of specialization. Rather than pursuing this matter, we would like to consider more carefully a specific issue: the social context of language and the role language plays in learning and performing commonplace Kpelle tasks.

It is curious that in spite of all the cultural variations in childrearing practices, there are almost no data describing how children in different societies learn such basic skills of living as those discussed above. Studies of toilet training, weaning, authority patterns, and other aspects of the parent-child relation presumably relevant to personality development have pre-empted the field (see Hsu, 1961). The reported data, including our own (Gay and Cole, 1967), indicate that children learn more from observation than from situations specifically designed to transmit information orally.

Although monographs and articles on "traditional education" abound (see for example, Fortes, 1938; Raum, 1940), the emphasis in most of this work has been on socialization and enculturation. Perhaps the invisibility of learning vis-à-vis the technological domain is another reflection of the fact that this is not a talked about, problem-situated, enterprise.

N. Miller (1928), for instance, culls data from many anthropological descriptions, the burden of which is that the child is treated as a "little adult," who is expected to contribute to the family larder in proportion to his strength and skill. Even the very small child is frequently to be seen carrying a still smaller child on his back, chopping wood with a tiny ax, or scratching a small portion of the rice farm. The degree to which such activities are seen as a part of the group's work, rather than an opportunity for the child to learn adult behavior, is emphasized in Bruner's discussion of the cultural context of learning and its implications for cognitive development. Speaking of filmed observations of the Kung bushmen, Bruner observes:

What the child knows, he learns from the direct interaction with the adults' community, whether it is learning to tell the age of the spoor left by a poisoned kudu buck . . . or to dig a spring hare out of its burrow. Yet in thousands of feet of film, one sees no *explicit* teaching in the sense of a "session" out of the context of action to teach the child a particular thing. It is all implicit. . . . The only exception is the well-known teaching of rituals. . . . [Bruner, Olver, and Greenfield, 1966, p. 59]

Nor are such observations limited to interactions between adults and children. Beryl Bellman, an anthropologist who has worked among the Kpelle, describes his first day as a member of a Kpelle cooperative work group (*kuu*), clearing an area of bush for a rice farm:

The leader of the *kuu* and two other men . . . worked with dancing steps and precise movements. It was actually from watching the *kulai-mii* work that I was able to observe the "correct" technique for brushing bush, viz., to cut straight into the bush and after coming several feet, turn to the right or left and cut in for several feet and then cut back rolling the cut bush along as it lays against your back. [Field notes, January 10, 1968]

No advice was offered, but when Bellman explained his new-found expertise to a *kuu* member who had some Western education, this member was able to add a few refinements to Bellman's description, helping him to cut more efficiently and with less danger of lacerations.

Although discussions between adults and children as a mode of teaching appears to be minimal, children communicate more among themselves. In what we may call "practice" sessions, children may often be seen in a Kpelle village practicing the skills they will use as adults. One group of children may scratch the ground with a stick, or another may cut tall grass. The children, moreover, will criticize each other's performance and techniques.

An apparent consequence of this "learning *in situ*" is that except for nonspecific criticism of the quality of performance or the willingness to work hard, such learning is an extralinguistic process. To quote Bruner, Olver, and Greenfield again: "But because so much of the 'meaning' of what is being learned is intrinsic in the context in which the learning occurs, there is very little need for verbal formulation" (1966, p. 61). Moreover, it seems that this relative absence of verbal formulation in Kpelle learning of basic skills makes it difficult to produce a verbal analysis of the problems involved. An example will make clear what we have in mind.

A Peace Corps volunteer of our acquaintance decided to build a house. The land assigned to him by the town chief was located on a rather steep slope. After viewing the location, the volunteer decided that he would make the floor of the house level by making the rear wall of the house much taller than the front to compensate for the slope. The interior would be filled with dirt to the level of the base of the front wall. The men who contracted to do the work complained that the house would be "ugly," but such is the power of the dollar that they agreed to do as requested. However, complaints continued to be heard. Thomas Ciborowski set about to find out what the objections to the house were, but at first he made little progress beyond the assurance that the house was going to be ugly. Considerable probing uncovered the difficulty. All those working on the house objected to the proposed method of leveling the floor because the long sticks of the rear wall, which would ordinarily be protected from direct rainfall by the overhanging roof, would be exposed to the rain at their base, thus weakening the wall and undermining the foundation.

Two points stood out concerning this incident. First, the workers plainly knew the critical elements of construction and the way in which structural features of the houses related to factors such as the weather. Second, no one offered the reasons just outlined in a coherent explanation. The inquirer had to piece together the elements of the complete explanation through a lengthy process of questioning.

A similar phenomenon has been noted in the case of swamp rice. Foreign experts have for years tried to convince the Kpelle to grow rice in the swamp rather than on upland hillsides. The yield is better; the same land can be used indefinitely, given proper techniques; after the initial year, less labor is required; fish can be raised along with the rice to provide a source of protein. And yet, most Kpelle resolutely resist growing swamp rice, despite the examples of successful non-Kpelle rice farmers.

It was only after John Kellemu extensively questioned a large number of traditional farmers that a pattern began to emerge, explaining the resistance to growing rice in the swamp. It is true that the process of farming is not much discussed and that the techniques are learned by observation rather than by oral instruction. But it is not mere conservatism, not mere resistance to change in what has been learned nonverbally, that keeps the Kpelle farmer growing his rice on the hillside. There are many other factors which he can explain, if pressed to do so.

Some of the reasons that Kellemu uncovered are based on the technology of farming. Swamp farming gives its best yields with imported and, to the Kpelle, less palatable strains of rice; rice farmers typically grow other crops among the rice shoots, and these crops are an important source of extra food and income; health hazards, such as snakes and tropical sores, are more prevalent in the swamps than in the uplands.

Perhaps even more important than these work-related reasons are doubts couched in terms of the social consequences of changing one's style of farming. Clearing and burning the bush, planting and tending the rice, and harvesting the crop are all communal events. The Kpelle value the occasion of cutting the forest, with its corporate rhythm of a group of men, spurred on by singers and drummers, laying into a piece of bush. Men show their strength and their zeal as they clear the field.

Harvesting is also a social as well as an agricultural event. There are tests of strength and speed, and the fastest worker receives a special hat for his labors as well as the largest portion of the food, palm wine, and cane juice which are integral parts of the process.

Swamp labor, on the other hand, is thought to be uncoordinated and dirty, not fit occasion for the display of strength in a corporate setting. Swamps, moreover, are thought of as the last resort for women whose husbands are dead or gone to another area. They sow their rice seed late in the season, when there is no hope of an upland farm, and they reap a small and uncertain harvest. By making a farm in a swamp, moreover, a man loses his claim to traditional ancestral farms, a fact that is certain to displease those who had farmed this area in the past and are now dead, but still present to the extended family as ancestral spirits.

Kpelle farmers do not articulate their objections to growing rice in the swamp unless pressured by a persistent (and thereby rude) inquirer, and even then not in abstract, narrative form. Furthermore, if the farmer is questioned by a government official impatient for change, he will almost certainly not quote the reasons mentioned above and will give the casual outside observer the impression of stupid, backward-looking recalcitrance.

These observations suggest that verbal formulations of the problems and activities associated with everyday work are not characteristic of the Kpelle adult. From the reports of others it appears that the Kpelle share this trait with other African groups. For example, in our earlier work (Gay and Cole, 1967) and the investigations of others (see Doob, 1960), a recurrent theme has been the difficulty traditional peoples experience when asked to speak about certain areas of their own behavior and culture. Yet, as Gibbs points out (1965, p. 209), Kpelle parents take great care in teaching their children to use the language well. The ability to speak well is a prerequisite to political power, and verbal skills, whether in telling a story or pleading a case in court, are greatly admired.

On the face of it, there appears to be a contradiction when the same individual has difficulty describing the process of making a bird trap, but is a skilled advocate in court cases. Yet the discrepancy may be considerably more widespread than is usually believed. Consider, for example, the average American male, who would have great difficulty describing how to tie his necktie without actually going through the process, or the grandma who is a marvelous cook, but can describe her techniques no better than "a bit of this and taste of that."

These observations and speculations suggest that as a part of our ethnographic enquiry, we need to consider the social life of Kpelle people as an important area within which a great deal of their thinking is manifested. Again we must defer to the general ethnographer for a complete description of social organization (see Gibbs, 1965, pp. 306ff.). However, we can describe certain major features of Kpelle social life that we think might yield clues to the kinds of problem solving and learning that being a Kpelle adult involves.

Social Interactions

Traditionally, an adult could use three resources to play the Kpelle status game, namely, wealth, age, and knowledge. For obvious reasons these three often go together. Wealth is the accumulation of goods or a large family, which were virtually the same process in traditional Kpelle life. At present, the accumulation of wealth is coming to depend more and more on participation in *kwii* society. Age makes a man closer to his ancestors and thus superior to those younger than himself. The elder embodies the traditions that form the core of Kpelle society. In the present changing society the elder is less and less respected. Knowledge is a key to status and power in several respects, and the social management of knowledge is closely bound up with the functioning of the secret societies. Yet new forms of knowledge, learned in Western schools, are winning grudging respect from members of the tribe. In any event knowledge is essential to possession and use of power in the community, as shown by the following example.

Basic to the quest for status is the question of who says what to whom. Beryl Bellman's field notes from 1967 and 1968 are a rich source of observations on Kpelle social interactions. Bellman made a genuine effort to be accepted in a highly traditional Kpelle town, and he became deeply involved in the matter of secrecy. He discusses how the concept *ifa mo* "do not say it" plays a central role in the secret society and in all Kpelle life. An example drawn from Bellman's field notes illustrates the point. The context is the initiation of a man into a secret society (not the all-important Poro society) of which Bellman was a member. Bellman states:

43

We had finished the man's initiation. Mulbah and the others left the house, leaving Yakpawolo and myself alone inside. Yakpawolo pulled some leaves from under his shirt and placed them in the meat to be cooked. He implored me not to talk saying that would be our portion. Suddenly Mulbah appeared. I wondered if he heard Yakpawolo and myself. It seems he didn't because his concern was with V. He ordered her into the house to cook the society food. Without arguing she proceeded to clean the rice. I was surprised as I knew that she was not a member of the society. She is the daughter of the number three man in the society and is *maleŋ* (translated "niece" and indicating a special relation with her uncle) to Mulbah, the *kali zoo* (leader of the snake society). Because of this and out of respect for Mulbah she proceeded to do all that he demanded. Soon the other members arrived. No one said anything and they pretended as if all was normal. After V. finished cooking Mulbah gave her a portion of the rice and she left. [Bellman, 1969, p. 24]

This scene is very complex. Under some circumstances V., the girl, could have been killed for being present in the house and preparing and eating the food. Yet both she and the members of the society who were present accepted her presence. Bellman determined later that she was not afraid of the consequences because she understood a complex set of rules that rendered her immune from blame, in particular, the rule requiring obedience to one's uncle. Moreover, the fact that she was already a member in a corresponding women's society convinced the men she would not talk about what she had seen and done. Her knowledge of the matters of the society was not so important—her willingness to maintain secrecy and obedience to her uncle were of critical importance.

Bellman shows how Mulbah was able to act as he did with relative impunity, incurring only a small fine by society members, because of the subtle manipulations of power and status within the social context. Mulbah was quite aware of these actualities when he asked V. to do his bidding.

Mulbah . . . (wanted) . . . to force V. to become a member of the society. She was reluctant to do so as for a woman to join she would be counterposed to her fellow agemates as being one who put much interest in the medicines and secret societies. The *Kali Sale* (snake society), although allowing female membership (two positions of the society are necessarily held by women), is almost exclusively a men's organization. For a woman to join she is openly setting herself apart from others. . . . When Mulbah ordered V. to cook the society's food he was offering her membership. [Bellman, 1969, p. 26]

44

Mulbah broke the rules of the society in order to achieve certain ends and was certain he would incur only a mild rebuke. Even more significant for our purposes, however, is that nowhere were these matters stated by the parties to the case. They continued to be bound by *ifa mo* in their dealings with one another.

In a society where secrecy is a major social phenomenon, asking questions is also a very delicate enterprise. For instance, the question "who are you?" is a common form of abuse in an argument. According to Bellman, "to ask a question is to demand the other make his knowledge public. This knowledge, when asked for, is counterposed to the other's knowledge either as a challenge or as a membership testing device" (p. 9). Because the Kpelle behave very much as if "knowledge means power" in a literal sense, asking questions about people is not the trivial matter that it usually is to us. (This is a fact to be remembered when one performs experiments that are preceded by a questionnaire concerning various items of information about the subject and his family!)

A further illustration of the importance of secrecy to status-conscious Kpelle elders arose when John Gay was asking a village blacksmith a series of questions about the sale of his goods. In one of these questions the blacksmith had to calculate how much he would earn from the sale of six axes. He gave the correct answer, but was angered when Gay asked how he knew the answer. He asked Gay in turn for his sources of information, implying clearly that such information is not for public consumption.

Secrecy is not, however, an either-or matter. Even where the injunction *ifa mo* is in force, it may apply only to direct and unequivocal speech. Indirect means are used to communicate messages that would never be stated directly. In the story previously told, V. and the others all knew the meaning of the request to cook and eat the food, yet none of them stated it. The request itself within the particular setting was sufficient to communicate Mulbah's desire for his niece to become a member of the society.

Certain special modes are commonly used for indirect communication. Foremost among these are tales and proverbs, which can be used to give instructions to children, warn persons against ill-considered behavior, sum up an argument, or convey information to members of a select group. Stories are told commonly in the evening; the child listens and learns, gathering a store of tales and contexts. Proverbs, usually with an explicit moral, are used on a wide variety of occasions. As a person progresses toward the status of an elder, he learns more stories and proverbs as well as more circumstances under which he can apply them.

An illustration of indirect speech seemingly used inappropriately occurred on an occasion when an old man came to the Gay family selling grapefruit. At that time the Gays spoke no Kpelle, and so a schoolboy who was working for them translated the old man's words. He had great difficulty doing so, because, as he explained later, the old man was speaking "deep Kpelle." Gay pressed the boy on the point, and it seemed that "deep Kpelle" consists of language that is complex, not so much because of intricate vocabulary or syntax, as because of an extensive use of proverbs. The old man may have been using proverbs because he believed the Gays were mature enough to understand them, but the boy who was the intermediary could not interpret them. Had this young man remained a part of traditional Kpelle culture, he would have learned the "deep Kpelle" over the course of years.

In addition to knowing *how* to use proverbs, the individual has to know *when* to use them. He would have to wait, for example, until he was old enough, since it is disrespectful for a young man to quote proverbs to his elders. A proverb illustrates the problem: "Sitting quietly will reveal alligator's tricks"—only by careful watching and waiting will the young person come to understand his elders and their ways; revealing himself too soon can do no good and may be counterproductive.

Great reliance is placed on clever speech as a means to attaining status in Kpelle society in institutional as well as informal ways. Disputes are settled by the chief and the town elders either by the relatively informal "house palaver" or by the somewhat more formal court case. Physical force, witchcraft, and sorcery are frowned upon. The formal arena for resolving conflicts is often the chief's "palaver house," a large circular structure with a thatched roof and low walls where people gather to discuss matters of interest and settle disputes.

If one member of the village lodges a complaint against another member, the quarter or town chief seeks to resolve the issue informally at first, by going with some of the elders to the house of one of the principals. There he uses his skill to reconcile the two parties, airing the issues and seeking by compromise to reduce conflict within the community without causing a change in the status quo. If he fails, however, to achieve reconciliation, the case moves to the more formal court. The intention of such cases is to restore village harmony by a decisive action, even if the status quo is altered. Court cases provide a setting for the exercise of argumentative skills. We will look more closely at one such case as an example of the use of logic and evidence in Chapter 6.

These examples, by no means exhaustive, suggest some ways in which rather subtle forms of cognitive activity occur in common, everyday situations. It is our impression that to a larger extent than is true in American society, among the Kpelle the acquisition of status and power are the result of the application of intellectual skills to social life. About a farmer, one can say only that he is hard working or lazy, his success being judged as the result of his effort. But in social matters a successful man is one who is clever in manipulating his fellow townsfolk and proficient in the careful use of wealth, age, and knowledge.

At present we can only point to the suggestive examples that we have collected. These indicate that social interactions are a source of data for the study of problem-solving skills that may not be evident in activities such as farming and house building. Until systematic data are available, however, examples will have to suffice.

The Encroachment of Kwii Society: Schools and the Schoolchild

Although traditions, particularly as enshrined in the secret societies and in the elders, are still very important among the Kpelle, the power of Western culture is becoming greater every year. Although its impact is felt everywhere in Kpelle society through the money economy and taxation, nowhere is Westernization's influence felt more than through the schools.

Yet schoolchildren are not necessarily *kwii;* specifically, a few years of school attendance do not constitute grounds for being considered *kwii*. Most of the children in Sinyee attend school for a few years. They learn to speak English and many become to some degree literate. However, their early schooling is likely to be interrupted for lengthy periods during which they are expected to help with the farming or other family business. They attend secret society initiation school, but at present only during school vacation.

The elementary schoolchild in a village such as Sinyee is thus the locus of the struggle between traditional Kpelle society and the *kwii* way. Traditional Kpelle upbringing is ranged against the new institutions, personified by the government school and its teaching, in a struggle for the child's allegiance. As a rule, the school is physically outside the traditional boundaries of the town, along with the teacher's house, the Lebanese store, and other Western buildings. In the town Bellman studied, the "old town" is surrounded by a vine, outside of which there is said to be no law. The "new" institutions, such as the school and the clinic, are in the lawless portion, outside the tradition.

In many cases the competition between Kpelle tradition and the *kwii* way is won by at least a modified version of the traditional way. Statistics compiled by AID show that a very large percentage of all children who entered first grade in 1956 dropped out of school by the fourth grade and most dropped out by the seventh grade. Those who drop out may do so because they do not have the money to provide books and uniforms, because their families put inordinate pressure on them to work on the farm, because they are involved in an unexpected pregnancy, because they are expelled, or because they cannot maintain passing grades. The economic reason is probably the most important, since feeding, clothing, and supplying an economically unproductive and socially uncooperative schoolboy will eat up a high proportion of the cash income of a family, with no visible return. Children are frequently told to fend for themselves if they wish to remain in school.

A critical point for the child comes when he graduates from the sixth grade. A national examination administered at the end of the sixth grade determines promotion to the next level. Should he choose to continue his education, a child who passes this sixth-grade examination will probably have to leave his home in order to attend junior high school and will no longer be subject to traditional calls on his labor by his family or village. The child who does not pass this examination or who does not go to junior high school for some other reason will probably fall back into village routine unless he leaves to make his way at a mining company or urban center. Moreover, even if he does make an effort to enter the *kwii* world, whether by further schooling or by deeper involvement in the money economy, he remains tied to his family and the more slowly changing world of the partially educated Kpelle adult. He is expected to send home money, to care for relatives who visit him, and to continue his connections through periodic visits. He may even be expected to support younger brothers or sisters who follow him to school.

The School Environment

While the schoolchild shares most of the other influences from the *kwii* world with his parents, only he knows the school influence. It is to be expected that formal schooling will have a significant effect on his cognitive process, but before we can understand that effect, we must understand the situation within which that effect is achieved.

By American standards the rural elementary school in Liberia is marked by overcrowding, poorly prepared and poorly paid teachers, rigid and often irrelevant curricula, ill-equipped schools, lack of textbooks, parental indifference, and linguistic and tribal confusion. In the Sinyee school in a recent year 250 children were in the first grade, divided into four sections, depending on the child's knowledge of English. Two teachers taught two sections each, one in the morning and one in the afternoon. Children in the lower sections knew essentially no English and would not move to the upper section until their teacher deemed their performance satisfactory, a process that may take several years. High dropout rates mean that upper-level classes are less crowded, but the confusion of age levels consequent on the variations in time spent in first grade remains throughout the school system.

Older teachers in the elementary schools have often had only six years of school themselves, and their education may have been received under even more adverse circumstances than that of their pupils. An attempt is being made to increase the educational level of teachers through teacher-training programs. However, the methods used to prepare teachers are at times no better than those we have observed in the village schools. Teachers are paid poorly, and when questioned, many indicate that they stay in the profession only because they cannot get another better-paying job. A college graduate with a degree in education, for instance, can expect to earn only $125 per month if he enters teaching, whereas he can earn $250 as a clerk in a Monrovia bank. Teachers with less education may earn as little as $30 per month and thus may have to eke out a living by making a farm or by teaching in the morning in one school and in the evening in another.

The curriculum in the Liberian school is set by the Department of Education and follows very closely the pattern of American schools. Textbooks are almost always American, either castoffs or new books, and their content is at best marginally relevant to the Kpelle child's world. The national examinations at the end of the sixth, ninth, and twelfth grades determine the content of instruction, and the students greatly resent a teacher straying from the specific material upon which they will be examined. As a consequence, even well-trained teachers are pressured to provide rote teaching. Perhaps this is why rote learning of a set sequence of facts is the dominant style.

Not only are the textbooks largely irrelevant to Liberian experience, but also they are expensive and in very short supply. The government has been making serious efforts recently to find more books, but their cost is prohibitive to most children even when they are available. This means either that the child must work, must use the books of others, must leave school, or must have no books. The schools are generally ill-equipped in other ways, too; libraries are minimal or nonexistent, and teaching aids are rudimentary.

It is clear that useful teaching aids can be found in the village itself. Many elementary subjects can be best taught if local materials and experience are brought into the school. However, the isolation of school activities from the village is almost complete. Neither students nor teachers integrate or correlate the two domains. In Sinyee townspeople use the school yard as a place to dry clothing and otherwise never enter the buildings unless there is a special occasion to which they are called by the town chief.

Finally, there is a major linguistic confusion in the schools. Liberian English differs in many ways from standard English: (1) it has a different phonology, for example, the absence of final consonants; (2) it has its own syntax, such as a system with two future tenses, one immediate and one remote; and (3) its vocabulary varies widely from standard English. The teacher speaks one variety of Liberian English, children speak more rudimentary varieties, and the textbooks are written in standard English. This creates vast linguistic confusions, a situation made worse by the fact that most of the teachers do not understand the true state of affairs. Spelling, for instance, is made very difficult when the standard orthography differs widely from the speech patterns. (Compare, for example, the work of Labov, 1969, with black children in New York City ghettos.) We reported in our earlier work (Gay and Cole, 1967, p. 32) the difficulty caused by the English phrase "as many as," which was interpreted in Liberian English as "more than" for perfectly understandable phonetic and syntactic reasons.

The teacher, who may have the best of intentions, is faced with an overwhelmingly difficult job. To the young child the school probably seems completely without meaning. We thus must ask what constitutes a reasonable adaptation to this school environment on the part of the student. It is our feeling that the child would adopt what most observers would call rote learning. Given an extremely chaotic situation in which few concepts are clearly taught, and even then taught in an unfamiliar language, the best way to survive is to pick out certain salient features of the situation and simply memorize them. These features may be words, phrases, mannerisms of the teacher, or even more extraneous characteristics of school life. The extremes to which present schooling practices can lead is illustrated by a story from Hugh Bradley of the Education Development Center. A child who was asked to recite the multiplication tables for his teacher began "la-di-da-di-da, la-di-da-di-da," at which point the teacher interrupted to ask him what he was saying. He responded that he knew the tune but he did not yet know the words.

We are relatively certain that the same phenomenon appears in other, less amusing ways in many classroom situations; for instance, it is a standard procedure for graduating classes of sixth graders to memorize some heroic English poem as a graduation exercise. Although it is virtually certain that the children have little understanding of the poem, they give a reasonably accurate rendition, to the apparent satisfaction of all. One reason for the satisfaction is that completion of sixth grade carries with it status. This new status, in turn, creates new problems for Kpelle society.

The Social Context of the School

Of importance to the Kpelle child is not only his experience in school, but also the very fact that he *attends* school. Western-style schools are a relatively recent innovation in Kpelleland. They are a source of culture contact and culture conflict, and the child who attends school is the focus of both contact and conflict.

Discussions with the children and their elders reflect, sometimes poignantly, the problems which school causes—the cultural confusion of those choosing the *kwii* way, the stubborn conservatism of those who remain behind. Several elders in Sinyee were asked how they thought a child should change as a result of his education. They stressed that the child should learn (in descending order of frequency) right and wrong, the history, customs, and traditions of his people, respect for the elders of the community, and skill at making a living. The methods they suggested for learning were as traditional as the changes desired in a child.

These elders felt that a child who does not listen should be beaten or else told frightening stories of spirits or ghosts. He should be advised how to correct his mistakes and be allowed to watch his elders as they perform their daily tasks. The ideal educational product is one who will respect his elders, make a living, know the traditions, and be courageous.

We asked high-school students to record for us the kinds of things they learned from their parents and other elders before they entered the *kwii* world. They report learning to make mats, wash themselves, care for the house, cook their food, and whatever else is required for life. If they made mistakes, they were corrected, or, if the mistake continued, beaten. One student says:

When I was small as far as I can remember, the first major thing I learned was not to be too avaricious. I was also taught to thank people when they gave me anything. If I do a good thing sometimes by bringing wood or fishing for the house, I was rewarded with sometimes a big bowl of rice or with candy; so the reward of doing right is a good name or prize, and the reward of wrong is punishment.

The traditions of the Kpelle people concerning their ancestors were learned through songs and stories. One student says: "I suppose my grandmother and elders of our family taught us these not only as songs and stories, but also for their significance in our daily life, in order to teach people not to be greedy, not to be jealous, not to make trouble, and not to boast."

Students report how they listened with pleasure to the stories and instructions of their elders, how they went to the farm and enjoyed the work, even though it was hard, how they listened and learned while the elders discussed serious matters. They report their childhood as a time of joy and growth. Yet these same students left the traditional world and went to school. Somehow the old way lost its appeal and much of its meaning as they grew up.

Schools are an important focus of this change, which carries with it a clear devaluation of traditional culture. A Kpelle college student reported that, whereas he learned many things and came to his full tribal manhood in the year he spent in the initiation school, during the whole time he was concerned about his chances for a Western education. He found to his disgust that, when he returned to the government school, "my mind had fallen back into ignorance and I had to struggle most severely to keep up with the fourth-grade class."

The secret society bush school, which was formerly a major experience of the Kpelle boy or girl, has now become a pale imitation of its former self. The power of the experience has been lost, an experience intended by the Kpelle elders to shape the child into an adult. An account by John Kellemu of the closing ceremonies of the girls' bush school in two Kpelle towns makes the point very forcefully. He attended the ceremonies, only to find that much of what he remembered from his own childhood had been lost. He noticed a two-year-old girl in the group of initiates and asked himself what she could have learned. He looked more carefully at the others and saw that they too had only superficially been initiated into the Kpelle traditions. As a result, he says:

Without any hesitation I would say that the Poro and Sande bush schools in general terms have lost their former meaning. They are no longer performing their traditional function: to prepare the individual to be adjusted economically, socially, religiously, and even physically to his society.

The traditional economic life of the people has changed radically with the coming of the road and the Western society that the road brings with it. The secret-society bush school is losing its role as the place where one learns to live as a Kpelle man or woman.

Kellemu points out:

In this transitional period the emphasis (in bush school) is now placed on something that is social in character. That is, the mere sense of belonging. It is becoming quite clear that most matters concerning the community are no longer settled by the *zoo* and the traditional chiefs in Poro and Sande bush, but by government authority. As a result, most people are now interested in membership in the Poro and Sande merely for the fact that they become, by joining, respectable or acceptable members of their community, since everybody else accepts them as part of long-established social institutions.

Significantly, social etiquette seems to dominate the teaching in the much-abbreviated bush school. The girls have learned respect for their elders and the proper way to show this respect, and this respect is displayed in the ceremonies at the termination of bush school. The girls, moreover, are dressed in all their best finery, but the clothing and the ornaments are Western in character.

The Western way, the way of the *kwii* person, is changing the Kpelle way of life, and changes in the bush school reflect changes in the traditional way of life. Kellemu describes the conflict as follows:

The conflict is this. The Poro and Sande bush schools are all institutions of long standing, whose meanings and values are printed in the minds of our people. These values have become the center of the Kpelle culture. On the

53

contrary, the Western type of education is new to the culture. Its new standards of value tend to give new interpretations to the Kpelle standards, which in most cases are the opposite of the old standards. As such, it sometimes means a total change. As a result, the *kwii* way (Western culture, as it is called in Liberia) of life is in itself a paradox to our people. To them, it is good and yet destructive. The *kwii* way has broken up tribal institutions, disorganized native villages and the whole society, outlawed native laws and practices, and has made children disrespectful toward the traditional way of life. The *kwii* way is at times oppressive and demanding, giving little in return.

Kellemu says that the tribal elder cannot understand the long-term benefits of education or plantation employment. He only sees the short-term disadvantages, wherein he has to pay a crushing tax and is required to perform labor for the government. He sees the old ways as necessary in order to give him satisfaction in life. The bush school is the last symbol of that satisfaction. Even though the children do not learn Kpelle culture in depth, at least they receive the membership, and the manners that the elders treasure.

The pathos and the conflicts that are centered on the schoolchild are reflected in the answers to a series of questions we put to Kpelle students at an interior high school, in the town of Bolahun, itself far from Kpelle country. The very fact of their being in this high school shows their separation from traditional Kpelle life. These students grew up within the Kpelle culture, but left it to enter a new and different world. They look at both worlds as persons who belong to both, and yet do not belong to either. One student reports his fear of "war, generators, powers, Satan, and trouble," a combination of the old and the new. Most look forward to having money, power, and Western luxuries after they leave school. Yet, paradoxically, for all the boys Western goods are to be the means for success and influence among their own people.

All the boys look forward to the day when they will be important men in their own communities. They do not expect to live in the same fashion as the traditional Kpelle, but they expect to be part of their society. This combination, whereby tradition and Westernization together lead to a position of authority, is reflected in the comment of one boy: "I will change my family by showing them the right way to live if I have the opportunity. The relation is that we are all one." The right way to live is one in which Western improvements are brought into the Kpelle scene and integrated with it.

And yet this is difficult, as one boy pointed out:

54

There are many things I've done which have helped to change my family. I have encouraged my people to send many of my brothers and sisters to school. The relation between my family and me is quite different from what it used to be. Now I'm no longer able to communicate with my family as much as I used to do. There are many things my people do which I consider wrong, such as drinking dirty water, living in an area with lots of dirt around.

The estrangement between these boys and their families is not complete, but relations are difficult. One boy stated that he did not feel that any-one in his family cared for him because they did not provide him with the means of maintaining himself at school. Three of the boys report that they depend on a family from the *kwii* community to give them the support, advice, and help that they need in school. When the boys come back home for vacation, they report that they are received well, but that they do not feel a sense of belonging.

They look forward to the day when they lessen the estrangement be-tween them and their families by bringing others into the *kwii* world. All speak of sending their younger brothers and sisters to school. They announce with certainty that their own children will not have to be brought up as they themselves were brought up—no more carrying wood, walking from town to town, dressing in shabby clothes, working on the farm during school hours, marrying several wives, or believing in witchcraft and spirits.

Clearly, the ambition of some Kpelle high-school students is to live differently (most would say, better) than their parents and to reject as-pects of their traditional culture that they now view as difficult and con-fining. They look down on the uneducated country person and appar-ently accept many Western stereotypes concerning so-called primitive life. One spoke of the relations between the sexes: he tries to treat girls in a polite and educated fashion, not like the uneducated man who beats his girl friend so that she cries. Another says "uneducated people treat women different kinds of ways which I hate to see or hear about." All but one of the boys assert they will marry someone different from their family's choice, since they plan to choose a girl from the educated com-munity.

The high-school students are very hopeful about the power of the ed-ucation they are receiving. One says:

There are many things I know that will contribute to the changes of the world. If there is peace, love, good education, and moral kindness, and if people live in peace, there will always be progress. The things that will most change the world are good education and love for all men. The idea of kindness will not change, but the idea about things that are true today may change tomorrow.

Another says: "An educated man desires and gets things as he wishes." According to still another: "An educated man is able to get most of the things he needs and desires. He is able to ask people to help him by writing to them and asking for help."

The rejection of Kpelle culture goes deeper than merely the material affairs of life. One student feels more at home in English:

There are only a few words that stand for different things in my language, but in English there are numerous ways of expressing the same idea. All these ways make our language different from English. The only things that I am able to say or talk about more easily in my language are proverbs, and the name of trees and other things. Most of the time if I want to express myself more fully I speak English because this gives more freedom to say many more things that I am unable to express fully in my language.

Some students reject traditions about medicine and spirits and witch-craft. Concerning the traditional Kpelle medical practitioner, for in-stance, our informant said: "I know country doctors have medicine to cure things like worm tro ᵇble, headaches, and other small troubles. But I know they can't make me sick in any supernatural way, so I don't fear them." This is not, however, the majority opinion. Most tell of members of their family who have been killed through witchcraft or who have practiced witchcraft; many tell of seeing spirits in the night. A charac-teristically ambivalent story is the following:

One time my father was sick. They said that ancestors are making him sick because they were not satisfied with him and so were vexed with him. I went there and they told me. I told him to go to the hospital, but he said no. So they made a sacrifice and he got well. I didn't believe it.

Another boy tells of an experience on the trail:

When we were coming from the farm, I once saw a man in a hammock on the shoulders of the other men. When I told my uncle to look he looked and looked but he saw nothing. From that moment, I was unable to talk until we got to town. I bathed with cold water before I could talk.

The ambivalence extends to their relation with the Poro and Sande secret societies. Most report fearing their initiation into the tribal tradi-tion, and most also report a sense of community with others in the tribe as a result of the initiation. Yet one says, "I really do not know why my parents sent me there." He complains that he learned only "if you go to bush school we will be able to keep secrets, not to talk people's secrets outside."

However, the students look at the Western school system as itself a kind of initiation into an adult society. The boy in the bush school had to learn respect for the elders and traditions of the Kpelle people; schoolchildren now learn to respect new institutions. One student reports that as he learns civilized ways, he and his parents can no longer understand one another. He says of the elders of Kpelle society, "I don't believe in some of their ways of life, and there are some of them I really believe in."

Another student describes his respect for the elders, the chief, and the *zoo* in his village: "I feel that I should pay proper respect to them because I don't want them to feel bad about me. I don't want them to think since I am going to school I don't respect them any more." He rejects the ancestral traditions that shaped the lives and attitudes of his elders, even though he does not reject these elders as individuals.

The Influences of Education

Our overall impression of the schoolchild and his social environment is one of extreme complexity. The Kpelle schoolchild is a mixture of the traditional and the modern. Moreover, it is clear that not all of the "modern" elements would be considered to represent "progress" by even the most enthusiastic advocates of modernization.

We can offer some tentative generalizations about important ways in which the school affects the Kpelle child which may be relevant to our study of cognitive processes. First, the child is systematically exposed to an entirely new set of ideas and institutions, which are presented as *the* correct way to live, the wave of the future. As our interviews indicated, the propaganda of progress has had an effect on the child. Second, the child is exposed to writing as a form of expressing ideas and solving hypothetical problems that may exist outside the classroom. Both literacy and learning detached from the immediate situation are likely to have significant effects on cognition. In school the use of language is essential to all problem-solving activities, including the technological. In fact, the whole notion of technology becomes more complex and more analytic. The 4-H activities at the school, such as the introduction of swamp rice, which the children grow as part of a national competition, take farming out of the matrix of traditional social activities and make it a problem to be solved.

On the negative side we have the barren educational environment of the classroom. A great deal of the learning that occurs can hardly be characterized as problem solving in the usual sense, and it is possible that learning capabilities are actually retarded by incoherent or rigid instruction. Moreover, the negative and hostile attitudes that many successful schoolchildren develop toward their families and social groups are scarcely compensated for by the learning that occurs in six years of schooling. By virtue of the prestige resulting from the completion of elementary school, a man no longer considers rice farming a fit activity for his talents. But measured by the yardstick of the modern economy, he has no talents save rice farming. The result of this conflict is, to say the least, often a less than effective individual.

Our brief sketch of the ways of life and the thoughts of the Kpelle raised within the traditional and the Western educational systems suggests major differences between the two. Accordingly, the contrast between those with and without the experience of Western schools forms a basic feature of most of our experimental comparisons. Whatever the dimension of difference (literate-nonliterate; traditional-*kwii;* conservative-modernizing) that ultimately defines these groups, we can be assured that they differ on many ethnographic dimensions. Whether they differ on our cognitive tasks as well remains a matter of empirical concern.

THREE : Classification

A person behaves toward things in a
manner that is similar to the manner in
which he talks about the things that he
behaves towards.

V. STEFFLRE

Introduction

Our concern with the cultural context of experimentation led us naturally to a study of the Kpelle language as an integral part of our study
of learning and thinking processes among the Kpelle. But when we turn
to the study of language, we are faced with the same problem that con-
fronted us in presenting ethnographic background data on the Kpelle: to
present a complete analysis of the grammar and vocabulary of the
Kpelle language would be a giant undertaking and in some respects be-
side the point.

Among all the linguistic issues upon which we might have focused
our analysis of the Kpelle language, we chose to concentrate on the
classification of natural-world objects in the Kpelle noun system. Our
reasons for this choice were compounded of historical precedent, theoretical relevance, and our own skills in studying the relation between
language and nonlinguistic behaviors.

To begin with, we needed to have a basis for evaluating the anthropologist's claim that presumed differences in cognitive processes are reducible to differences in the way two cultural groups classify some areas
of experience (Boas, 1911; Rivers, 1926). This viewpoint leads the ethnoscientist to make the study of classification a keystone in the study of
cognitive anthropology (Romney and D'Andrade, 1964). A similar line
of reasoning motivates the Whorfian cultural relativist, who maintains
that distinctions coded in the individual's language will determine all
manner of thought processes, ranging from what seem to be perceptual
groupings all the way to ethics and a world view (Whorf, 1956).

As we tried to make clear in Chapter 1, inferences of cognitive differences such as those made by the anthropologist do not entirely satisfy psychologists, who require in addition that we relate linguistic differences to nonlinguistic behaviors. The issue is put quite succinctly by Carroll and Cassagrande.

. . . it is not sufficient merely to point to differences between languages and to assume that users of these languages have correspondingly different mental experiences. If we are not to be guilty of circular inference, it is necessary to show some correspondence between the presence or absence of a certain linguistic phenomenon and the presence or absence of a certain kind of non-linguistic response. [1958, p. 21]

Consequently, the psychologist must concern himself not only with naturally encountered linguistic categories, but must seek to relate these to various other kinds of linguistic and nonlinguistic behaviors.

For example, an understanding of basic categories is absolutely necessary for the interpretation of concept-learning and memory experiments. If we construct a task that requires a subject to classify objects into two classes, it is going to make a great deal of difference whether or not those classes are familiar to him; learning to identify a known class and learning a new classification are very different processes (Kendler, 1964).

A related problem occurs in research on memory such as that discussed in Chapter 4. In some of our early learning research, we had focused on the degree to which the Kpelle use noun classes to organize memory for common objects. Under circumstances where we had initially expected to find categorically organized memory, no such organization was to be found and performance was generally poor by American standards. In bygone eras such a performance difference might have led to the conclusion that the Kpelle are incapable of "normal" memorizing. While rejecting such a conclusion, the lack of categorical organization posed an important problem of interpretation: was category organization absent, or had we merely incorrectly understood the way in which the Kpelle categorized this material?

A related factor that is important in the cross-cultural experimental study of thinking is the possibility that an accepted classification in one culture is not recognized in another. If an Anglo child classifies an eagle as a land animal he would be considered wrong, but not so the Osage Indian child. Similarly, when one looks for categorical organization in memory, he had best understand what categories are used by his subjects.

The approach we have adopted in this chapter represents our effort to combine techniques that have traditionally been used by the linguist, anthropologist, and psychologist in the study of classification. To begin with, we investigate basic classes and their relationships for the very general domain of "things" as coded in the Kpelle language, using two techniques borrowed from linguistic anthropology and one from psychology. Each of these techniques relies on face-to-face interactions between a trained observer, or experimenter, and an informant (sometimes we will use the term *informant,* sometimes *subject*). Each takes verbal behavior as its sole datum.

Once the basic categories have been determined for a variety of situations in which people talk about things, we turn to the task of determining the relation between the way things are classified in verbal behavior and the classifications that occur when objects are presented for classification. In addition, in several instances our study of classification is carried out independently on different subgroups of Kpelle people as those subgroups are defined in Chapter 2.

The *Seŋ* Chart: Classification of "Things"

We began our study of classification with the term *seŋ,* roughly translatable as "thing," the most general noun in the Kpelle language. Our first approach was to attempt to elicit specific examples of *seŋ* in order to obtain a taxonomy for the term. Our hope was that this taxonomy would provide an organization of visually and spatially definite objects in the Kpelle language on the basis of which we could then undertake studies of the cognitive uses of this domain. This work was carried out by John Kellemu, who was himself raised in the traditional Kpelle town of Parakole and who has retained much of his concern for Kpelle culture, despite his sixteen years of Western education.

In seeking a technique that would elicit a semantic classification scheme (if such existed), we finally settled on a watered-down version of the technique arising from the work of Metzger and Williams (1966). The basic question we used to elicit subclasses of the general term *seŋ* was of the form _____ káa à _____, which can be translated _____ is a _____. In some uses of this question, the first slot was filled by the name of an object and the second with a question word, as, for example, "banana is a what?" answered by, for example, "banana is a food." In others the object name was in the second slot and a question word in the first slot, as, for example, "a what is food?" answered by, for example, "a banana is food." A possible ambiguity lurks in this second formulation, but we were able to establish our usage as "what is an example of food?" rather than "what is the meaning of food?"

This question was repeated in many ways, using many terms, in order to find examples of class inclusion and subordination. At some point in the questioning procedure, the elders would be unable to name a special case for a particular term, indicating that we had reached a minimal species. An example of this is the series of questions and answers: "what is a thing?" "a tree is a thing," "what is a tree?" "a corkwood tree is a tree," "what is a corkwood tree?" No answer is given to the last question, indicating that the informant has reached the lowest level of generality.

At other points it seemed that the informants had leaped over several levels of generality. For example, in the exchange "what is a thing?" "a corkwood tree is a thing," clearly several levels exist between "thing" and "corkwood tree." In order to verify the existence of these intermediate levels, Kellemu reversed the questioning order and asked "a corkwood tree is what?" and if the subject said merely "a corkwood tree is a thing," asked "a corkwood tree is what else?" This question generally elicited other examples of the general term in question.

Kellemu began developing a first approximation to a classification scheme by close questioning of a small group of Kpelle elders. He suggested what seemed to him appropriate class headings and subclasses. The men agreed on most of the categories but refined and modified Kellemu's original intuitions. The revised framework was then used as the basis for questioning other Kpelle elders. They were not asked if the structure was correct, but rather the terms that had emerged from the informal interviewing were used in the first and second slots of the basic question _____ is a _____ to determine the correctness of the classification scheme which had been set up informally as a first approximation.

Where there was disagreement among several informants, Kellemu opened the question to group discussion. In some cases the men were able to resolve the questions in unambiguous fashion. In others they continued to disagree. He checked the resulting chart of class relations by opening it to general discussion in which the meanings of the particular terms were discussed in terms of their place in the organization of classes.

After this phase of the inquiry was complete, Kellemu went over the entire set of results very carefully with Yakpalo Doŋ, John Gay's Kpelle informant. Between them they found many more examples of each class, so that the lowest level on the chart was as complete as possible. They did not change the organization of classes at this stage, but maintained the basic structure elicited by the elders.

The subclasses of *seŋ* elicited and constructed by John Kellemu are given in outline form in Table 3–1. This table shows the ordered system from the most general term down to the most specific objects. Although we were seeking a taxonomy of the domain of things, Table 3–1 can best be considered an approximate taxonomy, because the table includes certain ambiguities in that several subclasses are members of more than one main class (a description of the major subclasses is contained in Appendix A).

In many, if not all cases, the ambiguities in classification arose because of the enormous complexity of classifying, subclassifying, and cross-classifying such a large domain of objects. As a consequence of the diversity of things being classified, the basis of classification often shifted in subtle ways.

The following example may serve to make these difficulties understandable. Suppose that someone asked an American college student for a classification of things. He might answer all things are living or inanimate. How then would he classify such things as a farm, or the earth, or food? Clearly, the choice would depend on ad hoc criteria made up for the purpose. At several points in working out the various subsets of things and their relations, Kellemu encountered the problem of shifting criteria of classification leading to the overlapping categories in Table 3–1. For example, a banana is a *town thing* insofar as it is a kind of food, but a *forest thing* insofar as it grows on a tree in the forest.

As a consequence of these difficulties, we were not content to accept the organization of Kpelle nouns as represented in the *seŋ* chart of Table 3–1 as a definitive picture of Kpelle noun classes and their organization. In addition to the ambiguities arising from shifting bases of classification, we were also concerned about the propriety of the technique we applied to elicit the chart; how much of John Kellemu's *kwii* education is contained in the structure of the *seŋ* chart? How much acquiescence (as contrasted with lexical knowledge) did he elicit from his

63

TABLE 3-1

Things

	TOWN THINGS					FOREST THINGS									
PLAYING THINGS	PEOPLE	TOWN WORKS	TOWN ANIMALS	WORKING THINGS	THE EARTH[a]	THE EARTH[a]	TRAPS[c]	ANIMALS	ROOT CROPS	WATER FOODS	MUSH-ROOMS	VINES	TREES	SHRUBS	EVIL THINGS[b]
dancing equip-ment	children	houses	walking animals	vehicles	dirt	dirt		hoof (two-part)	wild	water		wild	wild	wild	poro head
dancers	adults	sheds	birds	medicines	stone	stone		hoof (four-part)	planted	oil		planted	planted	planted	sande head
drums	good people	fences		herbs	sand	sand		claw		honey					fearful things
horns	evil people	bench		charms	mud	mud		dragging							witches
games	workmen	loom		societies				snakes							genii
	status			evil				snails							dwarfs
	appearance			divining				fish							spirits
				western				nonscaly							
				household things				scaly							
				sleeping things				worms							
				beds				crawling							
				cloths				edible							
				mats				nonedible							
				tools				water							
				clothing				burrowing							
				cooking things				tree							
				utensils				leaping							
				foods				edible							
				prepared forest[b]				nonedible							
				traps[c]				flying							
								birds							
								insects							
								edible							
								nonedible							

[a] The earth is a major subclass of both town and forest things.

[b] The edible forest things within the dotted lines are also a subclass of town things as indicated.

[c] Traps are a major category of forest things and a subcategory of town things.

informants? Would alternative classification schemes emerge if other eliciting techniques had been used?

Because an accurate assessment of the basic categorical structure of material used in our learning studies was critical to a correct interpretation of cultural differences, we undertook the detailed study of noun classes presented here.

Sentence Substitution

As a first step toward assessing the *seŋ* chart's representation of the structure of Kpelle noun classes, we chose a technique designed to minimize the inquirer's influence on the informant. Using class names selected from the *seŋ* chart, informants were asked to make up sentences employing each of these words. Then he was asked which of the words could sensibly be used in which sentences. The resulting data matrix, reflecting the degree to which words could be used interchangeably in different sentences, was analyzed, using a technique developed by Steffire (1963), in which the set of words was rearranged so that those that substituted in a similar manner into the various sentences are placed near each other. Our concern was to determine if words classified together on the *seŋ* chart would appear as groups according to this sentence-substitution method. In general, classes defined by the *seŋ* chart appeared again in the results of this study.

The sentence-substitution method is described in more detail in Appendix B. In order to understand the rationale for its use in the present context, however, it is probably sufficient to know that it arrives at its classes by determining the similarity in the way nouns are used in Kpelle sentences and that no substantive restrictions were placed on the kinds of sentences that people used. These features led us to hope that the method would be free of difficulties that might have existed in Kellemu's elicitation of the *seŋ* chart.

Several studies were undertaken to explore the relation between the class structure depicted in the *seŋ* chart and the class structure produced by the sentence-substitution method. Subjects for these studies were traditional Kpelle adults between the ages of eighteen and fifty years. Whenever possible, a sentence-substitution matrix for a given subject was elicited in a single session. However, if the informant showed signs of fatigue, the work was completed on the following day. Each study included data from five to ten informants, questioned individually. Each informant within a given study was presented with the same set of words, although the order of presentation was generally varied from one informant to the next. Informants made up their own sentences, except that completely general sentence frames (of the type, "I saw a_____") were discouraged if they occurred with great frequency. After the data had been collected from a group of informants, the individual data matrices were coded on data-processing cards, summed over subjects, and subjected to analysis.

The first study using this technique (details are included in Appendix B) employed thirty-five terms from all parts of the *seŋ* chart. Its major features can be summarized as follows: The major split between *town* and *forest things* and most of the classes at the next level of specificity are approximately maintained. However, ambiguities masked by, but present within, the orderly presentation of the *seŋ* chart appear. For example, *working things* does not appear as a unitary category; its ambiguous status in the chart is reflected by its tendency to divide into clumps that attach to other classes on the chart. *Cooking things* and *town animals* appear in a group next to *foods,* reflecting what seem to be natural relations that are suppressed in the search for order in the dichotomy between *town* and *forest* in the chart. Likewise, *structures* appears together with *clothing, tools,* and *sleeping things,* all of which are kept in the houses that compose the village.

Additional elicitations following the same procedure were subsequently made to evaluate relations within the two major groups, *town* and *forest.* In one case the terms were all *town things,* and in a second the terms were all *forest things.* In these studies the terms used included names of minimal species as well as general class names. In all these cases we observed ordering of the stimulus terms that was generally consistent with the ordering in the *seŋ* chart but often *seŋ*-chart distinctions failed to be reflected, and occasional large discrepancies were encountered (see Appendix B).

Free Association

In order to reduce the remaining ambiguity about class membership and interclass relations, one further kind of study was introduced, the free-association experiment. This technique for eliciting information about the structure of noun classes requires people to associate to words or other stimuli. For example, a person can be asked, "what do you think of when I say, 'cars'?" Properly analyzed, the free-association technique can provide evidence on the extent to which the set of stimuli (in our case, words from the *seŋ* chart) elicit each other and other words as associations. The strength of association among a set of stimuli, as well as class membership, can be evaluated, using both common associates (*cat* and *dog* both elicit the associate *hair*) and direct associations (*cat* and *dog* elicit each other) as indicators of the relationships among words (Deese, 1962). The details of this work as applied to the classes of the *seŋ* chart are contained in Appendix C. Once again the general result was a replication of the content of classes contained in the *seŋ* chart, although as was the case when the sentence-substitution method was used, the pattern of relationships among classes was often different, and in some cases class membership was different (for example, snake is grouped with items that fall in the class of *medicines* rather than the class of *animals*).

Discussion of Alternative Verbal-Eliciting Techniques

Before considering a more detailed exploration of a limited domain of nouns that we will use in connection with experiments to be described in later chapters, we would like to comment on the significance of the three general studies of the Kpelle domain of *seŋ*. Each of the techniques we used (formal elicitation, sentence substitution, and free association) has certain virtues and certain drawbacks. At first glance the formal inquiry carried out by John Kellemu would appear to be the most direct way to obtain information about class membership, class inclusion, and class subordination. At the same time our informants experienced some difficulty in keeping classes discrete because class membership is determined by the attributes considered important, and these central attributes shifted from time to time. Agreement about class membership once given the class name was not a problem, but items often were included in more than one class.

As the elicitation was made less constrained (using the sentence-substitution and free-association techniques), the ambiguities of class relation were more clearly expressed and the resultant structural description was less definite. The free-association task even gave rise to instances where the preferred responses to category names were members of different categories. All in all, our impression is one of considerably more variability and ambiguity than customarily appear in reports of linguistic elicitations of the type studied here.

To some extent the greater heterogeneity in our work with the *seŋ* classes is the result of our own relatively informal approach to elicitation and the overly ambitious attempt to describe the contents and relations among such a large set of classes. In addition the kinds of responses produced in each of the eliciting situations certainly depends upon subtleties of the way in which the informants interpret the aims of the elicitor. Considering all the possible sources of variation among the tasks, we have been impressed by the fact that the major contrasts and most of the specific classes of the *seŋ* chart repeatedly occurred in the different studies. However, the hierarchical relations among classes at lower levels of the chart probably represent only one of several possible ways in which various subclasses of *seŋ* can be related.

A Detailed Look at Words Used in Experimentation

For most experimental purposes the *seŋ* chart is too large a conglomerate to work with, although two studies described in Chapter 4 (pp. 94–96) are specifically concerned with organizational features of Table 3–1. In most of our memory and verbal-concept learning studies, we concentrated our attention on a relatively small subset of the things described in the *seŋ* chart.

Our experimental aims called for us to obtain two lists of twenty items each. Both lists had to consist of common nouns naming physical items that were small enough to be easily transported by our research assistants. One set of items (the categorizable list) was to consist of twenty words divisible into four closely knit classes (we chose *foods, tools, clothing,* and *utensils*), while items on the second list (hereafter referred to as the noncategorizable list) should have only minimal semantic connections with any other items on that list.

Our first objective was to obtain a set of common clusterable items. We hit upon the following informal listing procedure to generate the list. Our assistant walked around the local town recording the answers of adult informants to questions such as the following: "If you were to go to the market, what kind of things could you buy?" or "What kinds of things can you buy in Ukatu's store?" We assumed that objects named by a majority of the people questioned were relatively common. From the most commonly named objects, the list of twenty terms presented in the left-hand column of Table 3–2 was constructed. According to the *seŋ* chart, these twenty words fall into four separate semantic categories. Three of these are subheadings of the general heading,

TABLE 3-2

*List of Items Used in Kpelle Free-
Association and Experimental Studies*

CLUSTERABLE	NONCLUSTERABLE
plate	bottle
calabash	nickle
pot	chicken feather
pan	box
cup	battery
	animal horn
potato	stone
onion	book
banana	candle
orange	cotton
coconut	hard mat
	rope
cutlass	nail
hoe	cigarette
knife	stick
file	grass
hammer	pot
	knife
trousers	orange
singlet	shirt
headtie	
shirt	
hat	

household things (*clothes, tools,* and *utensils*), while the fourth consists of five instances from the general heading *food*, two from the subheading *root crops* (*onion* and *potato*), and three from the subheading *tree fruits* (*banana, orange,* and *coconut*). In terms of our desire to obtain clearly discrete "clusters," these classes do not appear to be optimal since three of our classes are subheadings of the general category, *household things*. But since we needed not only classes that were discrete but a list of common, familiar objects as well, our overall purpose seemed to have been fulfilled, although judgment about class discreteness had to await verification by verbal-elicitation studies.

A corresponding list of noncategorizable items was constructed in a different and slightly more haphazard manner. Working with two informants, we constructed a list of sixteen items that our informants claimed (1) were common objects known to everyone in Kpelle culture; (2) were small enough to be easily transported by our research assistants; and (3) if compared with our clusterable list and with each other, were judged to be dissimilar to the objects on the clusterable list and would themselves be dissimilar.

The list of sixteen noncategorizable items obtained in this informal manner is presented in the right-hand side of Table 3–2. For experimental purposes we added four terms from the categorizable list to this list to complete the set of twenty items.

The informal manner in which these lists were constructed was clearly not an adequate foundation for our experimental work. Not only did intuition play a large role in their construction, but what little evidence we had cast doubt on the cohesiveness of one class on the categorizable list. Consequently, the entire list of thirty-six items (the twenty categorizable and sixteen non-categorizable items) was subjected to the sentence substitution-analysis previously applied to the *seŋ* chart as a whole. The rearranged ordering of words from this analysis is presented in Table 3–3.

At the left side of Table 3–3, from top to bottom, are listed the thirty-six words in the order of their similarity to each other as defined by the technique. This list is separated at intervals defined by our a priori hypothesis that *utensils, clothing, food,* and *tools* would tend to group together in the list. Inspection of the table indicates that such groupings in fact occurred. There are three kinds of evidence for this in Table 3–3. First, in the rearranged order based on similarity scores (which reflect the extent to which two stimulus words substitute in a like manner into a variety of sentences), all of the hypothesized categorizable classes occurred in groups, separated by items from the noncategorizable list. It should be emphasized that these words were presented in different random orders to each subject. Hence the reordering was clearly not predetermined. Second, the average similarity number (which can vary from zero to one) for all the relations within a semantic group are consistently higher than the corresponding numbers between groups or between noncategorizable words. Third, the similarity among the items from the noncategorizable list is lower than among the categorizable items. These average similarity numbers are listed beneath the class name in the case of within-class scores, and between hypothetical classes in the case of between-class scores. We should note that Table

TABLE 3-3
Rearranged Experimental Terms

ITEM	SUBHEADING	HEADING
calabash bottle pot pan cup plate	utensils .814	household
. . . . .773		
box animal horn .797 book		
. . . . .756		
trousers singlet shirt headtie hat	household clothes .817	household
. . . . .693		
cotton rope .702 stick grass		
. . . . .689		
onion potato banana orange coconut	root crops .893 tree fruit .830	food .821
. . . . .684		
cigarette .766 nail		
. . . . .712		
file hammer hoe knife cutlass	tools .810	household
. . . . .656		
hard mat candle stone battery .679 chicken feather nickle		

3–3 reflects only the relative degree of "categorizability." The absolute size of the similarity score is affected by several factors. An important determinant of the overall level of similarity is the generality of the sentence frame used. This is why we emphasize the relative nature of "categorizability."

The results contained in Table 3–3 suggest that we have indeed hit upon two lists, one of which consists of relatively cohesive, distinct classes, while the other does not.

Free Association and the Experimental Terms: The Kpelle

One further study of the properties of the classes, *tools, utensils, food,* and *clothing* was undertaken, this time using free association as the eliciting device. The results are discussed here because up to now we have presented no data for Kpelle groups other than traditional adults and no data employing similar materials with American subjects.

In working with young subjects neither the formal eliciting procedure employed by Kellemu nor the sentence-substitution technique are easy to use. They both require periods of data collection considerably longer and more arduous than children are likely to cope with. The free-association technique, on the other hand, is quickly and easily administered. With proper analysis free-association data can yield information about category grouping that is comparable to the information yielded by the sentence-substitution technique.

Based on these considerations, free associations to the experimental words were studied in samples of subjects drawn from each of the following three Kpelle groups: (1) eighteen- to twenty-year-old students enrolled in the ninth to eleventh grades; (2) eighteen- to twenty-year-old nonliterate adults, who spoke little if any English; (3) ten- to fourteen-year-old children enrolled in the second to fourth grades. Each group was presented a list of twenty-four words one at a time (the twenty clusterable terms detailed above, and the four appropriate category names, *food, tools, clothing,* and *utensils.*) The lists were presented in a random order, and each subject was required to give at least four responses to each stimulus word if possible. All responses were tape-recorded for later transcription; then the data were analyzed according to the technique described in Appendix C. Because the results for the three groups were quite similar, with an average correlation between group performance of .89, we present only the data for the group most similar in age and educational level to the American groups to be described, the ten- to fourteen-year-old schoolchildren (Table 3–4).

TABLE 3-4

*Kpelle Free-Association Overlap Scores
for Twenty Experimental Words*

	FOOD	CLOTHING	TOOLS	UTENSILS
Food	.468	.010	.016	.010
Clothing	XXX	.268	.020	.033
Tools	XXX	XXX	.620	.182
Utensils	XXX	XXX	XXX	.731

NOTE: Entries on the diagonal represent within-class overlap scores, while entries above diagonal represent between-class overlap scores.

The data in Table 3–4 indicate the degree of similarity in the associational responses to stimuli within a given category and between categories. The actual numbers are average "overlap" scores reflecting the extent to which the various stimulus words elicit common responses (see Appendix C for a discussion of this measure of similarity).

As can be seen from Table 3–4, the four categories from the clusterable list emerge as readily recognizable groups; the average similarity (overlap) among scores within each of these groups is considerably higher than the overlap between groups. *Tools* and *utensils* produce quite high similarity scores and appear to be relatively tight, compact clusters, while *food* and *clothing* appear to represent somewhat looser groupings. In addition, a relatively high interrelation appears to exist between *tools* and *utensils* when they are compared with each other, while there is virtually no interrelation between any other of the possible pairs of classes.

A convenient graphic method for representing the way in which these items group themselves according to their overlap scores is presented in Figure 3–1. Using a technique introduced by S. C. Johnson (1967), Figure 3–1 represents the hierarchical grouping of the twenty four words according to their similarity scores. The greater the similarity between items, the closer to the right-hand side of the figure is the point where they are connected by a line. The numbers at the top of the figure represent the degree of overlap represented by items that intersect at that

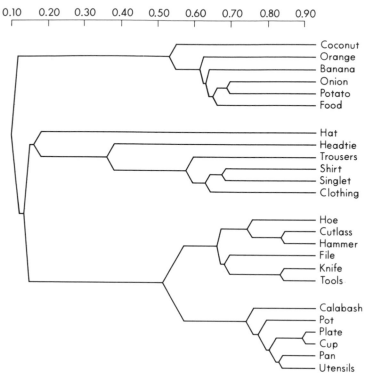

FIGURE 3–1 Results of Johnson Hierarchical-Clustering Program Applied to Free-Associations of Clusterable Stimuli; Kpelle Subjects

point. Both the distinct nature of the groups and the way in which *tools* and *utensils* come together to form a higher-order class are represented in the graph; each individual class clusters prior to the point where any items between classes meet, and the *tool* and *utensil* classes meet at a relatively high level of overlap.

Free Association and the Experimental Terms: The Americans

Since much of the experimental work to be reported later involved American comparison groups, we felt it necessary to study American free associations to these classes. In conjunction with this phase of our work, we studied three groups of American schoolchildren (grades one and two, three and four, and five and six) from the Newport-Costa Mesa, California school system.

Each subject was seated in front of the experimenter and given the following instructions:

_____ (child's name) I am going to say several words. Each time I say a word I would like you to tell me the words that come into your mind. For instance, if I say "cat," you could say "dog," or "mouse" or "fur" or anything else you think of. Do you understand?

The stimuli used in the American studies are listed in the left-hand column of Table 3–5 and appear comparable to those used in the African studies both in the nature and the membership of the classes. But such "face validity" is less compelling than hard evidence that the stimuli are behaved toward in similar ways by the two cultural groups. Children

TABLE 3-5

*List of Words Used in American
Free-Association and
Experimental Studies*

CLUSTERABLE ITEMS	NONCLUSTERABLE ITEMS
glass	candle
pot	book
pan	pot
cup	bottle
plate	cotton
	cigarette
hammer	box
knife	feather
ax	stone
saw	mat
file	battery
	nickle
banana	knife
orange	shirt
lemon	stick
potato	nail
onion	orange
	rope
sox	horn
shoes	grass
shirt	
hat	
pants	

NOTE: All are high frequency items from the Thorndike-Lorge (1943) tables.

were read the stimulus words one at a time and were asked to give at least four responses to each. The responses were recorded in order on separate data sheets and analyzed in the same way as the Kpelle free-association data.

Results of the hierarchical grouping analysis are presented for the combined age groups in Figure 3–2 and the average similarity scores are presented in Table 3–6. The results presented in Figure 3–2 and Table 3–6 resemble those for the Kpelle subjects as reported in Figure 3–1 and Table 3–5 above. All four categories emerge as readily identifiable units with relatively high within-class overlap scores. As shown in Table 3–6 between-class similarity scores are generally low. However, all the intergroup scores are not equal, and there appears to be some relation between *foods, utensils,* and *tools,* unlike the Kpelle data. This interrelation between categories is reflected not only in the average sim-

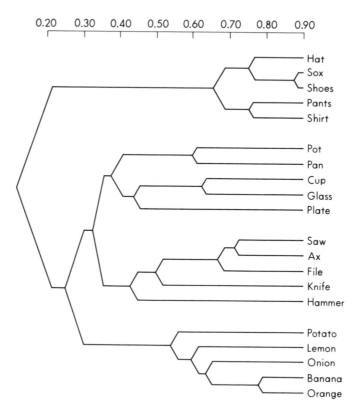

FIGURE 3–2 Johnson Hierarchical Output for All Three American Groups Combined for Word Stimuli

TABLE 3-6

American Free-Association Overlap Scores
for Experimental Words

	FOOD	CLOTHING	TOOLS	UTENSILS
Food	.547	.014	.048	.104
Clothing	XXX	.626	.021	.025
Tools		XXX	.466	.100
Utensils			XXX	.394

ilarity numbers of Table 3–6, but also in the order in which the categories join in the tree diagram of Figure 3–2 (first *tools* joins *utensils,* shortly after, that pair of classes is joined by the *food* items).

Kpelle and American Free-Association Data Compared

Perhaps the major generalization to emerge from a comparison of the group performances is one of cross-cultural similarity: in both cases the four basic categories which we have labeled *tools, clothing, food,* and *utensils* emerge. However, the similarity is not an identity because the relation among categories seems to differ: *tools* and *utensils* form a higher-order grouping for the Kpelle, while *foods* joins *tools* and *utensils* in the American data.

Other aspects of the free-association data also indicate that there may be important differences in the associations evoked by the stimuli, which are not reflected in general measures of similarity. With the exception of the category *clothing,* overlap scores are higher among the Kpelle. The greater average similarity among responses evoked by these stimuli among the Kpelle arises from several more specific characteristics of the associated responses. For one thing there is better agreement (more stereotypy) among Kpelle subjects in the particular words that they choose as associates; the first four most common responses to each word constitute 55 percent of the Kpelle data but 44 percent of the American data. Another indication of higher stereotopy in the Kpelle responses was that 89 percent of their responses fell within the same semantic class. The American subjects, on the other hand, generally gave fewer responses within the same semantic classes, and there was a clear difference between the children in grades one to four and grades five to six in this regard (no major differences among Kpelle groups were detected). The younger American subjects gave within-class responses about 73 percent of the time, while the fifth to sixth graders did so only 35 percent of the time.

On the basis of verbal-classification data presented thus far, it would not be profitable to speculate on the significance of the second-order differences in response patterns. We will return to these data, however, after we have studied how the various groups respond in other classification situations.

For the moment several conclusions are suggested by our examination of the materials to be used in experiments. First, the categories of *tools, utensils, food,* and *clothing* emerge in both the Kpelle and American settings. Second, there seem to be differences in the way in which these categories are produced by different groups: the Kpelle responses are much less variable, tending strongly to be "other examples" of the class to which the stimulus word belongs. The American responses show greater variability both in the particular words chosen and semantic class to which they belong. Finally, the three Kpelle groups yield very similar associational patterns, while there is an increase in response variability with increasing grade (age) among the American subjects.

Looking ahead to experimental studies using these stimuli in learning problems, we can be confident that we are dealing with categories that are recognized and used by both cultural groups. However, the secondary differences in the way the items are grouped into categories may present problems of interpretation.

Nonverbal Measures of Classification

We have thus far discussed techniques for discerning categories implicit in the organization of verbal responses. We found that each eliciting technique revealed a generally orderly set of categories, yet with sub-areas of ambiguity and cross-classification. We now consider the relation between semantic classes as elicited by verbal techniques and classes manifested in nonverbal behavior involving sorting of the objects themselves. Does semantic organization as measured verbally describe the actual manipulation of the objects?

When we consider the question of the relation between linguistic categories and nonverbal behavior, we are moving into an area of great current interest for the study of the relation between language and thought. For example, J. B. Carroll and J. B. Casagrande's (1958) studies referred to earlier, involved sorting objects that are categorized differently in Hopi and English; Greenfield (Bruner, Olver, and Greenfield, 1966) used a sorting task with Wolof children in order to assess the role of linguistic and educational factors on classification behaviors.

Our emphasis in this chapter differs from that of the authors cited. We know, on the basis of our linguistic elicitations, that certain stable semantic classes exist in the Kpelle language and are expressed in various verbal contexts. We wish to determine the ways in which these categories control the nonverbal behavior of our subjects.

Sorting

Our first study in which we asked subjects to classify objects was conducted before we had settled on a set of coherently, semantically classified items. In order to test subject's responses to the request to classify objects and to work out instructions, we gathered together a set of items that were potentially classifiable in a variety of ways— according to function, semantic class, length, size, color, and so forth. These objects were laid out on the floor in front of the subject, who was asked to sort them into piles that made sense to him.

The dominant mode of classification in this pilot work was what we have called "functional entailment." A pair of objects was selected so that the first went with, or operated on, the second. For example, a potato and a knife were put together because "you take the knife and cut the potato." Very rarely was a large group formed, and we virtually never had a classification justified in terms of the way things look or their common membership in a taxonomic category. This work is discussed in J. Glick (1968).

When we had settled on the set of clusterable items listed in Table 3–2, we used them to pursue the question: what control does category membership exert over the classification of objects? Two features of this work differed from our pilot studies. First, the entire set of objects could be classified according to membership in a semantic category (in our pilot studies, no single criterion of classification could exhaust the list). Second, we constrained the number of classes that the subject could make.

The task of sorting these twenty objects was given to three groups of

Kpelle subjects: ten- to fourteen-year-old schoolchildren in grades two to five, ten- to fourteen-year-old children who had never attended school, and nonliterate, Kpelle-speaking adults aged eighteen to fifty years.

When the subject entered the room where the experiment was conducted, he saw the twenty experimental items arranged on a table before him in a manner that was intended to be haphazard. In addition there were chairs (two for half the subjects and four for the remainder) arranged against one wall of the room with a two-foot distance between chairs. Subjects were then instructed as follows (in Kpelle):

These things that are on the table, we are going to divide them into four (two) groups. You should find some sense to divide these things. Here are four (two) chairs around the table. Each chair is for one of the groups. (After the subject is finished you say): What sense did you use to divide these things?

Ten subjects from each of the basic population groups were included in the two-class and four-class conditions, a total of sixty subjects in all.

It seemed to us reasonable to assume that the provision of four chairs (classes), in the presence of objects belonging to four linguistic categories, might be a powerful cue to sort according to these categories. The data did not confirm these expectations. The subjects frequently put objects from one class on more than one chair. Using as our measure the number of different chairs that members of a given category were placed on, Table 3–7 shows the distribution of items from each category for each subject group.

TABLE 3-7

Chairs per Category — Four-Chair Sorting Experiment

GROUP	CATEGORY				
	CLOTHES	UTENSILS	TOOLS	FOOD	AVERAGE
Ten- to fourteen-year-old schoolchildren	2.2	2.4	2.6	2.8	2.50
Ten- to fourteen-year-old nonliterates	2.9	2.2	2.8	2.3	2.55
Adult nonliterates	2.8	2.8	3.1	2.7	2.85
Average	2.63	2.47	2.83	2.60	

It is clear from Table 3–7 that each category occurs on an average of two or more chairs, and hence we are not observing perfect, semantically based sorting. As was the case in the free-association work among the Kpelle, there were no statistically reliable differences among the three groups in the way they sorted the objects.

If the subjects were not performing perfectly according to the previously elicited category system, there remains the possibility that some alternative category system better describes the data. In order to test this possibility, we computed a score for each item based on the proportion of times it occurs with each other item on a chair. This co-occurrence matrix was then analyzed using Johnson's hierarchical clustering program described earlier in connection with our free-association work (Appendix C).

The Johnson method forces the co-occurrence data into a hierarchy, possibly even one that we might consider inappropriate. If groups and hierarchies different from those predictable from categorical membership are produced, we have evidence for an alternative organizational scheme or perhaps the absence of a consistent scheme.

The hierarchical organization of these twenty items is presented in Figure 3–3 for all three groups combined. This figure should be interpreted as follows (the interpretation is similar to that applied to the free-association data). Two items have co-occurred to a degree indicated by the number on the top of the figure at the point where they are joined. For example, *trouser* and *cap* were sorted together nineteen times. Since the maximum is thirty (the number of subjects in the combined groups), this would be a relatively strong association between these two items.

Inspection of Figure 3–3 indicates that the items are, in general, organized with respect to category membership—although inspection of the strength of the association suggests that this mode of organization is not strong. A reasonable conclusion seems to be that there is an absence of any general violation of categorical expectations because there is no strong alternative way to categorize the items. The linguistic categories are weakly expressed, but are stronger than any other system when the items are sorted onto four chairs.

In the two-chair condition, sorting according to categorical membership appeared at first glance to be much stronger than in the four-chair condition: most commonly two complete categories were placed on each chair. In interpreting this finding it should be remembered that with only two chairs on which to place the objects, there is a greater chance possibility of perfect sorting. Taking the four-chair condition as a basis

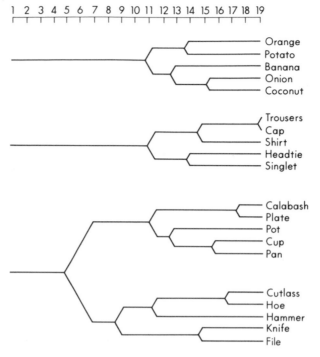

1 2 3 4 5 6 7 8 9 10 11 12 13 14 15 16 17 18 19

Orange
Potato
Banana
Onion
Coconut

Trousers
Cap
Shirt
Headtie
Singlet

Calabash
Plate
Pot
Cup
Pan

Cutlass
Hoe
Hammer
Knife
File

FIGURE 3–3 Hierarchy Generated by Sorting Clusterable Items onto Four Chairs

for estimation, we might expect a dispersion measure for the two chairs that is half that presented in Table 3–7. The expected score would be approximately 1.25 chairs per category, with an ideal of 1.0 chair per category, a difference that is too small to allow statistical comparison.

Accordingly, some other means was needed in order to study the apparently better categorical performance encountered in the two-chair condition. To do this we shifted our attention to the justifications given by subjects after they had sorted the objects in either of the two conditions. Two kinds of reasons were frequently offered by our subjects: (1) justification in terms of categorical membership, and (2) justification in diffuse, noncategorical, terms. Typical noncategorical classifications were "I divided them into groups" or "Because my Kpelle sense told me." We calculated the distribution of types of reasons for each of the conditions (since there are not between-group differences of any consequence, the groups are combined for this analysis).

In the two-chair condition, twenty-eight of a total of thirty reasons were categorical in nature, while in the four-chair condition, less than

half (twelve of thirty) are of a categorical nature. This difference between the two-chair and four-chair conditions is statistically reliable
($X^2 = 16.2$, $df = 1$, $p < .01$).

We have no way of explaining this difference at the present time, but
it raises a point to which we will return repeatedly: in trying to assess
people's competence with respect to a particular task, one has to be
very careful to consider more than one form of the task. There is no
general answer to the question: can the Kpelle describe their categorizations? The answer, as we see, depends upon the particular conditions of
categorization.

Similarity Mediation: Constrained Category Construction

The pattern of results we obtained when subjects were asked to categorize the full set of twenty items seems to indicate that greater constraints placed on the mode of categorization produced results more
consistent with the underlying semantic category structure. The procedure followed in the present experiment imposed a maximum of constraint under conditions where, it was hoped, the actual basis for grouping objects could be assessed.

We began the experiment by selecting fifteen of the twenty items
listed in Table 3–2, the *tools, foods,* and *utensils.* These items were
spread haphazardly on a table at which the subject was seated. According to a prearranged list, pairs of items (the "constraint pairs")
were placed before the subject about twelve inches apart. The subject
was then instructed as follows:

Do you see these things on the table? I want you to place one of these
things between the (Item 1) and the (Item 2) so that the thing you choose
and the (Item 1) are alike in some way and at the same time the thing and
(Item 2) are also the same thing in some way.

When the subject had selected an object for placement, he was asked
why that object belonged with the constraint pair.

These instructions and paraphrases thereof were difficult for the subjects to understand. Moreover, several subjects were unwilling to give
full justification of their selections. Nevertheless, we felt that sufficient
understanding was achieved for the experiment to continue, and as we
shall see, consistent categorizing behavior was observed.

The pairs of objects were presented one at a time and ample opportunity was given for subjects to respond. Different subjects were presented

constraint pairs in different orders, the only restriction being that the categorical makeup of the pair changed on each trial. The selection of constraint pairs (presented in Table 3–8) represented all possible combinations of the categories *food, tools,* and *utensils* (food-food, food-tool, food-utensil, tool-tool, tool-utensil, utensil-utensil). Three pairs were chosen to represent each combination of classes by a random selection procedure.

TABLE 3-8

Object Pairs by Category Used in
Similarity-Mediation Experiment

CATEGORY PAIRS	OBJECT PAIRS
food-food	onion-orange potato-orange banana-coconut
tool-tool	hoe-cutlass hammer-knife cutlass-hammer
utensil-utensil	pan-cup plate-calabash plate-pot
food-utensil	coconut-calabash orange-cup potato-pot
food-tool	orange-hoe banana-cutlass coconut-hammer
utensil-tool	calabash-file pot-cutlass calabash-hoe

Approximately thirty subjects were chosen from each of four groups. Three populations were the same as those in the free-sorting study: ten-to fourteen-year-old schoolchildren in grades two to five, ten- to fourteen-year-old nonliterate children, and nonliterate traditional adults. In addition a group of high-school students, ranging in age from sixteen to twenty, was selected from the Lutheran Training Institute and the Zorzor Rural Teacher Training Institute.

RESULTS

We looked first at the kinds of items subjects used to mediate between the two given objects. Two major conditions need to be considered separately: the cases where the constraint items were from the same class (intraclass groups), and those where the constraint items represented two different classes (interclass groups).

Table 3–9 shows the category of the item chosen to complete each trial when the constraint objects belonged to the same class. According to this table, all groups except the high-school students made choices in very similar ways. The dominant choice of an object placed between two food items was a tool of some sort. In 94 percent of these cases, the tool was a cutting implement, either a knife or cutlass. In most cases these groups chose food items to mediate between two utensils. Where

TABLE 3-9

Category Membership of Mediating Objects for
Like-Class Constraining Objects

SUBJECT GROUP	CONSTRAINING OBJECTS: FOOD-FOOD MEDIATING OBJECT		
	FOOD	TOOL	UTENSIL
NC[a]	1	30	2
A[b]	6	22	2
SC[c]	6	27	0
HS[d]	28	4	1

	CONSTRAINING OBJECTS: TOOL-TOOL MEDIATING OBJECT		
	FOOD	TOOL	UTENSIL
NC[a]	1	32	0
A[b]	1	29	0
SC[c]	1	32	0

	CONSTRAINING OBJECTS: UTENSIL-UTENSIL MEDIATING OBJECT		
	FOOD	TOOL	UTENSIL
NC[a]	12	0	20
A[b]	16	1	13
SC[c]	7	1	25
HS[d]	4	0	28

[a]Ten- to fourteen-year-old nonliterate children.
[b]Nonliterate traditional adults.
[c]Ten- to fourteen-year-old schoolchildren, grades two to five.
[d]High-school students, age sixteen to twenty.

both constraint objects were tools, all groups overwhelmingly chose another tool to complete the set.

On the whole it appears that only high-school students used consistent categorical grouping. The other groups choose mediating objects in different ways, depending on the constraining pairs. Even in the case of tools where the grouping appears to be categorical, as we shall see, the high-school and other groups chose the mediating tool for different reasons.

The nonliterate children, nonliterate adults, and schoolchildren also tended to make the same specific choice of an object to mediate between two tools. The set of objects that constituted the choice set consisted, after these tools had been removed, of thirteen objects, three of which were tools. Any of the three remaining tools satisfied the criterion of category membership. We might expect then that subjects' choices of mediating object would be randomly distributed over the remaining tools. In fact, in 93 percent of the cases, the non-high-school groups chose the file to mediate between all pairs of tools. In contrast the high-school group chose the file only 34 percent of the time—thus accurately reflecting its probability of occurrence if category members were treated in an equivalent manner.

Similar, though less dramatic, deviations from randomness appeared for other cases where the object was chosen from the same category as the constraint pair. Since, however, in other categories the percentage of intracategorical choices was relatively low for the non-high-school groups, analysis comparable to that offered for tool-tool relationships was not possible.

The reasons subjects gave for their choices were important in understanding this pattern of categorization. There are many ways to describe the subject's choices, but we found that two main categories of justification include most of the data. First, there are static responses which group the items in some fixed class. Typical are statements of a common category ("They are all food") or a common function ("They are all used in rice farming"). Second, there are dynamic responses which link the items in an action sequence that we earlier labeled functional entailment. In some cases the item chosen may act on the constraining items ("The knife can cut both the banana and the orange"); in others one constraining item may be said to act on the mediator and the other constraint item ("Soup from the calabash goes in the pan and the cup"); in still others the three items may be linked in a sequence of actions ("I can take the knife and cut the orange and drink the juice from a cup").

This type of response seems most natural when the constraining items belong to different categories.

In virtually all cases the high-school students justified their choices in static, categorical terms, while the choices by the non-high-school groups were not justified according to static rules of classification even in those cases where the object chosen was a member of the same class. An examination of the actual objects chosen for the tool-tool pair suggests the process involved. It will be recalled that a file mediated between two other tools in 93 percent of the cases for these groups. In virtually all these cases, the reason given was of the form "the file and the hammer sharpen the cutlass (knife)." In other words, the pragmatic use of the tools rather than their class membership was the basis for selection.

In general the same pattern of results appears in an analysis of the responses to the intercategory constraint pairs (see Appendix D). The high-school students handled an ambiguous situation by choosing a mediating item that shared one category relation with one of the constraint items and a different category relation with the other constraint item. For instance, one high-school student said that he placed a knife between a cup and an orange because the cup and knife are made of iron, while the knife (handle) and orange both come from trees. The other groups used dynamic, noncategorical justifications in virtually all cases. (The data are presented in Appendix D, Table D–3.)

Replication of the Similarity-Mediation Experiment with American Schoolchildren

These results obtained among the Kpelle naturally raise the question of how American schoolchildren would respond to the same task. Unfortunately, we only have data collected from children six to nine years of age (kindergarten, first and third grades) so that comparisons are only legitimate with the Kpelle schoolchildren. However, certain patterns in the American data are sufficiently striking to warrant mention.

Two major contrasts between the American groups and the Kpelle groups stand out. First, the American children, especially those in kindergarten and first grade, often justified their responses in terms of only *one* of the constraint pairs, even though prompted to relate their choices to both objects. Moreover, static categorical reasons dominate when only two of the objects are related.

Second, younger American subjects have a strong tendency to give static categorical justifications in terms of a visual attribute of the stimulus, such as color or form. On the other hand, the African groups gave, at most, 1 to 2 percent of their responses in terms of such attributes, a fact in strong contrast to results we will report in later chapters. These modes of justification, particularly the frequent restriction of a justification to pairs of objects instead of the triplet, make the American subjects appear to be considerably more adept at static classification than all but the high-school Kpelle. But such a conclusion would overlook the major point that the two groups, faced with the same task, *respond to it quite differently.* It might be, for instance, that our young American subjects, by responding only to pairs, reflect their implicit recognition of a "demand" for a static category. Conversely, the Kpelle subjects, for whom no special mode of classification seems "right," comply better with the instructions to consider all three objects in their choices. This raises an additional question: are there situations where the Kpelle do respond as if there was a "right" kind of classification?

The following section provides an illustration of one traditional Kpelle activity which seems to foster a particular kind of categorizing activity.

Sorting Leaves

The Kpelle play a game in which twenty to thirty leaves are tied to a rope. The object of the game is to name and describe the function of each leaf without hesitation—a long pause or an error and the player is "out." Since we remembered the importance of leaves in Kpelle medicine, this game suggested to us an experiment on classification in which both the materials and the procedure would be relevant to traditional Kpelle culture. We asked Akki Kulah, a Kpelle-speaking college student, to select twelve forest leaves, six from vines and six from trees. These twelve leaves were presented to ten nonliterate adult Kpelle farmers and ten American adults working in the Cuttington College area in the following manner. The leaves were spread out on a table in front of the subject, who was told: "I have some leaves here. I want you to sort them into two piles according to which ones you think go together. There should be six leaves in each pile." The experimenter then recorded which leaves were placed in each of the two piles.

As an index of the degree of category separation, the six vine leaves were assigned the numbers one to six and the six tree leaves the numbers seven to twelve. Then the averages of the numbers of items in piles were computed. If a perfect score was obtained, the averages would be 3.5 and 9.5 for the vines and the trees, respectively, yielding a difference between the scores for the two piles of 6.0. The average difference between the two piles for the Kpelle subjects was 4.90, 84 percent of the maximum. On the other hand, the average difference for the American subjects was 2.48, roughly half that for the Kpelle.

Here is an instance where the Kpelle were asked to sort objects that have previously been sorted under similar circumstances. The task closely resembles the sorting tasks discussed previously in this chapter. Kpelle performance would be difficult to improve upon.

There should be little surprise at the American performance except insofar as the American subjects manifest any ability at all to distinguish the two unnamed categories. Their relative inferiority simply underscores the necessity of relevance and familiarity for successful performance of an act of classification.

Summary

We have now completed the presentation of our data on the classification of Kpelle nouns as reflected both in verbal tasks and in tasks that require subjects to classify objects. It should be apparent that even restricting our analysis to Kpelle nouns, the pattern of results is quite complex.

On the surface, at least, it appears that we have successfully identified rather stable class groupings in the way our Kpelle groups use nouns in the verbal tasks. When explicitly asked to identify class membership and to indicate superordinate labels for particular words in the eliciting technique that generated the *seŋ* chart (Table 3–1), we obtained a fairly orderly set of classes with seemingly well-defined relations of subordination and superordination. We also noted some conflicts in the chart caused by changes in class membership stemming from consideration of different attributes of objects at different times.

Evidence from the other two verbal-eliciting procedures reflected both the class structure of the *seŋ* chart and the fact that alternative groupings were possible, depending on context. Using the sentence-substitution technique, we found that in some cases (for example, subclasses of *town things* and *working things*) similarity of the way the words were used in sentences better reflected everyday similarity in the use of the objects than the category relations of the *seŋ* chart. The same kind of relationships were to be found in the free-association data, although semantic category relations dominated.

Our interpretation of these data is that semantic classes can serve as a means of organizing verbal behavior, but the extent to which this happens in naturally occurring contexts is very much open to question. It is quite possible that in our desire to find "the" classification of Kpelle nouns, we overlooked situations where quite different kinds of classification would dominate.

For example, in conducting interviews prior to beginning the work that generated the *seŋ* chart, John Kellemu tried out a number of informal procedures designed to elicit ideas of category membership. The first few of these procedures produced interesting results but not a taxonomic classification system. In one, the men were given an example of a general class and asked to group all the examples they had named into subgroups. This technique elicited what Kellemu called "informal classification"; the men organized the objects according to *function* and *use* rather than according to a formal semantic system of classes.

Three other techniques also resulted in functional schemes of classification. In one, persons were asked to name all the things they had seen in a given day and then to group these things. A second technique was to have the men name all the things visible in a given scene and then to group them. The third asked them to name all the things similar to a given thing. In each case the subject drew on immediate experience.

The use of alternative classification principles emerges from our studies of the way in which objects are sorted. In pilot work using a large array of objects bearing no salient class relations to each other, functional pairing was a dominant means of classification. But when objects bore a class relation to each other, and when only two classes were permissible, semantic class relations were strongly expressed. Finally, where taxonomic relationships are habitually used as a basis for classification (such as was the case for the leaves that we asked our subjects to sort), the recognized taxonomic class was the dominant basis for classification.

In short, we have demonstrated to our own satisfaction that the Kpelle know and use taxonomic class relationships to structure their verbal behavior. But we have also established that the use of this kind of structuring is neither universal nor obligatory for the situations we have studied. The question then becomes: how do cultures lead people to adopt different kinds of classification systems under different circumstances? This is a very broad and difficult question to which we will turn in the concluding chapter of our book. In the remaining chapters we will pursue a closely related question. Under what circumstances do classification schemes enter into various situations where the subject is required to learn something new?

FOUR : Classification, Learning, and Memory

> To study the mind as a transformer, you have to ask subjects to do more than denote and define.
>
> ROGER BROWN, 1964, p. 251

The techniques described in Chapter 3 can be viewed as alternative ways to express habitual, well-learned relationships among things. The data reported there should reflect linguistic usage and its relation to the referents of words. Subjects are not asked to form any new categories but only to use familiar categories. We tacitly assumed that any learning that occurs in the elicitation or categorization situations does not change the nature of the subject's longstanding semantic habits.

In the present chapter we will reverse the direction of our attention. Based on what we have discovered about the Kpelle organization of nouns, we can now ask, "Does such organization affect the way in which subjects learn tasks whose successful performance is aided by the use of their lexicon, their store of 'things'?" In pursuing this question, we must be aware of such issues as the degree of structuring in the task, the nature of the stimulus materials, and the experiences of the subject populations. We have shown in Chapter 3 that such factors materially affect habitual categorization.

Verbal-Concept Discrimination

The question asked in this set of experiments is whether subjects use semantic categories when asked to learn a particular classification scheme. An alternative to the use of categorical information would be to learn the system by memorizing each item rather than using information about the class to which it belongs. An example will clarify what we mean by these distinctions.

In each case we told the subject that we would name a series of pairs of things and that he should indicate each time which one of the two "we are thinking of." We would then tell him if he were right or wrong. Suppose that the kinds of things that appear in these pairs are either items of clothing or items of food, but the subject is not told this. One example of each class is presented on a single trial. When the first pair is presented (say, "orange-shirt") the subject has no way of knowing which item we have in mind. But if he learns that we had shirt in mind on the first trial, and if he is presented with "lemon-hat" on the second trial, he might infer that we always select clothing and, therefore, choose the hat on the second trial. On the other hand, he might merely memorize the correct item for each pair (shirt instead of orange, hat instead of lemon) and never recognize that it is always members of one particular semantic class that are correct. In this way he can only guess an item until it appears for the second time. The experiments discussed below continued a given series of pairs until the subject was correct ten times in a row or until forty-eight trials were completed. We then asked the subject how he knew which word we had in mind.

Using the basic technique outlined above, a series of experiments was designed to investigate two questions. First, how are these sets of conceptually orderable materials learned? Are they learned by rote or by a rule-governed process? Second, will the processes of learning or the speed of learning vary with features of the concepts, such as their interrelation as measured by the *seŋ* chart or their grammatical class?

Each subject had six different problems, selected from a large set of problems. The order for presenting the six problems was randomized across subjects so that we could independently determine whether categories in the material influence the rate of learning, whether or not subjects learn to learn this type of discrimination (by comparing performance across successive problems), and whether or not different types of concepts differ in their difficulty (by comparing performance across problem types regardless of presentation order).

Experiments Dealing with *Seŋ* Chart Organization

The first experiments use the concept-discrimination technique described above to investigate some possible implications of the *seŋ* chart (Table 3–1). Any conceptual hierarchy can be looked at as having both a vertical and horizontal dimension of organization. The vertical dimension refers to the fact that classes "higher up" on the chart are quite general and include classes lower on the chart. Looking at the *seŋ* chart, for example, we see that *town things* subsume such subclasses as *playing things, people,* and *town works,* which in turn subsume their own subspecies. The conceptual classes that we used in our experiments represented different levels of generality. If there is strong dependence of conceptual learning on the specificity or generality of the classes to be contrasted, then an experiment using the vertical organizational feature of the *seŋ* chart would indicate the influence of this particular aspect of class structure on learning.

The horizontal organization of the *seŋ* chart provides different evidence on interclass relationships. Here the question is not one of subordination but rather the relationship between specific classes according to the general class to which they both belong. In the *seŋ* chart, for example, the classes of *children* and *adults* are equally specific and are both subsumed under the category of *people.* Since they are subsumed under the same relatively low-order category, one might expect them to be rather closely related classes. The categories of *children* and *houses* are also equally specific, but they are related through the more general class of *town things,* since children belong to the class of *people,* houses belong to the class of *town works.* The "distance" between *children* and *houses* might be expected to be greater than the distance between *children* and *adults* because the former pair is related at a higher level on the *seŋ* chart. Note, however, that the classes involved are all equally specific, in that all are minimal species.

If the discriminability of classes is related to their distance from one another and learning is affected by discriminability, then an experiment making use of different levels of horizontal distance might provide independent evidence of the organization posited by the chart. Two experiments in which to-be-discriminated classes varied in their vertical and horizontal distance from each other were performed as a means of learning about the situations in which class relations, such as those re-flected in the *seŋ* chart, influence performance.

The first experiment investigated the identification of twelve classes: *food, clothing, utensils, tools, town animals, forest animals, insects, birds, trees, mats, town things,* and *forest things.* This group of items can be divided grossly into two general levels of specificity, as defined by vertical organization. Ten of the classes are relatively unitary and specific, while the two remaining categories (*town things* and *forest things*) are composed of a general selection of items that might be found within these major classes. Each class was represented by five examples which on a given problem were randomly paired with the five examples from one of the other classes.

The primary measure of performance was the number of trials re-quired to attain a criterion of ten successive correct responses. In addi-tion, we noted whether or not the subjects (nonliterate adults) could correctly verbalize the basis of their solution once they had attained it.

The learning we observed in this first experiment was extremely rapid, ranging from two to five trials required to obtain the criterion for different classes. More interesting than the bare fact of rapid learning are certain more detailed results.

For one thing, we found that the more specific classes were learned significantly more rapidly (an average of 2.8 trials) than the general classes (4.9 trials). In addition to supporting our characterization of these classes as "specific" and "general" in the Kpelle lexicon, these re-sults suggest that the learning process needed to describe these results is *concept*-based and in some way related to the vertical organization of the *seŋ* chart. We can infer this because the number of items to be learned is the same in each problem. The fact that the more specific classes are learned more quickly suggests that the subjects are able to make prompt use of the more specific concepts. The fact that the gen-eral classes are learned in approximately five trials indicates that one presentation per pair is sufficient for learning. The fact that less than three trials are required to learn five pairs is rather convincing evidence that in the case of the specific categories the category rule governs learning.

Another aspect of the data warrants mention here. Not only were the general classes more difficult to learn, but also they were more difficult to describe following solution. Subjects were able to describe the basis of solution only 10 percent of the time for the two most general classes, but about 25 percent of the specific classes were described successfully.

The second experiment concerned with organizational features of the *seŋ* chart studied additional classes and investigated questions related to *horizontal* organization. Three major groupings of classes, representing different degrees of horizontal distance, were used. The least distant relationship (grouping 1) selected classes from within the same relatively low-order category (for example, *animals that drag themselves* versus *animals that crawl,* both being subclasses of *animals*). An intermediate distance was represented by classes that were related one step higher on the *seŋ* chart (for example, *children* versus *dancing things*). The greatest distance is represented by pairs of classes that fall on the one hand into *town things* and on the other into *forest things* (for example, *town animals* versus *shrubs*) and hence only share the common class of *things*. In all cases classes were at the same vertical level, low on the *seŋ* chart.

Each class was paired against three other classes, one from each of the distance groupings. In contrast to the first experiment, each class was composed of eight items. We felt that more clear-cut results relating to the operation of categorical structures could be obtained if the number of items within class were increased from five to eight so that simple rote learning of the items would be made more difficult by the greater number of items to learn.

One hundred and forty-four nonliterate adults each solved six problems representing all possible pairings of class distances. As before, our primary measure of performance was the number of trials required for the subject to attain the criterion of ten correct successive responses.

As in the initial experiment, learning was extremely rapid, ranging from 1.9 to 5.8 trials before the last error was made. More significantly, learning varied as a function of horizontal distance between contrast classes. The means for closest, intermediate, and most distant contrasts were 4.2, 3.7, and 2.9 trials respectively, suggesting that ease of learning is inversely related to distance as measured by the *seŋ* chart. The closest and hence presumably least discriminable pairings produced relatively slower learning than the most distant and most discriminable pairings.

Both experiments reported in this section point to the potential influence of semantic organization on learning, demonstrating that learning varies with both the specificity of classes and the distance among classes represented in the material to be learned.

96

Experiments Contrasting Rule-Based
and Random Classes

Although suggestive and instructive, the results of the previous experiments dealing with *seŋ*-chart organization could be strengthened by a stronger investigation of the operation of categorical systems. In the first two experiments there was no control over the initial ease of learning the items involved in each of the contrasts. In order to achieve this kind of information, we sought a direct comparison of semantically grouped classes with random classes, made up of the same kinds of items. By random class we mean a set of items made up in systematically random fashion of members of both classes supposedly being discriminated. Assuming that there is no accidental order in such classes, the only way that subjects can discriminate the sets is to learn each correct item individually. A comparison between the rate of learning random and rule-based classes provides a way of evaluating the control that class membership exerts over learning. If subjects are learning in a stimulus-specific manner, which we can call rote learning, we would expect the learning rates for the random classes and rule classes to be identical.

With these thoughts in mind, we undertook another study, which was intended to sample a wide range of possible bases of classification and, in each case, to compare rule-based with randomly constituted classes. The domains selected in this experiment were the following:

Animals: nocturnal-diurnal, carnivorous-herbivorous, land-water, mammal-egg laying, and harmless-dangerous
Grammar: singular-plural, adjective-verb, third person-first person, marked complement-unmarked complement, conjunction-implication
Logic: past tense-progressive tense, affirmative-negative, stressed-unstressed, question-statement, transitive-intransitive
Names: initiation-birth, men's-women's, middle-first, first-last, Western-Kpelle
Sounds: unvoiced-voiced, fricative-stop, vowel-contrast, tone-contrast, consonant-contrast
Zoology: flying animals-flying insects, jumping-crawling, claw-dragging, insects-mammals, forest animals-town animals

With each of these domains two random classes were made up, containing eight items each selected in matched fashion from each of the other classes. By making up random and rule classes from the same domains, we can control for differences in familiarity and ease of learning between domains. Any differences in rates of learning can be attributed to the fact that all the items do or do not come from a single semantic or syntactic class.

It should be noted that only the classes listed under the heading "zoology" are drawn directly from the *seŋ* chart. The other classes were chosen on the basis of our analysis of the Kpelle language and our general curiosity about the range of rule-based learning. The learning of these kinds of classes provides a useful contrast with the learning of nouns from the *seŋ* chart.

One hundred and forty-four adult subjects participated in this experiment, each receiving six subproblems, including one random problem, in a completely counterbalanced order. Each subproblem contained eight items. At the top of Table 4–1 are listed each of the dependent

TABLE 4-1

*Class-Based Learning for Semantic and Syntactic Classes
in the Verbal-Discrimination Experiment*

COMPARISON DOMAIN	TRIALS TO CRITERION	DIFFERENCES IN TRIALS TO CRITERION: RANDOM-RULE	SUCCESSFUL VERBALIZATIONS
Animals	20.8	11.6	11
Zoology	15.5	10.7	11
Names	16.1	10.8	17
Grammar	24.4	6.6	6
Sounds	23.0	5.9	11
Logic	23.6	5.5	9

variables, trials to criterion, a measure of the difference in trials to criterion between the random conditions and the rule conditions, and the number of successful verbalizations. The new measure, the difference between the randomly constituted classes and the rule classes, was arrived at by subtracting the trial number for the average trials to criterion for the rule class from the corresponding random class.

From the column labeled Trials to Criterion, it is clear that there are differences in difficulty associated with the different domains. Moreover, difficulty of learning seems to be paralleled by the results indicating the difficulty of verbalization, although verbalization is, as in many such experiments, very poor.

One way of conceiving of the difference among the domains studied is to view grammar, logic, and sounds as all involving some linguistic feature not explicitly named in the Kpelle language, and animals, names, and zoology as embodying different taxonomic classes nameable by the Kpelle. Based on this distinction, the data can be viewed as supporting the following generalizations: (1) nameable items are easier to learn than those nonnameable items that make up our various linguistic classes; (2) verbalization of nameable discriminations is easier than verbalization based on classes that are difficult to name; (3) learning of nonnameable discriminations is much closer to learning of the corresponding random discriminations.

One disturbing feature of these data is that learning was in general slow, compared to that observed in the earlier experiments. Perhaps such slow learning occurred because the discriminations are, in general, more difficult than those presented in previous studies. However, in line with our general philosophy, we are less concerned about the differences *between experiments* than we are about the relations *between conditions within experiments*. The important point is that for a certain group of classes (the nameable nouns), learning seems to be of a concept variety, whereas for another group (the linguistic class), rule-based classes are only slightly (although consistently) easier than random classes, implying that the subjects must, at least in part, be learning particular items rather than recognizing general concepts.

We did not contrast the learning rates of various subgroups among the Kpelle in this particular set of experiments. Some of the class distinctions we asked the subjects to make are matters of general knowledge, such as the distinction between materials used in building a house and clothing items. Others are known primarily to traditional specialists, such as the distinctions among various types of root plants and mushrooms. Still others are Western distinctions, not made by the Kpelle, such as the distinction between nocturnal and diurnal animals. Some distinctions are linguistic in character. And finally some distinctions are random.

John Kellemu sorted the entire set of class pairings into these five groups. After he had sorted the class pairs, we computed the mean trials to criterion for each group of distinctions for the second and third experiments. We found in the second experiment, that the successive means for traditional-familiar, traditional-specialist, *kwii,* linguistic, and random distinctions were 5.6, 7.4, 9.0, 10.2, and 13.3, respectively. All of these differences were statistically reliable except that between *kwii* and linguistic categories.

We conducted further experiments of this type, the results of which in general confirm what we have reported thus far. An interesting feature of one of these experiments was that it included different groups of subjects: Kpelle educated adults (high-school students), Kpelle schoolchildren (ten to fourteen years old, second to fourth grade), and nonliterate adults. In general, the results support the conclusion that education is positively related to the use of classification in learning. Over a large variety of problems educated adults, schoolchildren, and nonliterate adults learned in an average of 6.0, 7.0, and 9.3 trials, respectively.

One further fact to be noted in all these experiments is an overall tendency to improve in learning from the first to the subsequent problems. There is, on the average, a three-trial improvement between the first and second problems, while thereafter learning remains relatively constant. Educated subjects show a slight tendency to improve their learning beyond the second problem, whereas nonliterate subjects seem to confine all their "learning to learn" to the step from the first to the second problem. We interpret these results as indicating that the task requires some familiarity in order for subjects to do their best, a familiarity that is generally acquired by one performance of a problem.

In summary, where the materials to be learned are organized in nameable semantic categories, discriminations are aided by the presence of those semantic categories; that is, we are dealing with true concept learning and not rote learning of particular items.

Transfer of Classes

A related concept-discrimination experiment was conducted with two purposes in mind: (1) to determine the extent to which learning the distinction between two classes would facilitate learning to distinguish between other, closely related classes according to the *seŋ* chart; (2) to link the class-identification experiment to the free-association data from the previous chapter. The procedure differed slightly from that employed previously. The subject was instructed that he would be told the names of two things, one of which belonged with one of two chairs and the other to the other chair. Pairs of names were presented to the subject until he made correct assignments of items to chairs on ten trials in a row. The subjects were 108 nonliterate adults.

After a subject had reached criterion on this first phase of the experiment, the experimenter immediately shifted to new classes, which were also to be identified with chairs. In some cases, these new classes were very close (according to the *seŋ* chart) to the old ones. For instance, one distinction to be learned was between *big persons* and *claw animals*. After reaching criterion on this verbal discrimination, the subject was required to distinguish *children* from *jumping animals*. In other cases the classes presented in the second phase of the experiment were more distant from the original ones. For example, some subjects were required to distinguish *town animals* from *evil things* after learning the distinction between *big persons* and *claw animals*. We hoped to show that transfer of the discriminations to closely related classes would be easier than transfer to distantly related classes.

In fact, we showed nothing of the kind. There were no significant differences between the learning of related classes and unrelated classes on the second phase of the experiment. Learning of a second distinction did not seem to be influenced by learning a closely related prior distinction. In fact, learning the second discrimination was in no detectable way different from learning of the first one.

A further modification of this experiment produced results that seem initially to contradict those described above. The first half of the modified experiment proceeded as before. In the second half, instead of being asked to solve a second, related, discrimination problem, the subjects were asked to name five things that could be assigned to each of the two chairs. Under these conditions, additional members of the same class were given in a very high proportion of the cases.

Their performance on the discrimination tasks shows that the subjects had clearly learned the distinctions between the classes, and previous evidence indicates that category membership influenced that learning. Yet, when asked to learn a closely related class, even though they were able to name other members of the class, they showed no transfer of knowledge from the first task to a closely related one.

One possible cause for the lack of transfer is suggested by the results of our free-association studies. In that work subjects persisted in a strategy of giving particular instances of a class rather than names of closely related classes. For example, the responses to "farm tools" were particular tools used in farming. Our earlier analysis of free-association responding leads us to suggest that the free-association responses in this concept-discrimination experiment produce little overlap between classes. This specificity and lack of overlap may well be the cause of the lack of positive transfer. It seems likely that if we had set up problems where the second-phase problem was made up of items selected from a subclass of the classes named in the first problem, rather than a class that seemed similar on the basis of the *seŋ* chart, positive transfer could have been obtained. Unfortunately, data are lacking on this point.

Verbal Discrimination:
The Twenty Clusterable Objects

For any given concept-discrimination problem of the type described in the previous section, the subject is asked to deal with two classes at a time. A central question of interest is the degree to which category structure aids learning of the particular items designated correct.

In the present experiment the subject's task is somewhat more complex with respect to the categorical structure of the learning situation. However, the essential problem remains the same: will the presence of categorical structure in the materials to be learned facilitate learning?

We adapted for this purpose the standard paired-associate experiment which has been used for many years by psychologists interested in verbal-learning processes. The textbook model for paired-associate learning is the process by which beginning language students learn the vocabulary of a foreign language. For such students each term in English serves as a stimulus term and, a corresponding term in, say, French serves as the response. Thus, a student might prepare a card for each pair, on one side of which is written the English word, on the other side the French word. In the experimental study of this learning process, the stimuli are usually presented on slides or cards and the responses are either written or verbal. All manner of stimuli and responses have been used, for example, common nouns, numbers, letters, pictures, and nonsense syllables.

Our Kpelle adaptation of the paired-associate experiment was to use the twenty clusterable terms (tools, food, containers, and clothing), contained in Table 3–2 as stimulus terms and four chairs as response "categories." The subject's task was to learn which objects were assigned to which chairs.

This modified technique, in which the stimuli are in effect "classified" according to response "categories," represents a kind of halfway point between the concept-discrimination experiments of the previous section and completely unstructured learning tasks, a variety of which we will consider in the next section. In the American experimental literature on verbal learning, this kind of problem is called a verbal discrimination. We call it a paired-associate task simply to distinguish it from the experiments in the previous section.

By a suitable arrangement of the way in which the stimuli are assigned to chairs, we can determine whether or not semantic classification exerts control over the paired-associate learning process. In this particular experiment we manipulated the possibility of semantic control by having some conditions where five items were assigned to each chair in such a way that each group had at least one item from each of the four categories. Using this kind of comparison, we can reformulate the question of the role of semantic classes in learning. When objects are assigned to chairs on a semantic basis (rule condition) do subjects learn faster than when objects are assigned to chairs at random (random condition)?

We used this experiment not only to learn about the role of semantic classification in learning, but also to study the way in which feedback about the correctness of choice affects the rate of learning. This issue arose during pilot work for the experiment, when our informants indicated that it was very unnatural to learn item by item as the paired-associate technique demands. Rather, they thought that study periods followed by evaluation periods seemed more natural. We used this suggestion to develop a series of specialized ways of presenting material for learning. Also, because some of the techniques for comparison had no counterpart in the Western literature on paired-associate learning, we ran an experiment with comparable conditions in the United States to give us some basis for comparative judgments about the effects of various presentation schemes.

Our variations in the structure of the learning opportunities were designed to evaluate a series of hypotheses (perhaps intuitions would be a better word) about conditions that our Kpelle subjects would find most congenial. In some conditions the subject was an active participant on every trial. For example, he might have to guess which chair was paired with each object before he was told the correct pairing. In other conditions all the information about pairings was given to the subject, who was merely asked to repeat the name of the object before recall was tested. The details of these conditions are somewhat complex and are not described here because the results failed to justify the elaborateness of our procedures.

The subjects were 140 nonliterate Kpelle adults (most of them men) between the ages of eighteen and fifty years. All of the subjects lived in the general area of Cuttington College and most were traditional rice farmers who spoke little or no English.

Half of the subjects were run under the rule condition, where items were assigned to chairs on the basis of their category membership as shown in Table 3–2. The remainder were run in the random condition where the same items were assigned to chairs according to a set of four randomly chosen categories. Within each of these two main groups, there were seven subgroups consisting of ten subjects each. For present purposes it suffices to say that conditions where the experimenter presents the objects for learning followed by responses on the part of the subject proved easier than conditions where the subjects were required to guess the assignments of objects to chairs and then be corrected by the experimenter.

All subjects were presented the set of items fourteen times or until they were able to place them all on the chairs correctly on a single cycle through the set. Subjects were scored according to the number of errors on each trial.

In reviewing the results obtained from our Kpelle subjects, the most striking features of the data are that learning was relatively rapid and that the rule conditions were significantly superior to the random ones.

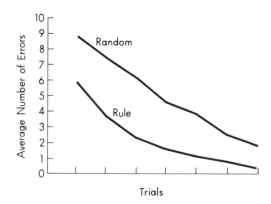

FIGURE 4–1 Average Number of Errors on Each of the First Seven Trials for Average Rule and Random Conditions. (Subjects who achieve an errorless test are credited with zero errors thereafter.)

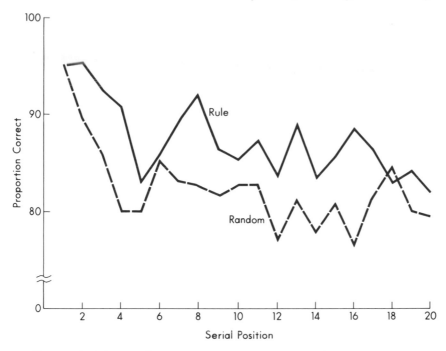

FIGURE 4–2 Proportion Correct as a Function of Serial Position for Kpelle Rule and Random Groups

The learning curves representing the relation between performance and the first seven learning trials are shown in Figure 4–1. In addition to the overall superiority of the rule conditions, it should be noted that the rule subjects were correct on fourteen out of twenty items on Trial 1, suggesting that they had learned the rule and were applying it from the outset. Statistical analysis indicated that superiority of the rule over the random procedure was constant across the various presentation conditions.

A detailed study of the results reveals an interesting relation between response accuracy and the serial position of the object-chair pairing during presentation. Figure 4–2 shows this serial-position relationship, beginning on the left-hand side of the figure with the first item in each list. It is important to remember that list order was changed from trial to trial, so that Figure 4–2 plots the first and subsequent ordinal items rather than a specific series of items. From Figure 4–2 it is clear that performance is best for early items on the list and that the decline as a function of serial position is monotonic (this is referred to as a "primacy" effect in the Western literature on verbal learning).

In order to determine if the pattern of results obtained with our Kpelle subjects is in some way peculiar to the population and materials we were working with, we undertook a replication of the experiment with a group of 140 American sixth graders. The procedures used with these American subjects were designed to be analogous to those used with the Kpelle. The following changes were made in the details of the experiment: (1) the subjects were shown pictures of the twenty clusterable objects from Table 3–2 (this change seems immaterial on the basis of our research which indicated that pictures and objects are responded to similarly by American schoolchildren [Cole, Frankel, and Sharp, 1971]); (2) a specially constructed board divided into four distinct sections replaced the four chairs; (3) a maximum of seven trials was presented because of time restrictions imposed by the school schedule.

Before describing the results of this replication, we wish to emphasize our interest in the pattern of results observed in the two groups. It is clear that the procedural changes and the multiple differences between nonliterate Kpelle adults and American sixth graders make absolute comparisons of performance in many ways specious.

With these provisos in mind, it can be reported that in two major respects the American and Kpelle data are markedly similar. First, for the American subjects the rule condition (2.8 errors per trial) was far easier to learn than the random condition (6.8 errors per trial). Second, the American subjects showed the same order of difficulty for the various presentation conditions as the Kpelle. In particular, the American subjects also found it more difficult to learn if they had to begin the learning sequence by guessing the correct response slot, instead of being shown the correct alternative and asked to recall it on a later cycle of the experiment. Similar findings reported by W. K. Estes (1969) suggest that this result is to be expected in a larger range of situations.

We chose the various presentation conditions in the first place because of our informant's intuitions about special problems that the Kpelle were likely to experience with the paired-associate task. Thus the similarity of the response patterns in this regard between Kpelle and American subjects is strong evidence of a significant *similarity* in the learning processes of the two widely divergent groups.

In one respect, however, the American data are unlike the Kpelle. As shown in Figure 4–3 there is no relation between serial position and accuracy for the rule condition among the American schoolchildren. For the random condition we observe both the primacy effect noted in Figure 4–2 and a corresponding recency effect in which American sub-

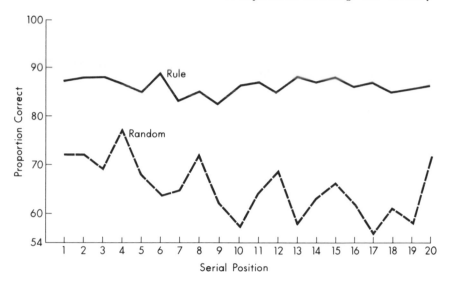

FIGURE 4–3 Proportion Correct as a Function of Serial Position for American Rule and Random Groups

jects are more accurate for the last item presented. Figure 4–3 also dramatizes the large difference between rule and random conditions for the American subjects, leading us to surmise that the lack of a relation between serial position and accuracy in the rule condition occurs because the semantic categories are so strong that their use in organizing learning completely swamps the factors that lead to serial-position differences.

Taken together, the American and Kpelle results of this experiment point to one important difference and one important similarity between the learning mechanisms of the two cultures. Both groups find it easier to learn when they are given sufficient information about stimulus-response relationships so that they can do more than guess on early trial. Both groups use the semantic structure of the list to aid learning, but the Americans make relatively more use of semantic information than do the Kpelle.

It is unfortunate that we do not have more data on this point from other populations of Kpelle people. We can only surmise on the basis of our previous results that the rule-random difference for children with a good deal of schooling (seven grades or more) would look more like the performance of the American children, while the preference for the full presentation of information would remain unchanged.

Category Discrimination: Leaves

In Chapter 3 we presented evidence on the ease with which Kpelle adults sort leaves into piles that distinguish between vines and trees, whereas American subjects fail to make the vine-tree distinction. The outcome, in that context, indicated that in situations where classification activities with common objects were familiar to the Kpelle, clear taxonomic classes emerged.

We can again ask under what conditions a categorical distinction, this time between tree and vine leaves, will control learning. Simply because the categories are applicable to learning does not mean that they will be applied.

Our materials for this study were fourteen leaves—seven from vines, seven from trees. These included the twelve leaves used in the experiment on sorting plus one additional leaf from each class. The subjects were thirty American and Canadian college students who were working in the Cuttington College vicinity and thirty nonliterate Kpelle adults ranging in age from twenty- to thirty-one years. Each group of thirty was divided haphazardly into groups of ten who were run under one of three different conditions, each designed to assess a different aspect of the relation between categories and learning. The three conditions are well described by the instructions read to the subjects who were seated at a table across from the experimenter.

Condition 1: (All the tree leaves are assigned to one name, the vine leaves to the other.) I have several leaves here. Some belong to Sumo and the others belong to Togba. I will hold up a leaf at a time, and tell you whom it belongs to. Then I will ask you to tell me as I hold up each leaf whether it belongs to Sumo or Togba. I will tell you each time whether you are right or wrong (continue until the subject has correctly named all the leaves in one trial).

Condition 2: I have here several leaves. Some are from trees and some from vines. I will tell you which leaf is from vine and which from tree. Then I will hold up each leaf after this, and I want you to tell me whether it is from tree or vine. I will tell you each time whether you are right or wrong (again continue until the subject has named correctly all the leaves in one trial).

Condition 3: (Three vine and four tree leaves for Togba and four vine and three tree leaves for Sumo.) I have several leaves here. Some belong to Sumo and some to Togba. I will tell you which belong to Sumo and which to Togba as I hold up each leaf. Then I would like for you to tell one at a time whether a leaf belongs to Sumo or not when I hold it up to you again. I will tell you whether or not you are right or wrong (continue until the subject has correctly named all the leaves in one trial).

Both Conditions 1 and 2 permit the subject to take advantage of the categories latent in the items, but in Condition 2 the categories are named, while in Condition 1 the subject has to discover them for himself. On the basis of the results from our experiment in sorting the leaves, discovering the classes should not be expected to be difficult for the Kpelle, but to be quite difficult for the Americans and Canadians. The third condition systematically violates the categories of the items.

The results of this study are summarized in Table 4–2 in terms of the number of presentations of the list required for one completely correct cycle with no errors. The really interesting point to emerge from Table 4–2 is that the tree-vine leaves distinction is helpful to the Kpelle

TABLE 4-2

Number of Complete Presentations of the Leaves Required to Make One Completely Correct Recall of the Set

| | CONDITION | | |
	1 SUMO-TOGBA RULE	2 TREES-VINES RULE	3 SUMO-TOGBA RANDOM
Kpelle	7.3	1.1	6.8
American	9.8	8.9	9.0

only if the instructions make clear that it is this distinction that the experimenter has in mind. By contrast, nothing proves of much use to the Americans. In spite of the slight indication that Americans were able to distinguish tree and vine leaves in our sorting experiment, this sample of subjects proved unable to make use of such distinctions in the context of a learning study. There seems also to be a factor relating to discriminability of the leaves; the Kpelle learn slightly faster than the Americans even under conditions where the tree-vine distinction does not seem to influence performance.

In our view the problems involved for the American and Canadian subjects are captured beautifully in an anecdote related by Eleanor Bowen (1954) in her book, *Return to Laughter.*

By nine o'clock that morning, I had several pages of words, and my tongue was limp from unaccustomed twisting. Unable to take in any more, I instituted a review by again naming the notables. I again got most of them right: the right man and almost the right sound. Kako looked at me with favor. Encouraged, I demanded the names of the women. They smiled, but Kako ignored my question and turned firmly back to the leaves. Rather reluctantly I began to name them. With every word Kako became more dour. I spoke more loudly; my pronunciation couldn't be that bad. Ikpoom's eyes grew sadder; the women seemed incredulous. The little boy could bear it no longer. He snatched from me the leaf I was naming and handed me another. The order had been mixed, and not once had I put the right name to the right plant.

These people are farmers: to them plants are as important and familiar as people. I'd never been on a farm and am not even sure which are begonia, dahlias or petunias. Plants, like algebra, have a habit of looking alike and being different, or looking different and being alike; consequently mathematics and botany confused me. For the first time in my life I found myself in a community where ten year-old children weren't my mathematical superiors. I also found myself in a place where every plant, wild or cultivated, had a name and a use, and where every man, woman, and child knew literally hundreds of plants. None of them could ever believe that I could not if I only would. [Bowen, 1954, pp. 15–16]

Miss Bowen is making the point that her hosts had learned to make the distinctions upon which rapid learning is based so that even in classes where they might not know the particular plant name, it is easily learned, while she could not even distinguish between the plants.

Such factors help to explain the results for the Canadians and Americans and, in fact, seem obvious. But what about the difficulty of the Kpelle subjects in "Sumo-Togba Rule" condition? Why weren't they aided by the categorical split in the response terms? One possibility is that they failed to notice that tree leaves or vine leaves could form the basis for learning; a second hypothesis would be that such labeling actually misled the Kpelle subjects. After all, why should Sumo have all the vines and Togba all the trees?

This is another instance where considerably more research is required. Looking ahead we can guess that our Kpelle subjects in fact failed to note that vine and tree could serve as tools for easier learning.

Learning and Memory: Free Recall

In the previous sections of this chapter, we dealt with a series of situations in which subjects were required to learn to distinguish taxonomic classes, or make use of particular classification schemes selected by the experimenter in learning tasks. The emphasis in our description of these studies was on *learning*—learning the class discrimination or learning the object-pair relation. But we could just as easily have described the processes involved in terms of the concept of *memory:* what conditions affect a subject's ability to remember which item from the pair was correct previously? How well does the subject remember the stimulus-response relationship? In fact, each presentation of something to be learned is evaluated in terms of what is remembered later. Little more than a choice of terms determines whether we talk about performance in terms of what was learned at the time the items were presented or remembered at the time that they were tested.

Nevertheless, it does seem that when we discuss memory in its cultural context, we probably are not thinking about the kinds of situations studied in this section. In fact, a small body of literature has grown up around the question of cultural differences in the processes of memory. The questions raised in this literature will serve as an introduction to a set of experiments designed to study the relation between various cultural factors and memory.

Introduction to the Problem

Early observers of nonliterate societies, in commenting on differences in intelligence and logical capacity, reported the existence of excellent, and in some cases extraordinary, mnemonic skills. Levy-Bruhl, for example, cites many examples of this apparent ability to memorize, claiming that "in every case in which their memorizing power, which is really excellent, could relieve them of the effort of thinking and reasoning, they did not fail to make use of it" (Levy-Bruhl, 1966, p. 25). Similar anecdotes and assertions are often reported by Westerners who have taught in Africa, the most usual form being that African students do very well with material that can be "learned by rote," but become poor or indifferent students when expected to do tasks in which brute memorization will not work.

Professional anthropologists also bring us reports of excellent memories, although very little systematic evidence relating to memory has been collected. For example, D. Reisman quotes the report of an anthropological colleague that among a remote people in the Philippines, "messages are conveyed orally . . . with an accuracy which is fabulous to us" (Reisman, 1956, p. 9). A similar point is made in a contrasting manner by Elizabeth Bowen in the example cited earlier in which she recounts the displeasure and consternation of her Nigerian hosts at her inability to remember the names of local plants which every ten year old in the village had long since committed to memory (Bowen, 1954, p. 16).

Other modes of inquiry support the anecdotal evidence, which suggests that members of a nonliterate, traditional society have developed mnemonic skills that are quite different from those of their literate, technologically advanced brethren. For example, philological and historical evidence led E. A. Havelock (1963) and others to maintain that an oral tradition produces special mnemonic devices, such as the epic poem, which function as an "oral encyclopedia" of the social, material, and historical aspects of the culture. This idea, recently popularized by Marshal McLuhan (1969), is echoed by Reisman when he suggests that members of a literate culture "can afford to be careless with the spoken word, backstopped as we are by the written one" (Reisman, 1956, p. 9). Nonliterates, unable to store their experience in print, must devote full attention to the spoken word. Reisman, in a manner similar to Havelock, adduced evidence that nonliterates (in this case New Guinea headhunters and Zuni shamans) have developed special mnemonic habits for the organization of cultural material.

The reports of anthropologists concerning the great importance that many tribal peoples place on learning of history, mythology, and traditions are consistent with Havelock's ideas about memory and literacy. For example, W. D'Azevedo reports that among the Gola of western Liberia, "An elder with a poor memory, or 'whose old people told him nothing' is a 'small boy' among the elders, and might well be looked upon with contempt by younger persons" (1962, p. 13).

In addition to philological and anthropological evidence, there is a very small amount of experimental, or quasi-experimental, evidence on the question of culture and memory gathered by psychologists. One such source is the evidence reported by the IQ testers, who frequently note that subtests depending upon oral or visual memory produce scores that are equivalent to, or in some cases superior to, Western norms, while subtests in which memory is not an important factor suffer by comparison. Analogous findings have been reported by L. Doob (1965) in a study of the ability to recall visual stimuli. His data indicate that eidetic imagery, or the ability to recall visual stimuli exactly, is encountered far more frequently in Africa than in the United States.

One quasi-experimental psychological investigation of nonliterate peoples was carried out by F. C. Bartlett (1932) among Swazi of South Africa. Having heard of the "marvelous word-perfect memory of the Swazi from his childhood up" (p. 248), Bartlett set out to find out under what conditions this phenomenal memory manifested itself. First he asked a young boy to carry a message to someone else in the village, and found that recall was comparable to that which more systematic experiments had shown for English children of similar age. He then tested a cowherder's memory for a series of transactions involving cattle that had been sold the year before. In this case, the herder's memory was found to be phenomenally accurate, although he had been only peripherally involved in the transaction. Bartlett attributed the herder's performance to the importance of cattle as a medium of exchange among the Swazi, and suggested that because of this "persistent social tendency," the performance was really not so remarkable. The cowherder's feat of memory seemed outstanding because what was socially important to him was irrelevant to the Western observer, who therefore found a good memory for cows and prices quite unusual. In fact, we might expect the Swazi cowherder to be equally astounded should he encounter two American ten year olds trading baseball cards with the intricate recall of players, teams, batting averages, and relative standings that a successful trader requires.

The many hypotheses that can be generated from Bartlett's demonstration have never been systematically followed up and tested. For example, in what specific ways does a "persistent social tendency" influence recall? Does it produce different *ways* of recalling as well as different *amounts* recalled? Bartlett himself, when comparing the Swazi to the Westerner, suggested that culture determines a difference in the way things are recalled. He hypothesized that rote memory is the preferred memory technique of nonliterate people and defined rote memory as serial memorizing. He concluded:

According to the general theory of remembering which has been put forward, there is a low level type of recall which comes as nearly as possible to what is often called rote recapitulation. It is characteristic of a mental life having relatively few interests, all somewhat concrete in character and no one of which is dominant. Is there anything in social organization which parallels this state of affairs in mental organization and so, on the social side, favors the rote recapitulatory method? I think there is, and it is largely to this that we must look for the explanation of the reputation for excessively accurate and detailed memory which the more or less primitive group possesses. [Bartlett, 1932, p. 264]

Unfortunately, Bartlett's research has had little impact on subsequent research. S. F. Nadel (1937) provided evidence that themes of great cultural interest are best remembered, but G. Bateson (1958) provided anthropological evidence that serial recall is not characteristic of primitive people in general.

In our opinion, Bartlett's phrase "persistent social tendencies" has at least three interpretations, which have not been sorted out either conceptually or experimentally: (1) there are different levels of interest and motivation; (2) there are particular memory skills that different environmental conditions might produce; and (3) there are differences in the extent and ease of use of relevant vocabulary. Any one, or a combination, of these factors could account for Bartlett's results.

As described in Chapter 2, we too have noted a heavy reliance on what appeared to be serial rote learning in the classroom (see also Gay and Cole, 1967, pp. 33ff.). Students often copied exactly and step-by-step what the teacher said or wrote and failed completely to grasp the principle involved.

Our few observations among the Kpelle, combined with the anthropologists' casual observations and the psychologists' few experiments, led us to attempt a detailed and systematic experimental investigation in the hope of isolating those factors that influence the ways in which members of various cultures use memory as a cognitive tool. In order to move beyond the level of casual observations, we had first to choose an experimental tool or set of tools that would more nearly fit our idea of a memory problem than the concept-discrimination studies. The experimental technique should be flexible enough to make possible the study of memory in nonliterate societies, and at the same time should enable us to evaluate hypotheses concerning the particular memory skills being used by our subjects.

The task we selected for detailed experimentation, the free-recall experiment, has several features that render it useful for our purposes. First, it is extremely easy to administer. A subject is presented a series of items, one at a time, and is told that he must try to learn them so that he can recall them at a later time. After the last item is presented, a period is given for recall. The list can then be repeated as many times as the experimenter wishes. Second, the task is unstructured; the subject is free to remember in any manner he chooses, and the order in which subjects recall items gives important insight into the mechanisms of memory. W. A. Bousfield and his associates (Bousfield, 1953; Cohen, 1963) stimulated interest in this procedure by demonstrating that when the items to be remembered came from easily identifiable semantic categories, recall tended to be "clustered" so that items from a given semantic category were commonly recalled together. More recently, E. Tulving (1966) has measured the organization of recall in terms of the consistency between successive attempts by one subject to recall the same list. Although many questions of fact and theory remain to be clarified, it is clear from the work of these and other investigators that North American high-school and college students show a strong tendency to reorganize material presented for memorization and that success in recall is related to the degree of organization the subject imposes on the to-be-recalled list (see summary article by Tulving, 1968).

Although it might seem a contradiction at first glance to employ a memory task to study cognition, the concern with the organizational features of free recall fits nicely with definitions that emphasize the constructive and organizational features of cognition. In terms of our discussion in Chapter 1 (pp. 19–20), our interest in free recall could be characterized as a concern with the extent to which cognition plays a role in the memory process of different cultural groups.

Procedures

The basic procedure in each of the free-recall experiments (all essential modifications of procedure will be discussed as they occur) was for the experimenter to read the list of items to be recalled at a rate of approximately two seconds per item. After the entire list had been presented, the subject was asked to repeat as many of the items as he could. Approximately two minutes were permitted for recall, during which time the experimenter recorded each word on a specially prepared data sheet. The subject usually indicated prior to the end of the two minutes that he could recall no more and the next trial was then begun.

Unless otherwise specified, each subject was presented the same list five times but in a different order each time. The only restriction was that no two items from the same category occur adjacent to each other within a trial. Furthermore, the order in which different list orders were used differed from subject to subject, thereby randomizing the effects of list order.

For the basic series of experiments the list of items to be remembered was composed of the twenty clusterable items contained in Table 3–2. When desired for comparative purposes, the nonclusterable list from Table 3–2 was used.

Measures of Performance

In justifying the selection of free-recall task as a method for studying memory, we emphasized the great freedom permitted the memorizer in structuring his recall. It is understandable, then, that our measures of memory will represent alternative ways of assessing different kinds of structure.

An example of one possible structure is implied by Bartlett's hypothesis that rote recapitulation characterizes the recall of traditional, nonliterate peoples. As he describes the process, rote memory entails always beginning recall from the beginning of the to-be-recalled sequence. An analogue of this theory for the free-recall task would be the case where the subject remembers the items in the same order that they were presented by the experimenter.

In order to measure this serializing tendency, we calculated the correlation between the order of the experimenter's presentation of the to-be-remembered items and the order of the subject's recall. This correlation statistic (Pearson's r) then became a datum characterizing the degree of one kind of recall structure for a given trial. It was possible to compare different groups on the amount of serial organization under various conditions.

A major alternative to serial organization is clustering, the tendency to group items that are part of the same class together in the recall list. The nature of the particular class can be defined in various ways, and recall lists can be evaluated for the degree to which the observed clustering exceeds the amount expected if the items had been drawn at random from the to-be-remembered list (semantic classes are the focus of most of our attention, but functional classes, for instance, could be studied).

The measure of clustering used in our work is a "standard deviate" (z score), which is a measure of the extent to which a particular recall list deviates from chance clustering. A perfectly random list corresponds to a z score of zero. Clustering is reflected in positive z scores. Negative z scores are also possible and reflect systematic organization that runs counter to clustering (such would be the case if the subject is showing perfect serial organization). A discussion of the measurement of organization in free recall is contained in Frankel and Cole (1971).

Finally, we consider the question of the amount of recall. The simplest measure of how much is remembered is simply the number, or proportion, of items recalled. We, of course, present this basic datum and, as we shall see, the relation between practice with a particular recall list and the number recalled will be a central problem for analysis.

In addition to total number recalled, we will also include analysis of the number recalled from different parts of the to-be-remembered list. In free-recall studies in the United States (Deese, 1957; Cole, Frankel, and Sharp, 1971) one typically observes a "serial position effect"; items near the beginning or end of to-be-remembered list are better recalled than those in the middle. This fact is widely interpreted (cf. Atkinson and Shiffrin, 1968) as evidence for the presence of two distinct memory processes: a short-term process (reflected in near-perfect recall of words from the end of the list) and a long-term process (reflected in superior recall of words from the beginning of the list). Since group differences may be localized in a particular part of the list (for example Cole, Frankel, and Sharp, 1971, found that older schoolchildren remembered more items than younger schoolchildren only in the early and middle positions of the list), serial-position analysis offers still another measure of structuring in memory processes. The inference of short-term and long-term processes from the kinds of structure that are involved in this measure of recall is still a very controversial matter, but the universality of the fact that differential recall is observed for different serial positions in American studies suggests the usefulness of including such analyses for cross-cultural comparisons.

Keeping in mind the fact that our measures of performance represent various indicators of possible cognitive processes entering into memory performance, we turn to the first of our studies.

Experiment 1: Are Clusterable Lists
Easier to Learn Than Nonclusterable Ones?

The opinion is fairly widespread among American psychologists who study memory that recall and organization are closely related; the better the to-be-remembered material is organized, the better it will be recalled (Mandler, 1966; Tulving, 1968). A prediction that follows from this generalization is that all other things being equal, clusterable lists should be easier to recall than nonclusterable, randomly constituted lists. C. Cofer reviewed the meager evidence up until 1966 and concluded that clusterable lists are in general easier to learn than nonclusterable lists (Cofer, 1967, pp. 181ff.). The cross-cultural generality of this finding was the subject of our first recall experiment.

SUBJECTS AND PROCEDURES

The subjects in this experiment all lived in the area of Cuttington College. Twenty subjects were obtained in each of the basic population groups: nonliterate six- to eight-year-olds, nonliterate ten- to fourteen-year-olds (first grade), and school ten- to fourteen-year-olds (second to fourth grade). Half of the subjects in each group were presented a clusterable list and half a nonclusterable list (Table 3–2). Using the standard procedure outlined above, each subject was given five recall trials of an orally presented list.

The experimental design thus includes comparisons of age, education, and "clusterability" of the stimulus list. Details of the procedure for this and the other standard free-recall experiments are given in Appendix E.

RESULTS

Each factor of concern in this first experiment affected the number of items recalled. For all subject populations, the clusterable list was slightly easier to recall than the nonclusterable list (8.7 items per trial versus 7.6 items). Recall increases slightly as a function of both age and education as shown in Figure 4–4. These results are shown as an average across trials because group differences were approximately the same at all stages of learning.

Two conspicuous aspects of the groups' recall performance, which are not represented in Figure 4–4, require comment. First of all, an average of 7.0 items was recalled on Trial 1 and recall increased only to 8.8 on Trial 5. Although this increase is statistically reliable, its magnitude is smaller than one would anticipate on the basis of previously reported American data. Second, there is very little variation in accuracy among items as a function of their position in the recall list. We reported superior performance near the beginning of the list in our paired-associate study. But no strong effects of this kind are evident among our Kpelle subjects given the free-recall task. Figure 4–5 shows

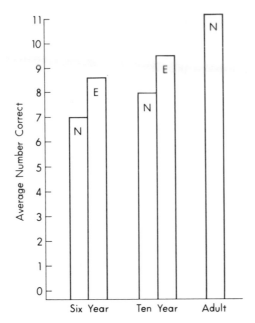

FIGURE 4–4 The Average Number of Items Recalled per Trial as a Function of Age and Education (E = educated, N = noneducated)

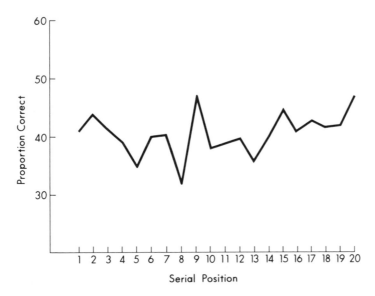

FIGURE 4–5 Relation between Accuracy and Serial Position of an Item during Presentation

the relation between accuracy and the serial position of the items at the time of presentation to be relatively flat.

The Kpelle also failed to organize recall according to semantic categories in the clusterable conditions where such clustering was possible. The average clustering z score was $-.13$ for all five groups taken as a whole; there was no significant variation among the groups. A similar lack of organization is reflected in the seriation measure. Far from showing rote learning, none of the groups studied showed any significant correlation between presentation and recall sequences, and the average for the experiment was $r = -.05$.

Thus, it would appear that for the populations studied, initial recall was anything but impressive, increases in recall with practice were negligible, and conspicuous organization either in terms of the presentation sequence or semantic properties of the list was absent. Moreover, the difference among populations and conditions, while reliable, were not of great magnitude.

Experiment 2: Do the Type of Stimulus Materials and Manner in Which the Presentation Lists Are Organized Affect Recall?

One of the first hypotheses that the relatively poor performance in Experiment 1 suggested (an hypothesis consistent with observer's comments about the "concrete mentality of the African," Cryns, 1962) was that presentation of the stimuli concretely instead of verbally would greatly enhance recall.

Evaluation of the relative effectiveness of concrete stimuli among the Kpelle is complicated by the fact that concrete stimuli such as pictures or objects are more easily recalled by Americans (see Paivio, 1968, for a summary of these data). Consequently, what we sought was to measure the *relative* amounts of improvements resulting from the introduction of concrete stimuli in the two cultures.

SUBJECTS AND PROCEDURES

The subjects in this second experiment were all drawn from the Cuttington College area. The basic populations were ten- to fourteen-year-olds in grades two to four, and nonliterate ten to fourteen year olds. The forty subjects from each of these populations were assigned haphazardly to four different experimental treatments, representing all combinations of two kinds of stimulus materials (spoken words or objects) and two ways of ordering the presentation lists. For all groups the lists consisted of the twenty items from Table 3–2 used in the clusterable groups of Experiment 1. For half of the subjects, this meant that no item from a given semantic class ever occurred next to another item from that class. For the remaining half of the subjects, the presentation orders were "blocked"; that is, items from within a semantic class always occurred together in the list. Blocks of items were arranged differently on each trial in a random fashion.

To summarize, the basic comparisons included in this experiment were educated versus nonliterate subjects, random versus blocked presentation orders, and objects versus words as stimuli.

RESULTS AND DISCUSSION

As was true in Experiment 1, our manipulations of the conditions for remembering produced only small effects on the average number of items recalled. There was no reliable difference between the children who had attended school and those who had not; there was only a slight advantage for the object over the word stimuli and for blocked over random presentation. Consistent with Experiment 1 results, we find no tendency for subjects to recall in serial order at any time in the training ($r = -.07$). There were, however, indications that the organization of recall differed between the educated and nonliterate groups and as a function of the experimental conditions (see Appendix E for a detailed discussion of these results). First, the educated subjects manifested a serial-position effect similar to that observed with American children. Second, we observed a significant amount of semantic clustering during the course of learning for certain of the groups. The development of clustering with successive trials is shown in Figure 4–6. It is clear from Figure 4–6 that for the blocked conditions, clustering begins at well above the chance level, while for the random groups, clustering only approaches nonchance levels toward the end of training. Presenting objects has a marked effect on clustering only in the case where stimuli are presented in a blocked order.

Several features of these results seem unusual if one uses typical data collected from American subjects as a reference point. The items seem common and distinct, yet memory is poor in terms of numbers recalled. Not only is performance initially at a low level, but there is little improvement with successive trials. There appears to be almost a total lack of semantic clustering except under very favorable circumstances (blocked presentation of objects) and virtually no relation between se-

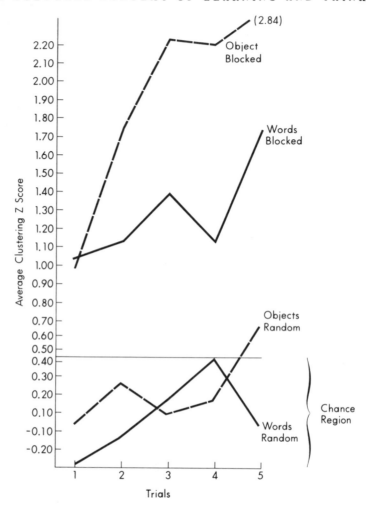

FIGURE 4–6 Average Clustering Score for Each Trial as a Function of Presentation Orders and Stimuli Presented. (The solid line at .44 represents the average score which reliably exceeds chance.)

mantic organization and amount recalled. Furthermore, alternative measures of organization (seriation and differential recall of items from various parts of the list) generally failed to indicate structure in recall.

In order to untangle the many factors that could be controlling this pattern of performance, we conducted a large series of studies, each of which was designed to evaluate a different hypothesis about organization and memory.

As one starting point in this research program, we conducted studies with various groups of American schoolchildren and young adults to obtain a clearer picture of the features of free recall that result from experimental manipulations such as those applied in Experiments 1 and 2 among the Kpelle. Because of several procedural variations that were introduced in Kpelleland, we undertook the studies in the United States to determine the influence of such variables as list clusterability, blocked-presentation order, and words versus objects as stimuli. The stimuli used in these studies were taken from Table 3–5, containing the lists used in our study of free-association responses. In addition, we collected data from groups of Mexican Indians living in Yucatan and another tribal group in Liberia. These latter data are included in Appendix E.

American Free Recall

The main features of recall performance among our American subjects are the following (see Cole, Frankel, and Sharp, 1971, for a detailed exposition):

1. For children in grades one to eight the number of items recalled on the first recall trial is comparable to our Kpelle results (seven to ten of the items). However, except for the youngest children, there is more improvement over trials than observed in Experiments 1 or 2.

2. College students recall many more words, and recall is essentially perfect by Trial 2.

3. All American groups are more sensitive to the serial position of the item to be recalled; averaging over trials, the last item presented is correct about 80 percent of the time across all groups. Recall scores for the different groups differ only in other positions. Trial 1 differs from the remaining trials in that on Trial 1 there is a large primacy effect (items near the beginning of the list are best remembered), but there is little recency (recall of late items from the list). On later trials, recency dominates.

4. On Trial 1 there is a significant positive correlation between presentation and recall order. On the remaining trials, this correlation is negative. The Americans begin by trying to rote memorize the list!

5. The relative increase in recall as a result of presenting objects instead of words is even greater than we observed among the Kpelle.

6. Except for the youngest children, there is considerably more semantic clustering among the American students. College students show almost perfect clustering in a very few trials.

In summary, there is an orderly development of free-recall learning among our American subjects. By the third grade, average performance is roughly at the level observed by our various African groups, but thereafter, performance among the Americans shows better recall and organization.

Summary of the Preliminary Experiments

The picture that emerges from these studies of free-recall performance in Liberia, the United States and Mexico consists of a set of regularities with some important divergences.

In all of the cultures sampled, the variables that control free recall seem to operate in very similar ways. There was a slight tendency for clusterable lists to produce better recall than nonclusterable lists, but this difference was statistically reliable only in the case of the Kpelle. Presentation of objects instead of words enhanced recall in each culture where it was tried. The same was true for the presentation of lists in a blocked rather than a random order.

A significant difference in the patterns of performance occurs when we compare changes in the Kpelle performance from Trial 1 to Trial 5 with changes observed for our older American subjects. The absolute level of recall would be very similar across cultures if we only considered Trial 1. Where large cultural differences in amount recalled are observed, the largest differences occur following Trial 1 and increase across trials.

In contrast with the number of items remembered, the way in which recall is *organized* differs across cultures from the outset of training. In general, the American subjects show primacy on Trial 1 (accompanied by a positive correlation between presentation and recall orders) and recency thereafter. There is also a significant amount of clustering from the outset, except for the youngest American groups. High levels of clustering and trial-related changes in serial-position responding are generally absent from the Kpelle data. For these groups conditions that are relatively favorable to recall and organization have their effect on Trial 1.

Hence, we return to a consideration of memory among the Kpelle with an orientation that differs significantly from the hypotheses that we started with. Considerations of "concrete versus abstract" learning, and ignorance about the major features of free recall among nonliterate groups have given way to a more precisely defined inquiry. Now we seek to determine why there is relatively little recall or clustering among Kpelle subjects, even after repeated practice. Are there experimental or naturally occurring occasions upon which the Kpelle will exhibit recall of the same quality as that typically observed in the United States?

Our approach to answering these and related questions can be divided roughly into two categories. First, we instituted a series of studies that were similar to Experiment 1 in terms of the basic procedures, but that varied characteristics of the subjects or the general conditions of the experiment. These studies were directed at such hypotheses as: perhaps the task seemed unimportant to the Kpelle subjects, so they were not trying; or perhaps one needs to have several years of schooling before free recall becomes organized.

Following our evaluation of hypotheses of this type, which involve no fundamental changes in procedure, we turn to a series of studies aimed at changing the basic *structure* of the free-recall tasks. The intent of these studies is to find ways of presenting the task that will evoke efficient, organized performance. After an analysis of the way performance depends on the structure of the task, we will try to make some educated guesses about the cultural factors influencing free-recall memory.

Experiment 3: The Effects of Different Motivating Conditions on Recall among the Kpelle

As an example of how one might come to consider lack of interest on the part of our Kpelle subjects as a determinant of their performance, consider the phenomenon of a *kwii* Liberian college student wandering into a hinterland village. This event is a little unusual, but hardly a matter of great moment to the villagers. If the student is a local boy, he is apt to be met somewhat patronizingly. The village adults will respect his book learning but will still consider him a "small boy" in the important matters of life. If he is a stranger, he might be met with some suspicion; and if he is thought to be a tax collector or government agent, suspicion might easily turn into enmity.

When the college student explains that he is visiting the town in order to talk with the people, it is likely to be some time before he can convince them that the outcome of this talk is likely to be harmless. It is emphasized that the project directors are teachers, interested in helping the children "learn book." Whenever possible, the town chief and his council of elders are consulted and shown traditional courtesies.

A possible outcome of this emphasis on the lack of a connection between the experimenter and the government, as well as the generally harmless nature of the tasks involved, might be to prevent the subjects from taking the experiment seriously. Although subjects were "dashed" a can of fish or a small amount of money for their cooperation, the knowledge that the outcome was relevant only to some far-off school-teacher could not have been of great concern. These doubts seem all the more plausible when we contrast the view of this would-be Kpelle subject with that of an American schoolchild, whose response to the experimental situation is likely to be, "Is this an intelligence test?" and whose desire to exhibit his intelligence often produces overt signs of anxiety.

Consequently, it was decided to determine the effect of providing monetary incentives for good performance on recall under certain of our standard conditions. Two such experiments were conducted at about the same time.

In the first incentive experiment, half of the subjects were told that they would receive at least thirty-five cents for their participation, but that they could earn up to twenty-five cents more if they performed well. The remainder were paid a flat thirty-five cents. Since rural Kpelle consider seventy-five cents a good wage for a full day's work and many workers receive only fifty cents a day, the promise of up to sixty cents for twenty minutes of a man's time was thought to be an adequate incentive.

The four groups in this experiment, each consisting of ten nonliterate adult subjects, represented the factorial combination of two incentive conditions (incentive versus no incentive) and two kinds of lists (non-clusterable and clusterable). In all other respects, the procedures were exactly like those used in the standard experiments.

The results conformed to those obtained earlier and there was no difference between the incentive and no-incentive conditions. If the Kpelle performances in the previous experiments were the result of motivational deficiencies, the incentive motivation used in this experiment was clearly inadequate.

A second experiment explored a slightly different motivating manipulation. Instead of simply telling the subject that he could earn more money by recalling more items, the subject was given a running account of his performance by the use of pebbles, which represented money. Each time that a word was correctly recalled, a pebble was added to the subject's pile, and he was told that he would get a penny for every four pebbles (five pebbles in the case of children). Pebbles are traditional markers used as counting devices in many situations and hence their function was thought to be clear in the context.

The results were, in all essential respects, the same as those obtained in the original free-recall experiment. There were small differences in the numbers of items recalled by the various groups, with the younger children performing worst. There was no noticeable improvement across trials and there was no reliable difference among the older children and the adults. Overall, there was no significant clustering.

One indication that subjects were not unaware of the consequences of increasing the number of items recalled was a marked tendency on the part of several subjects to say a great many items in their recall lists. The number of intrusions from repeated items or responses not on the original list was greater than we observed on other occasions.

On balance we can conclude that we have once again failed to affect the course of learning through a change in the incentives offered, and it seems that no qualitative changes are to be expected from this source. Granting the possibility that some other motivating manipulation might prove effective, we moved on to assess other plausible variables that might be at work.

Experiment 4: Recall among Nontraditional Kpelle Groups

One question that quickly comes to mind is whether or not Kpelle whose life experiences have taken them far outside traditional Kpelle culture will manifest the same kinds of recall phenomena as those described thus far. The data from the Vai (Appendix E) suggest that literacy or degree of Westernization might affect memory performance. The data from the second- through sixth-grade students seem to contradict such a conclusion, but further exploration is clearly in order. Initial steps toward answering this question were undertaken in three small studies.

Our first experiment on the recall of nontraditional Kpelle subjects compared ten- to fourteen-year-old schoolchildren who lived either in the area of Cuttington College or in Monrovia. We used schoolchildren in both groups so that only the fact of living in an urban setting or a semitraditional village would distinguish the two groups. The procedure used was that of the clusterable groups in the first free-recall experiment. The results are easily summarized. The urban Kpelle remembered slightly, but reliably more than the rural Kpelle (10.2 versus 8.7 items per trial, respectively). In all other respects, the data were virtually identical to the results of Experiment 1. There was little improvement over trials and no significant clustering. The magnitude of this difference is about equal to that between the Vai who knew Vai script and those who did not, suggesting that something to do with modernization is leading to the increase in recall. However, the lack of clustering among the Kpelle cautions us against judging the similarity of the underlying mechanisms, and in any event the major features of the data are quite unlike those observed in our studies in the United States.

In the next study, the clusterable list was presented to two groups of eighteen- to twenty-year-old Kpelle. One group consisted of ten nonliterate Kpelle from the town of Salayea, approximately sixty miles northwest of Cuttington College. Salayea is located on the main all-weather road running from Monrovia to the Sierra Leone border, but like the residents of Sinyee, these people were relatively traditional Kpelle rice farmers. The remaining ten subjects were Kpelle students attending two nearby high schools, the Lutheran Training Institute and Zorzor Training Institute. The students were in grades ten through twelve; in general they were living away from home, and as indicated in Chapter 2, they represent a nontypical population.

A second study contrasting nonliterate and high-school-educated subjects was conducted in the Cuttington area. An additional feature of this experiment was that training was continued for fifteen trials, instead of the usual five trials, in order to determine the effect of really extensive practice on recall and organization. The subjects were eighteen to twenty years of age. The high-school students were attending school in the county administrative center, Gbarnga. The nonliterate subjects lived in the town of Galai, a "feeder" town, many of whose citizens worked at Cuttington College. The first of these two studies was conducted by John Kellemu, the second by Paul Ricks. Except for the number of training trials given, the procedures for these two studies were identical to those used for the clusterable groups given oral presentation of the lists in the previous experiments.

The results of both experiments in terms of number recalled per trial are shown in Figure 4–7. The two experiments were consistent in showing a sizable superiority of the high-school students over the nonliterate subjects. This difference, significant from the outset, increased over trials; the high schoolers continued to improve with training, but the nonliterate subjects showed no improvement after Trial 3, and little improvement overall.

The same general relation between the two populations was observed in their clustering scores. As shown in Figure 4–8, clustering was similar for the two groups early in training, but the high schoolers show a

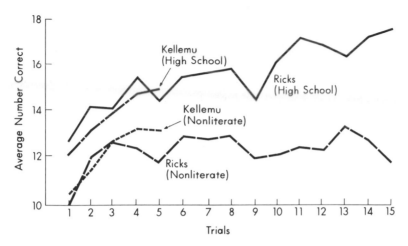

FIGURE 4–7 Average Number of Items Recalled per Trial for High School and Non-Educated Subjects. Replications by Ricks and Kellemu

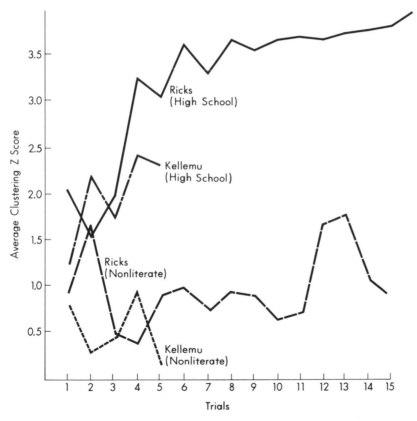

FIGURE 4–8 Average Clustering Scores as a Function of Trials Corresponding to Accuracy Data in Figure 4–7

clear improvement over trials, whereas there is little or no improvement for the nonliterate subjects for many trials.

In one general respect, these data differ from the data in our initial experiments; even for the nonliterate subjects, recall was a little better (twelve instead of nine items recalled per trial), and clustering was considerably better (.56 instead of $-.13$) than previously observed with nonliterate subjects run under the same conditions.

These discrepancies remind us once again that relatively small difference in the absolute levels of performance should not be given undue weight. It also reminds us that experiments that seek to compare performance for groups having dissimilar past experiences (like high-school-educated subjects versus nonliterates) must include both groups if the effect is not to be attributable to the experimenter or some other unknown factor, rather than to the variable in which one is interested.

On the basis of this scanty evidence, we can tentatively conclude that simply living in an urban environment does not qualitatively change the major features of free-recall learning, but that qualitative, as well as quantitative, changes in learning occur at the level of education represented by our high-school subjects. Some further evidence on the conditions under which education influences memory will be given in later experiments in this series.

What Produces Good Recall?

The results with high-school-educated Kpelle, combined with American data showing that increasing recall over trials and the occurrence of semantic organization begin after about three years of an American education, suggest that some features of recall may be the result of something connected with literacy when combined with the detached learning of the book and schoolroom. Unfortunately, we have neither grade-by-grade data for the Liberian student nor an independent evaluation of their degree of fluency in written English at different grade levels. Consequently, we will turn our attention in the opposite direction and ask: are there circumstances under which nonliterate, traditional people will manifest some or all of the organizational features produced by the Kpelle high-school students and older American groups?

One possible conclusion from such contrasts is that the high-school-educated, less traditional groups have acquired some general memory skill which the nonliterates lack. Another possibility is that the skill is in some sense specific; the nonliterate will manifest the same sorts of recall as the high-school student but under different conditions. It is these kinds of hypotheses that we sought to evaluate through a set of experiments that manipulate various facets of the recall situation in order to determine their effect on the recall of traditional subjects.

In two of the experiments attacking this problem we stumbled upon these two facts: (1) increasing the number of items to be remembered increased the number recalled; (2) asking the subject to place the items in a bucket, or to sort the items into cups, had a large effect on the number recalled and greatly increased the amount of semantic clustering. In the latter study, we seemed to have hit upon a mechanism for making the recall performance of the nonliterate Kpelle approximate the kind of recall we have observed in literate groups. The most likely candidate for the cause of the improved recall was the fact that subjects manipulated the items that were said to "go with the cups." Perhaps the cups served in some way to remind the subject of the items. Put in the language of contemporary theorizing about memory, these speculations give rise to the hypothesis that the cups act as cues, which aid the subject in retrieving the items from his memory.

The question then occurs: can the differences in amount and organization of recall that we have encountered in the studies reported thus far be accounted for on the basis of different retrieval cues? In particular, could it be the case that given the proper retrieval cues, the traditional, nonliterate Kpelle will show the organizational and recall features that we associate with our American subjects?

G. Mandler raises much the same issues in his recent discussions of organization and memory (Mandler, 1966). For example, he points out that it is necessary to make a distinction between the use of rules for effective retrieval from memory (such as semantic categories) and their discovery. In fact, Mandler goes so far as to hypothesize that the function of repeated trials in free-recall experiments, such as those we have been describing, is to give the subject repeated opportunities to discover the rule latent in the lists. Thus he says, "The free-recall situation demands a discovery by the subjects of some adequate rules that will allow them to make the input items accessible, and to retrieve them adequately" (Mandler, 1966, p. 41). Of clustering he says:

Obviously, a failure to find evidence of clustering might be due to the fact that the subject did not discover the specific rule that related members of subsets of the input list one or another. It is not equally likely, though it is possible, that subjects might discover the rule without being able to use it adequately. [Mandler, 1966, pp. 40–41]

It would seem that both in terms of an explanation of the results we observed with our Kpelle subjects and on more general theoretical grounds, it behooves us to make a systematic investigation of what kinds of cues might facilitate the use of, or the discovery and use of, retrieval rules.

Experiment 5: The Identification of To-Be-Remembered Items with External Objects: The Chairs Experiment

One of the first experiments we designed on the question of cues for recall was invented in the context of a discussion of the term *concrete*. It will be recalled that in introducing the contrast between objects and words as stimuli, we noted the suggestion that Africans have "concrete mentalities," and from this, we derived the idea that the use of concrete objects ought to enhance recall. When we failed to obtain the expected amount of improvement from the introduction of objects, one of our responses was to review the vague notion of a "concrete" stimulus and to hypothesize that what might be important is not the concreteness of the item to be learned, per se, but rather that the item have a concrete tie with some external object. In Mandler's terms, the subject might require such a concrete connection in order to discover the rule latent in the material. This idea fits in with our observations about sorting items into cups although the procedures we developed were somewhat different; the "concrete connection" was between items to be remembered and four chairs, with which the objects were said to "belong."

The first pilot experiment using chairs was run with two groups of ten- to fourteen-year-old schoolchildren in grades two to six. There were ten subjects in each group. The children all lived in Sergeant Kollie Town, a small roadside town located about two miles from Cuttington College. For both groups the experimenter stood behind four chairs, placed side by side, with a table on which the twenty objects were placed located behind him. The subject was seated facing the four chairs. The instructions used in earlier studies when objects were presented for recall were carried over unchanged to the present experiment, but the procedure was changed. On each trial when the experimenter held up an item to be remembered, he held it up over a particular chair for about two seconds, rather than simply holding it up where the subject could see it.

The two groups differed with respect to the assignment of items to chairs. In the rule condition, all items from a particular semantic category were held up over a particular chair. For instance, it might be that the items file, hoe, knife, hammer, and cutlass were held up over the chair on the far left of the subject; headtie, trousers, shirt, singlet, and cap over the adjacent chair, and so on. In the random condition, the semantic categories were broken up. A set of five items was always held up over a particular chair, but the selection of items did not constitute a naturally occurring linguistic group. It should be emphasized that the subject was not required to recall which chair an item had been held up over (as was the case in the paired-associate experiment discussed earlier), but only what items had been held up.

It is clear from Figure 4–9 that when items were assigned to chairs at random, the pattern of learning was very much like that we observed when objects were presented in the earlier experiments; recall averaged about twelve items, and improvement is restricted to the difference between the first two trials. For the rule condition, learning is more rapid and continuous, closely resembling the American pattern.

The same pattern emerges from an analysis of the clustering scores (Figure 4–10). There was significant *negative* clustering for the random condition (suggesting that subjects were clustering by chairs rather than by semantic categories), but highly significant clustering which increased over trials in the rule condition.

When these data were in hand, we felt that we had at last begun to approach an understanding of the dynamics of Kpelle memory organization. The replication sought to extend the basic findings of the pilot study by investigating such questions as the following: Would there be enhanced recall if there was only a single chair (perhaps using the chairs

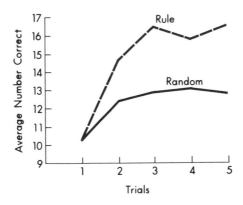

FIGURE 4–9 Average Number of Items Recalled per Trial for Rule and Random Groups in the Initial Study Using Chairs to Cue Recall

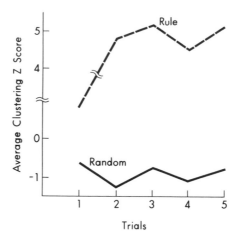

FIGURE 4–10 Average Clustering Scores as a Function of Trials in the Initial Study Using Chairs to Cue Recall

simply altered the subject's understanding of the task)? Would there be enhancement if items from a single category were always held up over the same chair, but the particular chair was changed from trial to trial?

To answer these and related questions, a large experiment was planned and executed. In view of the outcome, the strategy for conducting the replication could not have been conceived more poorly. A new experimenter was familiarized with the procedure. The experiment was conducted in a different area of Kpelleland than our previous studies, an area closer to the major population and rubber plantation center, and an area in which education was more widespread than it was around Cuttington College. The upshot of this experiment was that under *all* conditions, even one involving only a single chair, recall averaged seventeen to eighteen items per trial starting with Trial 1 and clustering was virtually perfect.

Further studies indicated that the effect produced by chairs as cues for recall depended heavily on specific features of the *experimenter's* behavior vis-à-vis the chairs.

However, this work was by no means a total loss; for one thing, *something* produced excellent recall in most of the studies using the chairs procedure. For another, our explorations of procedural variations in an attempt to track down the sources of variation go a fairly long way toward "explaining" (perhaps explaining away would be a better term) some of the gross differences in experimental outcomes.

We mention these experimenter differences in a series of experiments that we originally considered quite promising as an object lesson in the difficulties that can be encountered in research of any kind, but cross-cultural research in particular. The cases in which subjects' performance was all good or all bad speak only to the problem of experimenter differences. The cases where experimental treatments differ for the same experimenter indicate that genuine differential cuing effects can occur, but we do not know when they will affect both recall and organization and when they will affect only organization. (A general discussion of experimenter differences and other complications in conducting this kind of research are contained in Appendix F.)

Experiment 6: The Effect of Verbal Cuing on Recall

At the time of the first pilot study on the use of chairs as cues, when the subsequent experiments were not yet completed, we began to explore alternative ways of cuing recall. It seemed unlikely to us that cuing of the clumsy sort required by the use of chairs would be necessary to produce enhanced recall and organization. On both practical and theoretical grounds, we sought to determine if verbal cuing of any kind could influence recall in the way the chairs had in the initial pilot study.

Our first approach turned out to be much too subtle; we dropped one item from each category of the original clusterable list and inserted the category name instead. The results were identical to those obtained in the studies with the clusterable list and oral presentation.

Next we turned to a procedure based on the work of E. Tulving and his associates (Tulving and Pearlstone, 1966; Tulving and Osler, 1968). These experiments were concerned with the possibility that items might be remembered in the sense that they are stored in memory, but the subject cannot retrieve them at the time of recall. In Tulving's research, subjects were presented lists of words either with or without cue words present as a mnemonic aid. The cues were presented either at the time the to-be-recalled list was presented, or just prior to recall. It was concluded in the Tulving and Osler (1968) study that recall was enhanced only when cue words were present during learning, although it was considered possible that in the case of salient semantic groupings, the subject might provide the cue words (category names) for himself at the time of learning. The critical factor was thought to be the necessity for simultaneous storage of the item to be recalled and the retrieval cue.

Following the lead of Tulving and his associates, we sought to separate the use of cues during learning and during recall, and we varied the way in which these cues were presented: in some cases the subject was forced to recall by categories for part of the trials, in some cases this was optional.

The subjects were ten- to fourteen-year-old schoolchildren from the small road town of Wainsu, located approximately ten miles north of Cuttington College. The children were enrolled in grades two to six. Five groups of ten subjects each were run with the basic clusterable list for five trials. Presentation was oral.

The groups differed with respect to the point in each trial when category names were given as cues for remembering and the way in which recall of the items was elicited from the subjects. The basic four groups differed only with respect to when category cuing occurred; at the time the words were presented or at the time of recall. A two-by-two factorial design involving the four possible combinations of cuing at the time of presentation and recall represented the basic design. The instructions to each of these groups will make the group distinctions clearer:

1. Cued at both presentation and recall (cued-cued): "You and I are going to play. This play is about the things we work with. I will first call all of the names of these things. *The things will be clothing, tools, food, and utensils.* Listen to me carefully." (The items are then presented one at a time.) "Now I want you to name all of the things I told you; *they were clothes, tools, foods, and utensils.* When you are finished, tell me."

2. Cued at presentation, but not recall (cued-not cued): The instructions were the same except that the second italicized phrase was deleted.

3. Cued at the time of recall, but not during presentation (not cued-cued): The instructions were the same as the cued-cued condition, except that the first italicized phrase was deleted.

4. Never cued: Both italicized portions of the instructions to the cued-cued group were deleted.

5. Constrained recall: Subjects in this group were given the same instructions as the cued-cued group up to the point where recall began. Then for the first four trials, the subject was asked to recall the items by categories. For instance, he might be asked, "Tell me all the tools I named," then, "Now tell me all the foods I named," and so on. The order of recall categories was varied from trial to trial. When a subject had recalled all he could from a given category, the experimenter went on to the next until all four categories had been exhausted. This procedure was followed until Trial 5 at which time, without any warning, the procedure became that of the never cued group. That is, at the time of recall, the subject was simply told to name as many of the items told to him as possible.

RESULTS

In terms of the number of items recalled per trial, serial-position responding, and semantic clustering, the results for Groups 1 to 4 are entirely consistent with the results of previous experiments in which no cuing procedures were involved. There were no significant differences among the groups (which averaged about 11.5 items recalled per trial), very little improvement over trials, and a low level of clustering ($z = .49$). Although the absolute level of performance was slightly higher than that found in Experiment 1 where the same list and oral presentation were used, the level is typical of the experimenter for comparable experiments and of the same pattern and order magnitude as we found in Experiment 1. It would seem that giving subjects the category names as cues is not effective as a means for enhancing recall among our Kpelle subjects.

However, the results from the constrained-recall group indicate that verbal cuing *can* be effective under the proper conditions. Recall on Trial 1 was 16.6. On Trial 4 recall had improved slightly to an average of 17.6. Then, on Trial 5, when recall was completely unconstrained and uncued, recall for this group dropped only slightly to a level of 15.4, significantly better than the recall of the four other groups in the experiment (average = 12.9).

During the first four trials it was of course impossible to measure clustering for the constrained-recall group, which clustered perfectly by definition. However, on Trial 5 subjects in this group were free to recall items in any order they choose; clustering was the highest observed under any conditions in any of our previous experiments among the Kpelle ($z = 2.23$), except when chairs were used.

Thus, it would seem that a procedure that *forces* the use of cues has two effects on Kpelle free recall. First, it greatly increases the number of items recalled while the constraints are in effect. Second, it produces enhanced recall and semantic organization even after the constraints are lifted. How long such an effect would be preserved under unconstrained-recall conditions remains a topic for future research, but it seems that we have hit upon a way of "teaching" people to memorize more effectively in this short-term, free-recall task.

As interesting as the results from the constrained-recall group are, the question remains as to why the cued groups among the first four groups in this experiment failed to show any effects of cuing. The procedures we adopted were intended to be analogous to those used in similar cuing experiments in the Western psychological literature, but the outcomes were anything but similar.

A possible answer to this question may be contained in an examination of the adequacy of our "analogous" procedures. A re-examination of the work of Tulving and his colleagues indicated that their cuing was accomplished by providing the subject with a written list of the cue words during the appropriate cuing periods. Clearly, a procedure that relies on written words cannot be used with illiterates, but it is possible to use the procedures we developed in Liberia with literate American subjects. Although a comparison of Kpelle and American subjects using our procedure will not serve to specify the proper analogy between cuing procedures, it would serve the purpose of helping us to evaluate the effects of this cuing experiment. Consequently, a replication of this experiment was carried out with American subjects.

For our purposes here, the American replication of this experiment can be briefly presented. The subjects were third and sixth graders from the Laguna Beach, California, school system. The items to be recalled were the same as those used in the previously reported experiments where clusterable lists were employed with American subjects. Presentation and recall were both oral. The instructions were slightly elaborated versions of the instructions used for the comparable Kpelle groups. The experiment was conducted by Helen Wildwood.

In terms of the number of items recalled per trial and serial-position phenomena, the results obtained with our American schoolchildren were completely comparable to the results obtained with American schoolchildren reported on pp. 123–124. No significant effects were produced by the four cuing procedures used in Groups 1 to 4; a marked improvement took place over trials; a pronounced serial-position effect, dominated by recency was evident; and, a reliable difference between age groups appeared (the sixth graders recalled an average of 10.4 items per trial; the third graders, 8.2).

When we shift our attention to clustering effects, we find that overall there is no effect of the cuing conditions, but that late in training, the oldest subjects begin to show greater clustering in the cued-cued condition.

Most important, the American schoolchildren benefited from the highly constrained procedure of Group 5 in a manner quite similar to that observed with the Kpelle subjects. Recall was enhanced from the outset. However, in this case clustering, but not recall, was enhanced on

Trial 5, indicating that the conditions controlling transfer from the con-strained- to unconstrained-recall conditions need further study.

Experiment 7: The Effect of Embedding To-Be-Recalled Material in Natural Verbal Contexts

We next wanted to determine if there was some experimentally acces-sible, but natural, situation in which rule-governed retrieval processes would routinely be used by Kpelle subjects.

In most of the previous research that we know of, the paradigm for the study of memory in naturalistic situations involved recall of stories. The classic research in this area is described in Bartlett's (1932) mono-graph to which we made reference earlier in this chapter. However, to embark upon a study of recall of stories would fail to tell us how the free-recall situations we have been studying make contact with normally occurring recall for connected material. Consequently, we have chosen a middle course, which, we think, permits us to link recall for connected and disconnected material. The basic strategy that we adopted was to provide a continuum of story contexts in which to present the twenty basic clusterable items used in most of the previous studies. These con-texts varied from no context at all (our basic oral-presentation proce-dure) through a highly constrained story context in which each item was meaningfully linked to the neighboring item within the story. The sub-ject was told a story and then asked to recall the items that figured in the story and in one case the story itself (see Appendix G for details). Responses were recorded and analyzed just as they had been in the pre-vious experiments.

In one story a young man comes to the chief of a town and asks to marry the chief's daughter. He brings good bride wealth and the chief gives his daughter to the man. However, she soon discovers that he is a witch, and she wants to let her parents know where the man has taken her. So she leaves clues along the path as she travels to the man's farm. The clues (items) and their place on the path to the man's home make up the bulk of the story.

A second story involves four men who came to the town to ask for the chief's daughter. The first man brings five items of clothing; the sec-ond brings five items of food; the third brings five utensils; the fourth brings five tools. Once the story is told, the subject is asked what gifts were brought for the girl and then asked which man should get her.

The other stories contain the items in different arrangements designed to elicit differently structured recall.

In analyzing the results, it was found that the structure of the subject's recall mirrored the way in which the to-be-recalled items were structured within the story. If the items were structured in a linear manner (as in the first story described above), then a very high correlation between input and output orders was observed. However, if presentation structure was clustered, so was the structure of recall.

Discussion

Although by no means complete, the series of experiments presented in this chapter provides a wide range of situations in which to observe the influence of taxonomic categories on learning. And certain general patterns seem to emerge from the mosaic of results.

First, it is clear that under some circumstances all of the Kpelle groups studied were influenced in their learning by the presence of semantically definable categories. However, semantic control is neither uniform across groups nor across situations.

With respect to the various Kpelle groups studied, it appears from the evidence of our free-recall studies that semantic control (as manifested in clustering) became general in people with more than four to six years of schooling. How much more schooling we are not sure. Such control was not an inevitable consequence of maturation, because our adult populations differed little from younger groups.

The evidence from our American work shows really sizable amounts of clustering beginning to appear around the sixth grade, and it is possible that a similar finding could be obtained with the proper observations in Liberia. From Liberia we have the following pieces of evidence:

1. Comparisons of educated and nonliterate groups when the grades involved were second through fourth produced minimal clustering and slight differences in recall.

2. Comparisons of high-school students with nonliterate groups indicated rapid learning and significant clustering in the former.

Thus, it would appear that some time in the fifth- to eighth-grade range in Liberia, there is a change to a general use of semantic categories to control learning. We take it as no coincidence that these results parallel our findings in the similarity-mediation study in Chapter 3; the conditions that produce taxonomic "sorters" are most probably related to the conditions that produce taxonomic "rememberers."

The lack of a general influence of semantic participation in the learning process among those who have not had extensive schooling raises the question of what general statement can be made regarding the conditions under which such participation is observed. We offer the following formulation: the conditions in which the influence of semantic categories and rapid learning are observed are those in which the situation is structured for the subject. The conditions of structuring need not make explicit the categories (as when a single chair is presented, or the subject sorts items into cups without categorizing them), but when the structure of the categories is made explicit (verbal discrimination, the chairs, constrained recall), strong semantic involvement ensues. When the structure is strong and anticategorical (as in the case of certain of our story-recall situations), that structure will dominate.

This pattern of results is strikingly consistent with the account of the development of recall performance offered by J. H. Flavell and his associates. For example, Moely, Olson, Halwes, and Flavell (1969) in discussing the results of their study remark:

Both research findings and common sense lead one to suppose, for instance, that if a child of any age knows the name of an object he is instructed to remember, and if it also occurs to him to rehearse that name . . . then that rehearsal is very likely to help him remember the object. The problematical element in such a situation is precisely whether it will occur to him to rehearse, or for such situations generally perhaps, to engage in *planful* symbolic activity that is oriented towards and adapted to subsequent goal responses. [P. 32]

This description comes very close to characterizing the pattern of results from our Kpelle groups. The high-school student does not require specially structured situations in order to "have it occur to him" to use the semantic characteristics of the material to organize his recall—he produces that structure for himself. The nonliterate (and the same applies to those with little schooling) has not learned to spontaneously produce such structures under as wide a set of circumstances. He naturally uses them in some situations (when remembering stories) and can use them in a large variety of specially contrived situations (such as those provided by certain of our experiments).

In a number of instances we seemed to have tapped special organizing processes that permit the subject to retrieve the material he has been presented from memory. We have indicated certain naturally occurring situations in which such organization occurs spontaneously. We have laid to rest oversimplified ideas of rote memory and concrete mentality. But we have only nudged the iceberg that represents a full account of the processes underlying efficient and flexible learning (memorizing) and the cultural factors on which they depend.

We can look back on the verbal-discrimination studies as providing sufficient structure to induce the use of semantic information. Similarly, the chairs, constrained verbal cuing, and story experiments each, in its own way, provided such structure. But many of the simple free-recall studies did not, and hence learning failed to reflect the semantic structure of the to-be-learned material.

FIVE : Classification and Learning of Physical Attributes

"Why did you choose that one?" "Because
it was beautiful."
ANONYMOUS KPELLE SUBJECT

Especially to those unfamiliar with the history of psychology, it may seem strange that the vast majority of American studies of classification learning (called, among other things, concept learning and discrimination learning) do not involve natural-language classifications of the things of experience. Instead, psychologists have relied heavily on the study of classification based on *physical attributes* (color, form, size, number, and so forth), which characterize some aspect of the things of experience.

For example, L. S. Vygotskii (1962) in his classic studies of the kinds of concepts formed by children of various ages, used blocks that differed from each other in height, width, shape, and color. The blocks belonged to different groups (determined by Vygotskii), which were signaled by arbitrary labels which served as a sign of category membership. By carefully noting the way in which his subjects tried to form groups during their search for the "correct" way, Vygotskii was able to establish developmental trends which he then related to his theory of cognitive development. The details of Vygotskii's experiment are not essential to this discussion, but the idea that "a concept" represents the combination of certain values (wide, blue, etc.) of the attributes (size, color, etc.) that are used to describe the set of blocks represents a very basic tool of Western developmental psychology.

Why this emphasis on artificial materials? Although it might be possible to make a case for the general importance of color, form, and sim-

143

ilar physical attributes as the basis for classifications in Western socie-ties (traffic signs, signals of various sorts), it could hardly be argued that such categories play as important a role in everyday behavior (Bruner, Goodnow and Austin [1956] give excellent intuitive accounts of such processes). It is much less reasonable to assume similarity of processes when our subjects are traditional Kpelle rice farmers. For the American adult, the use of conventionalized symbols to "stand for" other situations is commonplace; not only his written language, but his whole education, are based upon such symbolic activities. The Kpelle, too, makes use of symbols, but not symbols of this kind and not for this purpose. Conse-quently, we are going to have to be especially concerned with the rela-tion between performance in our experiment and any underlying pro-cesses that we want to deal with in a speculative or theoretical manner.

A somewhat more subtle factor which enters into these experiments is that they almost all involve the use of materials that have no special meaning to the subject (blocks of wood or abstract designs on cards). This, of course, is a deliberate part of their design. But consider for a moment how rare a straight line, a perfect circle, or a pure, saturated red or green are in nature? In the Kpelle culture, which has no written lan-guage and only rudimentary pictorial art (such as patterns of cloth or painting on buildings), the standard classification of objects according to geometric form or pure, saturated color is not only a rare event, but probably contrary to experience.

A further problem concerns the relation between classification of the stimuli and the way in which the Kpelle language codes the particular dimensions involved. In the Kpelle language terms naming dimensions or attributes of experience are of several types, some of which seem to be different from English attribute names.

Number is one of the dimensions involved in our sorting problems, and our analysis of the language shows that numerical attribution is formed in a way very similar to that used in the English language (Gay and Cole, 1967; Gay and Welmers, 1970).

There are relatively fewer adjectives in Kpelle than in English. Of these, only the adjective translated "big" is a root word, while all the other adjectives are related to corresponding verbs. In particular, the adjectives naming colors are all related to verbs. There are three basic colors—white, red, and black. Each of these colors has a range of hue and saturation corresponding to it. Things are most frequently called white when they are of other colors, but are very low in saturation. The color red includes what in English would be named red, orange, dark yellow, and even certain shades of purple. Objects are identified as black when they are of high saturation; the color black includes what would be called green, blue, purple, brown, or black in English.

Adjectives naming geometric shapes are named in a variety of ways, but rarely in the same ways as in English. Adjectives such as *round, square,* and *triangular* simply do not exist in Kpelle. There are free nouns which name certain objects, and which refer by extension to those shapes found in other objects. One term applies to pot, pan, frog, sledgehammer, and turtle and indicates circularity. Another term indicates triangularity and is used for a tortoise shell, arrowhead, bird's nest and bow. The term for a path refers equally to a straight and a curved line.

There is also a set of adverbs that suggest various complex textures and shapes. These adverbs are translated by such English adjectives as *smooth, crumbly,* and *jagged.*

This brief survey of terminology naming the attributes and dimensions present in our experiments can perhaps set a context for interpreting certain of the results. Number is named in much the same way as in English. Color is named by fewer words than is true in English, and they have definite, high-salience conventional meanings in terms of the quality of experience. (For example, white is said to indicate generosity and friendship, black shows evil and the intent to humiliate, and red suggests both ripeness and foreboding.) It may be that behavior toward colors in our studies is influenced by these attributes, rather than by hue and saturation, but we have no specific evidence on this point. Form also is described in different words, in different word-classes, and with different referents than in English. Here, too, some of the behavior of our Kpelle subjects with respect to form may ultimately be shown to depend on such differences in usage.

The general point to keep in mind is that the American emphasis on classification according to physical attributes, such as color and form, and the dependence of our research techniques on pictorial representation and nonmeaningful stimuli play directly to an area of experience almost wholly lacking among the Kpelle, and one in which particular language differences may play a role.

As a consequence, the results of any such studies will be especially difficult to interpret. These experiments violate the principles of research that we have used in the previous chapters of this book, and it might well be objected that we have effectively ruled out this kind of research as a vehicle for cross-cultural comparisons. We have resisted such a conclusion, although we realize that by adopting traditional psychological methods for the study of concept learning, we are exposing ourselves to a series of difficulties in the interpretation of data. It is our belief that if we are careful in the way that we evaluate exactly what it is that our subjects do when we present them with a classification task and if we restrict ourselves to inferences warranted from the data, artificially constructed experimental tasks can be useful in cross-cultural research.

The situations we have chosen for formal experimental study are all relatively simple. They were not chosen as representative of common Kpelle problem-solving situations, but rather as possibly useful special situations in which the general processes underlying problem solving and concept formation could be manifested clearly enough to permit detailed analysis.

We will begin by reraising the issue of how stimuli are classified. Various techniques for classifying artificial stimuli commonly used by psychologists will be discussed. Among these are *sorting, matching,* and *discrimination-learning* procedures. Both sorting and matching provide evidence about the physical attributes that are likely to be the basis of classification. The discrimination-learning studies address themselves to a variety of problems. Prominent in our work are the following questions: how does ease of learning depend on the particular stimulus attributes comprising the problem? Under what conditions will a learned classification transfer to new problems?

All of our studies yield data about the influence of schooling on basic classification-learning skills.

A major distinction to grow out of the research reported in this chapter is between two ways of learning to classify a set of stimuli that differ in principle. The first of these learning processes we characterize as *stimulus-specific* or *isolated.* By this we mean that the subject, when he chooses (say) a red triangle instead of a blue triangle, does so because he learned that the specific red triangle in question was correct on a previous trial. The second kind of learning we characterize as *general* or *concept-based.* By this we mean that in choosing the red triangle, the subject is basing his choice on knowledge that red pictures are correct, although he may or may not have learned that the particular red triangle he chose was correct previously.

This distinction, which we first encountered in the early sections of Chapter 4, turns out in the present context to have broad implications for the course of learning across a series of similar problems. Because we think the issues raised by this series of studies are important for understanding cultural differences in cognition, we will present the course of our analysis in some detail.

Attribute Sorting:
The Classification of Artificial Stimuli

Just as we began our study of cognitive processes operating on the domain of everyday objects with an inquiry into the way in which the objects were classified, so we will introduce our study of concept learning of artificially constructed stimuli with a study of their classification.

Dimensional Preferences and Free Classification

Our earliest foray into the study of how the Kpelle classify artificially constructed simuli was reported in our first monograph on the Kpelle (Gay and Cole, 1967). Groups of subjects (six- to eight-year-old nonliterates, ten- to fourteen-year-old literates, nonliterate adults) were presented eight cards and asked to sort them into two groups so that the members of each group seemed to go together. The cards differed in the color (red or green) of the stimuli pasted on them, the form of the stimuli (triangles or squares), and their number (two or five stimuli per card); color, form, or number could serve as the basis for forming the two groups.

We found that there were no striking differences among groups when *first* asked to sort these cards. Color and number were selected as the basis for sorting somewhat more often than form, but the difference was not statistically reliable. A second study, in which the forms were traditional, stylized human figures (male and female), confirmed the results of the initial study.

A significant difference among the groups appeared when subjects were asked to *re-sort* the cards and to find a second way to form groups. When we first tried this task, we found that few of our subjects would arrive at a new principle for grouping the cards once they had hit upon one of the three possibilities. After several abortive attempts at making our instructions more explicit, we finally constructed a completely different problem, and the subject was given an elaborate demonstration of the way in which the task was expected to proceed (at this point in our research we were more intent on obtaining an idea of the order in which Kpelle subjects would consider various attributes than in classification and reclassification skills per se).

Even with this elaborate demonstration procedure as a preliminary instruction, only the schoolchildren were generally able to come up with an alternative grouping of the cards, and it took them almost a minute and a half to do so. The two nonliterate groups experienced a great deal of difficulty and only about a half of each of these groups arrived at a second grouping. Most schoolchildren did a second sort, but were generally unable to find the third regular grouping (only 36 percent did so); among the nonliterate groups the third sort was very rare.

The same general findings were obtained by M. H. Irwin and D. H. McLaughlin (1970), who carried out a set of similar observations with members of the Mano tribe, neighbors of the Kpelle in Liberia. One of the useful additions provided by Irwin and McLaughlin was a sorting problem that was analogous to the Gay and Cole problem, but that used rice as the material to be sorted. Working with this traditional, extensively measured, and familiar material, Mano adults were better able to find new ways to form groupings; at least some of the difficulty in reclassifying the pictorial material was apparently caused by the material itself and was not a general inability to reclassify.

Dimensional Preferences Measured by Other Techniques

Before discussing the implications of our initial study of classification, the results of two additional studies intended to elicit information about how various stimulus dimensions are classified need to be considered. In the first of these studies (presented in more detail in Appendix H) a matching procedure was used. The subject was shown cards containing pictures of three figures. He was asked which two of the figures belonged together. Individual cards were arranged to permit matches based on color (red, white, and black), form (triangles and squares), and size (small or large). In this study form was used as the basis of matching far more often than color or size; color dominated only if the choice was between color and size alone.

In the second study subjects were presented with two cards, each with a stimulus set printed on it. For example, the two cards might depict a single red triangle and two blue squares. The subject was instructed to name one of the cards so that the experimenter would know which card the subject had in mind. A set of twelve such pairs was constructed and presented to three groups of twelve subjects. The groups were six- to eight-year-old nonliterates, twelve- to fourteen-year-old schoolchildren (in grades four to six), and twelve- to fourteen-year-old nonliterates.

Among all groups the predominant response was for the subject to mention *only color* (for example, "It's the red one") in his response. Every subject mentioned color on every trial. Among the two nonliterate groups only two subjects mentioned number as well as color ("It's the two red ones") and only one mentioned form. Among the schoolchildren, five subjects mentioned number in addition to color, and only one mentioned form.

We present these data because they contrast so strongly with the results of our previous classification studies using stimuli of this type; color was not only dominant, it appeared to be the *only* dimension responded to by many of the subjects in the second study.

As a final complication these same stimuli were used in a sorting experiment analogous to that used by Gay and Cole (1967), and the results again indicated that color was far and away the dominant mode of classification.

Dimensional Preference?

If nothing else, this small set of studies of how the Kpelle will classify artificially constructed stimuli has amply demonstrated the validity of our warning that such material will present serious difficulties of interpretation. At the same time, the diversity of results with procedures that seem to be similar (and that generally produce similar results when conducted on subjects from Western countries) raises a number of issues that are central to our concern and about which we can offer a little evidence from the experiments presented in this chapter.

One conclusion seems fairly safe at this point: we are not going to be able to draw general inferences about the developmental significance of some particular order of classification (such as color over form) until we can specify the rules which lead one order to dominate under some conditions and another order to dominate under other conditions. In this respect we simply have to advise caution, although inferences based on dimensional preferences are widely used in cross-cultural research (Bruner, Olver, and Greenfield, 1966; Serpell, 1969). Second, any study of learning based on stimuli of this type must take account of the particular way in which the specific stimuli used are likely to be classified. It is not possible to make safe a priori assumption about color or form classification in general.

Problems in Re-Sorting
and the Transfer of a Discrimination

One of the more striking results from our earlier sorting experiments, as well as from those of Irwin and McLaughlin (1970), was the difficulty that our subjects, particularly our nonliterate subjects, experienced when asked to find a basis for sorting other than their original basis. This failure to reclassify is especially unusual when it is remembered that they had been given a demonstration problem in which the possibility of alternate modes of classification had been pointed out. Although striking, the difficulty in reclassification is very difficult to interpret. Even though we provided an example problem to our subjects, there was some question about how they interpreted the instruction to regroup a set of pictures which they had already been told was "fine." Even if there was no ambiguity about the instructions, and the difficulties with the second sort were the result of some deeper kind of misunderstanding, we cannot be certain what the extent of the problem was. For example, could subjects who experienced difficulty in spontaneously re-sorting these pictures learn to do so if a trial-by-trial *learning* procedure was used?

In order to answer this question we conducted a rather extensive experiment with five- to seven-year-old children who had not, for the most part, attended school, although some had entered the first grade to learn English. The stimuli were the same cards used in our original sorting experiment; they contained red or green figures that were triangles or squares, with two or five figures on each card. The procedure was quite different from that employed in the sorting studies. A subject was not presented the set of cards all at once, but rather was asked to discriminate between cards in terms of specific dimensions when the experimenter held up a pair of cards that differed along all three dimensions simultaneously (for example, two red triangles versus five green squares). The subject was instructed as follows:

I will show you two papers. Each time I show you these papers I want you to tell me which one I am thinking of. You must give me the one I am thinking of. If you are correct, I will say yes. If you are wrong, I will say no. You must try to be correct every time.

Each subject was presented a total of three problems. Every possible combination, including repetitions, of dimensions was sampled. When a dimension served as the basis for solution more than once, correct value was reversed between problems. For example, some subjects received a problem set where color was relevant on all three problems. In this case a particular subject might have the sequence: red correct, green correct, red correct. Other examples of problem sequences are color-color-form and color-form-number. This procedure yielded twenty-seven possible groups. Eight subjects were run in each subgroup for a total of 216 subjects. This extraordinarily large number of possibilities and subjects was included because we wanted to sample a large number of conditions under which subjects were required to switch the basis of their classification. Subjects continued responding until they were correct nine trials in a row or until forty trials had been presented.

On the first problem slightly more than half of the children were able to solve the form problem; in contrast, the color and number problems were solved by almost everyone. Ignoring the particular sequence of problem types, there was virtually no improvement for later problems in the three problem series. Only if the subject was presented a homogenous series of problems (for example color-color-color) was there any indication that learning on later problems was faster than learning on the initial problem. These results are graphically presented in Figure 5–1. On the left-hand side of the figure, we see the average number of trials to criterion (a score of forty was applied if criterion was not met) for homogenous problems. On the right-hand side of the figure, we see the results for completely heterogeneous problems (for example, color on problem two had been preceded by a form or number problem, and so forth). Even this rather crude representation of the data clearly indicates that there was a general absence of improvement unless the same dimensions served as the basis of solution throughout the experiment. Even under optimal conditions, there was very little improvement for the form problems.

Verbal justifications offered by the subjects, as we had come to expect from our earlier verbal-discrimination experiments, were very rare. However, they were qualitatively in line with the learning results. Only two subjects could verbalize the basis for a form solution—both said that they chose the "houses" (triangles). Twenty-two subjects identified

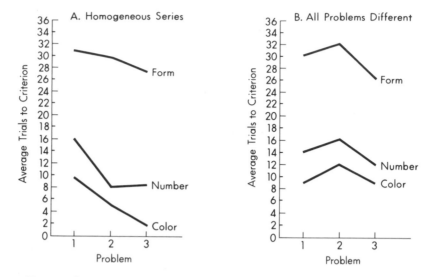

FIGURE 5–1 The Number of Errors Committed When Subjects Are Presented Problems Based on Color, Form, or Number. (In A, subjects have a single dimension relevant throughout training; in B, the dimension is changed from problem to problem.)

number solutions; in half the cases the number two was named and in most of the remaining cases the subject used the term *many*. Thirty-six subjects identified the color solution, using the term *black* for green and *red* for red.

These results suggest, first of all, that the failure to spontaneously sort along the form dimension persists even when an explicit training procedure is used. Before jumping to the conclusion that there is some general disability in understanding of form classes among this subject population, we need to consider additional facts. In the first place, there is no question that these children can make form discriminations—if they could not do so, they would be unable to function as human beings. The question is whether or not they can learn form classes with *stimuli such as those we have used here.* We know that under some conditions, at least, they can learn form discriminations of the kind presented here. In an investigation of discrimination among elementary geometrical-form classes (Gay and Cole, 1967, pp. 54ff.), children in the same general age range learned to discriminate the *class* of triangles from the *class* of squares in about thirteen trials.

But in the earlier work there were *no alternative dimensions on which the subject could base his response;* only the forms varied among the stimuli. This suggests that it may be competition among dimensions that is causing trouble for these subjects. A second suggestion from this study is that interproblem improvement in learning rate ("learning to learn") will occur only if the particular dimension serving as a basis for solution is maintained from one problem to the next. In order to clarify these issues, we need different, and, in general, simpler experimental situations, which will permit us to disentangle the possible processes involved.

Basic Procedure: Discrimination Learning and Transfer

As an example of one specialized approach, consider the following situation. The subject is shown two stimulus blocks, one a large black square, the other a small white square. These stimuli differ from one another on two dimensions; black versus white and large versus small. In a simple discrimination training procedure, this pair of stimuli is presented and the choice of one of the blocks is rewarded, that is, is said to be correct (for instance, the large black square). In this example the basis for the discrimination used by the subject is uncertain. Assuming that the blocks are presented on the left- and the right-hand of the subject in a random order, there still remains an important source of ambiguity. When the large black square is identified as correct, is it correct because of its largeness or its blackness? With the use of only one pair of stimuli, it is impossible to clarify this ambiguity. Therefore, in a typical experiment of this type a second pair of stimuli is presented on half of the trials, interspersed with trials on the first pair. This second pair performs the function of breaking up the ambiguity. In the particular case in point, one would introduce a large white square paired with a small black square. By evaluating the pattern of correct and incorrect choices on the two pairs, the subject can infer the dimensional basis for discrimination. If the experimenter designates (reinforces) both the large black square and the small black square on successive presentations, the subject could infer that "black" is correct. If, however, the experimenter reinforces the large black square and the large white square, the subject could infer that "large" is correct.

After the subject has reached some reasonable criterion of successive correct responses, there is still some ambiguity, but in this case the ambiguity rests in our inference about the basis for his selections. We might want to conclude that he has correctly analyzed the pattern of reinforcements and has acquired the concept in dimensional terms. For example, he may say to himself "black is correct" or "large is correct," or more complexly, "brightness is the relevant dimension, and black is the correct value of that dimension." However, there is another possibility: the subject may have acquired two separate choice responses, "large black square" and "small black square." These responses would imply that the two pairs of stimuli in the acquisition phase were learned as independent discriminations, and did not have a dimensional basis that bound them together.

One way to decide among these two possibilities (dimensional learning that includes both pairs of squares or learning of two independent discriminations) is to design transfer studies that indicate how the original discrimination was learned. The transfer conditions most widely applied for this purpose have been termed a "reversal shift" and "nonreversal shift" (Kendler and Kendler, 1967). A reversal shift is defined by a within-dimension change in reinforcement patterns (see Figure 5–2). For example, if a subject has been trained on "black" (either large or small square) we may shift our reinforcement to "white" (either large or small square). This change remains within the color dimension. What this means for the subject is that for *both* pairs in the original training, he must now shift his choice from the block that was previously correct to the previously incorrect block. A nonreversal shift, by contrast, involves a shift of reinforcement to a dimension that had not been previously employed, for example, a shift from "black" to "large." Considering block pairs instead of dimensions, this means that the subject must relearn only *one* of the previously learned discriminations. For example, if he had previously learned that the large black and a small black squares were correct, he can maintain his response to the small black square when shown small-black–large-white and must only change his response to choose a small white square when shown small-white–large-black. The subject must maintain his response on one discrimination pair but shift the response for the other. These relationships are shown schematically in Figure 5–2.

This analysis of reversal and nonreversal shifts would seem to indicate a clear advantage for transfer to a nonreversal condition if the subject is treating pairs separately, since he must only relearn one of the discrimination pairs. In the reversal-shift condition, he must relearn both. This pair-by-pair analysis, however, assumes that the two discriminations can be treated independently (by the experimenter in analyzing shifts in reinforcement and by the subject in relearning the discrimination). There is considerable evidence to suggest that rats (Kelleher,

Original Problem

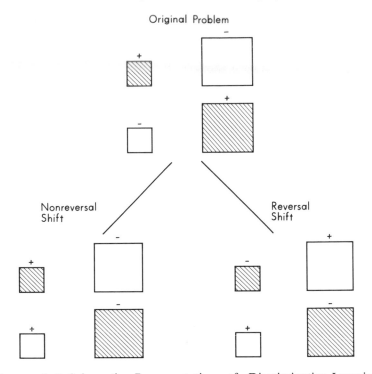

FIGURE 5–2 Schematic Representation of Discrimination-Learning Experiment in Which the Basis of Solution Is Shifted Following Initial Learning

1955) and young human children (Kendler, Kendler, and Wells, 1960) perform in exactly this manner.

However, our intuitive description of this problem is in terms of stimulus dimensions and attributes ("the black ones are correct"), and the pairs are treated as instances. What if subjects are, indeed, responding in terms of our casual description and using the stimulus dimensions to bind together their responses to the two subproblems? In this case making a double change might be easier than changing only one discrimination. We may, therefore, argue that reversal shift should be easier than nonreversal shift for people who approach the problem in this way, since a reversal allows the subject to make a *patterned* change to "the problem" as a whole.

Pursuing this line of argument, we may say that, if it is shown that reversal shifts are learned more rapidly than nonreversal shifts, the reasonable conclusion is that the subject is responding to the two pairs of stimuli in a common fashion; in contemporary terminology, he is using the stimulus dimensions to mediate his performance. The bulk of the evidence indicates that older subjects (beyond kindergarten) make reversal shifts faster than they make nonreversal shifts, lending support to the analysis presented here. (In somewhat different terms, this analysis and the data upon which it is based are presented in Kendler and Kendler, 1968.)

Recent analyses of the discrimination-transfer process, while supporting the general developmental trend that we have just described, suggest that the learning processes involved may be analyzable into a combination of elementary processes, which include, but are not exhausted by, our description of "typical" adult performance given above. As we shall see, we believe this analysis to be directly relevant to an understanding of cross-cultural differences in elementary concept learning.

The Pseudoreversal Paradigm: Stimulus Dimensions versus Response Patterning

Consider again the reversal-nonreversal paradigm diagrammed in Figure 5–2. In light of our previous discussion, we can see that two things are involved. On the one hand, there are two pairs of stimuli to be learned before we introduce the reversal of the subject's response to either one pair (nonreversal shift) or two pairs (reversal shift) of stimuli. The presence of multiple stimulus dimensions presumably influences the transfer (shift) learning. However, it is possible to learn this problem without using dimensional information by learning that two independent discriminations are presented, and continuing to respond in the successful manner until a clue is given that something about the problem has changed (for example, the previously correct member of a pair is now incorrect). A subject who learned in this manner might reason, "if this first pair has been changed, perhaps the other changed too." Further, he might do all of this without ever saying to himself that the two discriminations involve the same stimulus dimension—he may only be picking up response patterns.

The possibility of such pattern learning in young American subjects was investigated by B. Sanders (1971). Her experiment was exactly analogous to the reversal-nonreversal paradigm illustrated earlier, with the important exception that the two discriminations to be learned bore no obvious dimensional relationship to one another. One pair of stimuli consisted of two crosses—one red and the other black. The other pair consisted of a square and a triangle, both of which were gray. This arrangement makes a dimensional response to the first pair ("the red one is correct") of no help in learning the second discrimination ("the square one is correct").

With a two-component problem of this type, it is possible to investigate the effects of response patterning in shift behavior independent of the stimulus dimensions. If the subproblems are learned independently, we ought to be able to see this independence operate during the shift phase of the experiment. Continuing the analogy with the typical discrimination-shift experiment, Sanders changed the reinforcement contingency on one or both of the discriminations. Among younger children she found that changing only one pair (pseudononreversal) was an easier transfer problem than changing both pairs (pseudoreversal). These results parallel results obtained when dimensions are common to both stimulus pairs. Sanders found that the superiority of nonreversal among younger children was the result of their tendency to treat the discriminations independently. However, dependence between the two subproblems characterized the learning of the older subjects. That is, once the shift phase began, a nonreinforcement on one subproblem immediately led to a spontaneous change of choice on the second subproblem. This spontaneous shifting resulted in errors if the second pair was not changed (nonreversal) but immediate solution if the second pair *was* changed (reversal).

This evidence strongly suggests that in addition to (and even possibly instead of) any dimension-related mediation of responses involved in discrimination transfer, there are strategies of response-patterning which operate in this situation to unite subproblems. As the most elementary form of discrimination-reversal problem, we will begin our discussion of discrimination transfer among the Kpelle here.

Methods and Procedures

Two pairs of stimuli were used in the acquisition and shift phases of the study. Pair 1 consisted of two T-shaped cutouts of three-eighth-inch plywood of equal size; one was red and the other black. Pair 2 was a triangle and square of roughly equal size cut out of three-eighth-inch plywood. The triangle and square were left unpainted (and, hence, highly similar in color). The pairs were presented repeatedly throughout the acquisition series in a randomized order, which varied both the succession of pairs and the side on which the correct member of the pair appeared.

Subjects sat at a table facing the experimenter, who was a Kpelle college student. The subjects were told: "Each time I will show you two things. Every time I do this, you must tell me which one I am thinking of. If you are correct, I will say 'yes.' If you are incorrect, I will say 'no.' Try to be correct every time."

Each subject was run until he had made fourteen correct responses in a row (a rather stringent criterion, but one which seemed necessary, because two independent discriminations were to be learned); in most cases this criterion reduces to seven in a row correct on each of the two discriminations. After subjects had successfully demonstrated acquisition of the two discriminations, they were randomly assigned to either a pseudoreversal-shift or a pseudononreversal-shift condition. The reversal condition was defined by our shifting reinforcement contingencies on *both* of the discriminations. The nonreversal condition was defined by our shifting reinforcement contingencies on only *one* of the discriminations. Subjects were run to criterion of ten in a row on the shift condition.

Four groups of thirty-two subjects each were employed. These were six to eight year olds who had not attended school, six- to eight-year-old first graders, nine to twelve year olds who had not attended school, and nine- to twelve-year-old third graders.

RESULTS

In view of the results of the earlier experiment with color, form, and number solutions, where many of the children failed to learn a form discrimination and learning was generally slow regardless of the dimension, it is of some interest that learning for this problem was extremely rapid. The younger nonliterate subjects learned in an average of six trials for the two subproblems combined, indicating an average of only three trials per subproblem. The older children learned slightly, but not significantly, more rapidly. This result is one further bit of evidence that there is nothing inherently difficult about form classifications per se, but leaves open the question of when they are difficult and when they are not.

The basic question of interest in this study is, "are subjects treating the two discriminations independently, or are they in some way interdependent?" Regardless of whether the subject was in the reversal or nonreversal condition, we looked at his first response after no reinforcement as evidence relating to the question of independence.

Two possibilities exist. If the subject was treating the problems independently, his response to one pair would remain unaffected by his experiences with the other. In the case of a reversal shift (where the reinforcement contingencies are changed on both pairs), the subject should make an error on his first encounter with the second pair (since he is preserving his old response to that pair—which is now wrong). In the case of a nonreversal, the subject should respond correctly to the second pair, because the reinforcement contingencies on that pair are unchanged. This situation would produce a small, but consistent difference in favor of the nonreversal shift.

A second possibility, however, is that the subject has treated the two discriminations in nonindependent terms. He may see information gained from experience with one stimulus pair as being relevant to his performance on the other pair. In this case nonreinforcement on one pair would produce a "spontaneous reversal" on the other. This would lead to an error in the nonreversal condition, where the second pair has not changed, and a correct response in the reversal situation, where both pairs have been changed. In this case reversal would be easier than nonreversal learning.

Data pertinent to this analysis are shown in Table 5–1. Statistical

TABLE 5-1

Percentage of Subjects Who Spontaneously Shift

AGE	EDUCATIONAL STATUS	
	SCHOOL	NONLITERATE
Six to eight years old	33	28
Nine to twelve years old	57	25

analysis on the data in Table 5–1 (using the chi-square test) revealed the following:

1. Older children tended to make more spontaneous shifts than younger children, and the schoolchildren made more spontaneous shifts than those who had not been to school.
2. Older schoolchildren did better than their nonliterate age mates, to a greater extent than did younger schoolchildren.

The pattern of results from this study strongly suggests that younger children, and children who had not attended school, tended to treat the individual instances in simple discrimination problems as if there were no relation between instances. Older children, especially if they had been to school, treated the individual subproblems as instances of some more general problem.

Looking back to the complex transfer problem that began this section, we can speculate that one of the difficulties that the subjects were experiencing (recall that they were quite young and had not attended school) was that they were not sensitive to the relation among separate pairs of instances. But before settling on that conclusion, we need to consider another simple discrimination-learning problem where common dimensions do, potentially, unite instances.

Standard Two-Dimensional Discrimination-Transfer Studies

When we first began our research using the discrimination-transfer experiment, we did not distinguish the response- and dimension-learning aspects of subjects' performances. Basing our work on extant theory (particularly that of Kendler and Kendler, 1962), we began by using the more or less standard discrimination-transfer design upon which the phylogenetic and ontogenetic sequence we outlined earlier rested. Our first experiment (described in more detail in Gay and Cole, 1967, pp. 84ff.) included sixty-four nonliterate Kpelle children between the ages of six and eight years. The stimuli were four 1″ x 1½″ wooden blocks that varied in height and color. Two of the blocks were 5″ high (T-tall), the other two were 2½″ high (S-short). One of each size was painted green (G) and the other white (W).

The children were tested individually by a Kpelle-speaking college student who was drilled in the proper techniques. All work was done in Kpelle. The experimenter and the child sat opposite each other at a table or on the ground. The experimenter then read the following instructions (in Kpelle): "I will show you two blocks of wood. Each time I show you these blocks, I want you to tell me which one I am thinking of. You must give me the block I am thinking of. If you are correct, I will say, 'yes.' If you are wrong, I will say, 'no.' You must try to be correct as often as possible."

The experimenter presented the pairs of stimulus objects in a predetermined order which he read from a mimeographed score sheet. Each cue appeared an equal number of times on both sides. No stimulus pair appeared together on more than two consecutive trials. The criterion of learning was nine out of ten successive correct responses.

During training, the subjects were presented with SG-TW or SW-TG pairs, as shown in Figure 5–2. For half the subjects height was relevant; for the other half, color. Each value of the two dimensions was relevant for half of the appropriate subgroup.

The discrimination-transfer phase of the experiment was begun as soon as the training criterion was reached without interruptions or change in instructions. The four subgroups from the training phase (as defined by the positive dimension and attribute) were split, with a randomly selected half of each subgroup given a nonreversal shift while the other half was given a reversal shift.

In view of our later experience, one detail of the procedure used during the shift phase of the experiment must be described. Following acquisition, the pairings of the blocks were changed so that only a single dimension varied at a time. Thus, if the acquisition pairs were SW-TG and SG-TW, and if during the shift phase the correct response was "green," the shift pairs were TG-TW and SG-SW. This procedure, which was adopted to make the results as comparable as possible with those obtained by Kendler and Kendler (1959), precluded responses during the shift phase that were based on acquisition-phase *pairs,* since the acquisition pairs never occurred together.

RESULTS

The children learned the initial discrimination in approximately six trials, which is comparable to the speed of learning reported in American experiments using stimuli of this type and children in this age range. The only difference among groups was a strong learning-rate bias in favor of the size dimension (3.1 trials to criterion) over the color dimension (9.5). A similar bias was found by Kendler and Kendler (1959). In view of our earlier results showing a preference for color classification, this result serves to remind us once again of the situation-bound nature of dimensional preference among the Kpelle.

Performance on the transfer discrimination averaged 7.8 trials to criterion for both the reversal and nonreversal groups. This lack of differential transfer, when we first encountered it, appeared to be confirmation of the Kendler and Kendler findings that there is a transition point at about seven years of age at which the two kinds of transfer tasks are learned with equal ease. Also in line with their results was the fact that an analysis which separates the performance of fast and slow learners on the initial problem reveals the fast learners excel at the reversal shift, while the slow learners perform better on the nonreversal shift. As we reported in our earlier monograph (Gay and Cole, 1967, p. 87), we found that fast learners did, in fact, learn the reversal shift more quickly while slow learners learned the nonreversal shift more quickly. Unfortunately, subsequent analysis indicated that the fast learner–slow learner dichotomy was confounded with the rates of learning on the different dimensions, so that all that we now want to conclude is that nonliterate Kpelle children in the six to eight year range learn reversal and nonreversal shifts with equal ease for this set of stimuli.

If the Kendlers' analysis were correct, however, it would still be possible to show a developmental trend in response to the various kinds of transfer tasks by studying older and younger children. Consequently, we embarked upon such an enterprise, and for good measure, we included comparisons of nonliterate with school-attending children of the same ages.

The upshot of several studies using groups from four to fourteen years of age and zero to six years of schooling was that in virtually every case, reversal and nonreversal shifts were learned with approximately equal ease. The only regularities that stood out from this series of studies were a strong preference for the size dimension and a tendency for the older children to learn *more slowly* than the younger children. Neither of these findings could be considered hopeful bases upon which to build a developmental explanation of Kpelle problem-solving processes.

At approximately the same time as this initial study began (using the four blocks and nonliterate six to eight year olds), we undertook a similar study using considerably more complex materials with adults and young teen-agers (Cole, Gay, and Glick, 1968). The materials used were copied from a study by Kendler and Mayzner (1956) in which the authors were interested in studying discrimination transfer in American college students. The task required subjects to match each of sixteen response cards to one of two stimulus cards. There were several possible principles for matching—one of which the experimenters had arbitrarily chosen to reward. Once criterion had been reached on the initial discrimination, the basis of solution was switched in either a reversal or nonreversal fashion.

In this case we found that: (1) nonliterate adults showed positive transfer (learned more quickly) when presented a reversal shift and negative transfer when presented a nonreversal shift. This finding is similar to that obtained by Kendler and Mayzner (1956) for their college students. (2) Schoolchildren showed the same pattern as the adults. (3) Nonliterate children learned the reversal shift at the same rate as the initial problem and a nonreversal shift slower than the initial problem. Clearly, there are conditions under which the gross pattern of Kpelle discrimination-transfer processes is very similar to that of educated American adults. But such was not the case in our initial studies, and we are left with the problem of identifying the processes at work in the simple four-stimulus situation with which we began this investigation.

Returning to the outcome of the pseudoreversal experiment, it will be recalled that our analysis of that experiment considered each training pair as a separate problem and determined empirically the degree to which learning of one pair influenced learning of the other. The procedure adopted in our study of the four-stimulus, two-dimension problem did not permit us to follow learning of the individual pairs during reversal because we had carefully rearranged the pairs in order to preclude pair-specific transfer.

In the last two experiments in this series, we returned to the straightforward procedure of using the same stimulus pairings in the shift phase that were used in the training phase; assignments of correct stimuli within each pair were simply changed in accordance with the shift procedure desired. In all other respects the procedure was the same as that employed in the previous experiment (pp. 160–161) with which we introduced the four-block, dimensional experiment.

The subjects in the first of these experiments were 128 illiterate Kpelle children, half of whom were six to eight years old, half of whom were ten to fourteen years old. Within each of these age groups, subjects were assigned to various subgroups on the basis of availability (reversal or nonreversal shift, color or height correct, and so forth). For the major comparisons (age and type of shift), this arrangement meant that there were thirty-two subjects within each group.

The initial discrimination was learned in an overall average of 10.9 trials with the older children learning somewhat faster than the younger ones. The transfer phase was learned in 10.6 trials on the average. In this case reversal learning (9.2) was slightly, but not reliably, more rapid than nonreversal learning (12.1). Thus in its gross features this experiment produced results that are similar to those of our initial four-block problem, although the procedures were slightly different during the shift phase.

Because the stimulus pairings were not changed between initial learning and transfer, it was possible in this case to trace learning for each of the pairs separately. Consider once again a concrete example. Suppose that in initial learning, a subject is presented pairs consisting of tall-white versus short-green and short-white versus tall-green and the white blocks are correct. If a reversal shift follows, the correct block for each pair becomes incorrect; both pairs involve a change in the choice of blocks for solution. If a shift to choice of the tall blocks follows (nonreversal shift), solution of the tall-white versus short-green pair remains unchanged, but choice on the remaining short-white versus tall-green pair must be reversed.

If our analysis of the pseudoreversal learning problem is applicable (at least in part) to an analysis of this dimensional problem, we ought to expect different patterns of learning on the changed and unchanged pairs; the changed pair should suffer greatly during transfer, the unchanged not at all. Predictions concerning reversal learning are not so clear except that initial performance ought to be poor on both pairs. As a basis for discussion of the pair-by-pair learning that occurred during the transfer phase of the experiment, we have plotted the proportion of correct responses for the changed and unchanged pairs of the nonreversal condition and the two pairs for the reversal condition in Figure 5–3. This comparison is carried out only for the ten trials of the transfer phase because our practice of using a criterion of nine out of ten correct responses, combined with rapid learning on the part of many subjects, insured complete representation of all the subjects only through nine trials and almost complete representation with ten trials. With pairs interspersed, this arrangement meant that the first five trials for each pair were represented in the analysis. Since there were no important age differences, the two age groups were averaged together for this analysis.

From Figure 5–3 it is clear that for the nonreversal condition, performance on the unchanged pair remained at a very high level, although it was by no means perfect. Learning of the changed pair began at zero (there was no way for a subject to know that the basis of solution has changed for this pair until he had experienced it once during the shift phase) and increased rather slowly so that by the end of five trials with the changed pair (ten trials overall), performance was equivalent on the two pairs.

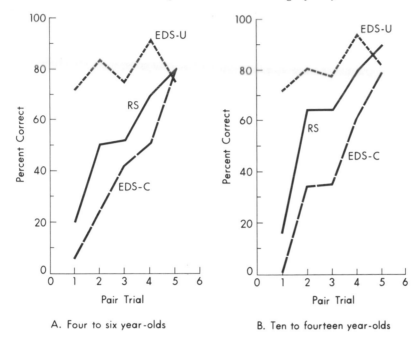

A. Four to six year-olds

B. Ten to fourteen year-olds

FIGURE 5–3 Trial-by-Trial Learning of the Discrimination-Shift Problem: Kpelle Nonliterate Children

The separate analysis of the two pairs suggests that they *were* being learned relatively independently. However, this result raises a puzzling problem: if changed pairs are learned so slowly, why don't we observe extensive negative transfer for the reversal group? After all, in this condition *both* pairs are changed. The answer provided by Figure 5–3 is that the learning rate for the two changed pairs of the reversal problem was greater than that of the single changed pair of the nonreversal problem. Moreover, a comparison of the initial trials with each of the pairs provided solid evidence of the *nonindependence* of the pairs. For the first pair presented, there were no corrected responses; this trial was simply a continuation of initial training from the subject's point of view until *after* he had been told he was wrong. For the second pair presented, 34 percent of the subjects responded correctly, although on their previous experience with that pair, the opposite block was correct. Thus, it appears that we have witnessed another manifestation of "spontaneous shifting," which clearly indicates that at least in terms of response-learning strategies, the two pairs were in some way connected.

To complete the picture we have obtained comparable data from two groups of middle-class American children tested on the same problem with very similar procedures (courtesy of T. Tighe). The older American group average ten years of age, the younger about four years of age (the data are from Tighe and Tighe, 1967). The results of our pair-by-pair analysis is shown separately for each of the American groups in Figure 5–4. Looking first at the right-hand panel, we see that the non-reversal performance of the younger American subjects looks like the nonreversal performance of both of our African groups; performance on the unchanged pair remained quite good, while performance on the changed pair dropped to zero and then recovered. However, for these young American subjects performance on the reversal problem was just like that for the changed pair in nonreversal; the subjects did not show the intermediate rate of learning for the two changed pairs that puzzled us in the Kpelle performance. As a consequence, nonreversal learning as a whole proceeded more rapidly than reversal learning. When we look at the results from the older American subjects, a completely new pattern of performance appears. Here performance on both pairs under both shift conditions suffered, and recovery was faster in the reversal case where both pairs had been changed.

Several points about the relation between Kpelle and American performances are intriguing. First of all, the Americans showed much more clearly than the Kpelle a distinction between independent learning of pairs (the younger children) and nonindependent learning where pairs were learned as "examples" of a more general problem (the older children). The Kpelle seemed to show both tendencies in some measure, as if they could treat the problem either way, depending on the circumstances. Moreover, there was no age-related trend among the Kpelle; both age groups showed the same pattern; as a consequence the younger children seemed precocious, the older children, retarded. Unfortunately we have no educated children run under these conditions, although results of the pseudoreversal study indicate that educational experience may affect the pattern of performance.

Further, these discrimination-transfer problems bear a direct relation to a question of major concern to us—under what conditions will learning one problem speed learning of a later problem? These data and our analysis of them suggest that only under special conditions are we going to find Kpelle children learning simple classification problems faster because they have learned a similar problem previously. More rapid learning occurred only when the relevant stimulus dimension exerted control over learning (in the Cole, Gay, and Glick 1968 study with six-

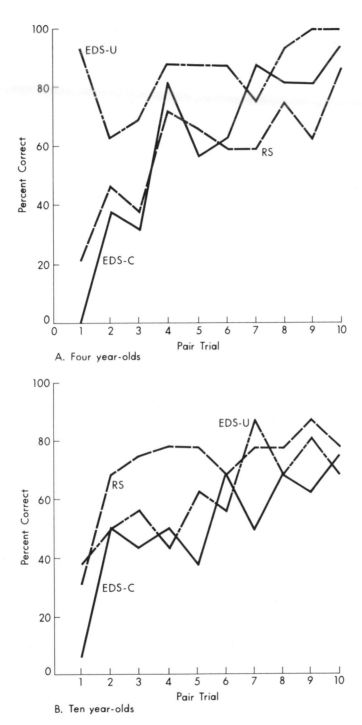

A. Four year-olds

B. Ten year-olds

Figure 5–4 Trial-by-Trial Learning of the Discrimination-Shift Problem: American Schoolchildren

teen response cards), but we have found this generally not to be the case. In the absence of dimensional control (when subjects treat subproblems separately), the new problem, even if the same dimension is involved, is in effect a *new* problem. Thus, questions of subproblem learning and dimensional control seem to underlie the more general problem of learning to learn. We also have to reject the idea that we are dealing with learning mechanisms (linguistic mediation, abstraction, and so forth) that are not universal among the Kpelle. We know that under some conditions learning will occur under generalized dimensional control. For example, such a process is implied by the results of the Cole, Gay, and Glick (1968) experiment described briefly on pp. 162–163 where twelve- to fourteen-year-old nonliterates learned a reversal shift faster than a nonreversal shift. Still lacking, however, is any specification of when learning will occur in the instance-specific manner implied by the independence of the subproblems in our simple discrimination studies and when it will occur under general dimensional control.

Transposition

One classic situation used by American psychologists to study both the question of stimulus-specific versus dimension-based learning and the role of linguistic mediating processes is the so-called transposition experiment.

As first used by us among the Kpelle, the procedure was to present a subject with two blocks, varying in size. On each trial the subject guessed which of the two blocks was "correct." Assuming for the moment that the larger of the two blocks was always correct (exactly the same logic applies to the choice of the smaller block), the experimenter continued to reinforce the choice of the larger block until the subject identified it as correct on nine successive trials. Then a new pair of blocks was presented in which two larger blocks (or the originally correct block and one larger than it) were presented, and the subject indicated which of these new blocks was "correct." The central question of interest is whether, when the new pair of blocks was presented, the subject chose the block that was previously correct (or the member of the pair nearest in size to the correct block) or the block that was larger than its mate. In other words, does the subject base his discrimination on the choice of a particular block, or does he base it on the relation of the two blocks along the dimension of size?

Regardless of what kind of test pair was presented and regardless of whether the initially correct block was larger or smaller than its mate, the subjects responded *relationally* (see top curve in Figure 5–5 and see Cole, Gay, Glick, and Sharp, 1969, for details of the experiment).

This experiment was repeated exactly using a color continuum. For one condition the training cards were two shades of gray, with the darker of the two always being correct. For a second training condition, three shades of gray were presented, with the middle shade always correct. Subjects run under these conditions (six- to eight-year-old or twelve- to fourteen-year-old nonliterate Kpelle children) gave the results in the lower two curves in Figure 5–5 (there were no substantial differences among age groups, so the curves are an average of all subjects who were presented a particular problem). Consider first the curve indicating transposition of the darker-than relation. From Figure 5–5 it is obvious that in general there was less relational responding than we had observed in the case of size transposition (the average amount of transposition for comparable age groups on the size transposition was about 90 percent). Moreover, when dealing with color, the particular test pair

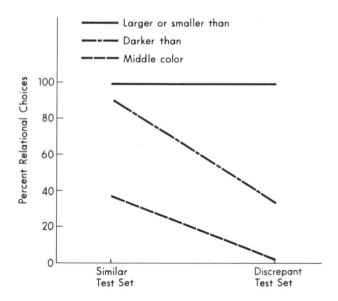

FIGURE 5–5 Average Number of Relational (transposition) Choices as a Function of Discrepancy between Training and Testing Blocks and the Nature of the Rule

made a difference; the pair which overlapped with the training pair was responded to as if the subject were choosing relationally, while the card nearest in color to the correct card during training was chosen most often if the test pair was discrepant from the training pair.

When we consider transposition of the "middle color" which is represented by the curve, relational responding was even less likely, but the effect of testing with a similar or disparate test set was about the same.

We do not propose to explain these results. We present them because they dramatically illustrate the fact that our Kpelle subjects can, for problems which seem very similar to us, respond in widely different manners that bespeak very different *ways* of learning.

Dimension Preferences, Concept Learning, and Learning to Learn

As a finale for this series, we will describe an experiment that unites several features of the disparate studies included in this chapter (a detailed report of this experiment is contained in Sharp, 1971). To begin this study, Sharp conducted the dimensional-preference study described on pp. 147–149, in which subjects were presented with pairs of cards differing from each other in terms of the color, number, and form of the figures printed on them. It will be recalled that when asked to describe these stimuli so that the experimenter could pick the correct card, subjects described the cards almost exclusively in terms of color, and when asked to sort these same cards, essentially the same results were obtained. Thus, in terms of two quite different measures of dimensional preference, it was found that color was a much more likely basis for choice than either number or form (the dimensions and values were color—red, blue, black; form—triangle, circle, square; number—two, three, four).

Then Sharp conducted a discrimination-learning experiment with the very same stimuli. His subjects were six- to eight-year-old nonliterates, twelve- to fourteen-year-old nonliterates, and twelve- to fourteen-year-old schoolchildren in the fourth to sixth grades. Seventy-two subjects from each subpopulation served in the experiment; within these groups, subgroups of twelve subjects each were run in specific experimental conditions.

Unlike our earlier experiment involving the learning of successive discriminations with multidimensional stimuli, Sharp arranged things so that the correct dimension remained from one problem to the next. However, the particular set of cards changed from problem to problem. For example, a subject trained on color might have to discriminate between red and blue on the first problem, blue and black on the second problem, and red and black on the third problem (the correct attribute never remained the same for two successive problems).

In addition to studying learning of each of the dimensions, Sharp created three degrees of variability with each problem. In some cases only the relevant dimension differed between the two stimulus cards (for example, when number was the solution, two red triangles versus three red triangles). Sometimes one of the irrelevant dimensions varied (two red triangles versus three green triangles), and sometimes both irrelevant dimensions varied (two red triangles versus three green circles). The purpose of this manipulation was to assess the possibility that the children in our initial discrimination study with these relatively complex stimuli were hindered in their learning by the complexity of the varying, irrelevant stimulus dimensions.

The major result of this experiment is shown in Figure 5–6 where learning curves for each of the groups are shown separately for each dimension. Considering first the performance of the six to eight year olds, we see that regardless of the dimension of solution, there was relatively little improvement across problems. The twelve- to fourteen-year-old nonliterates showed improvement for form and number, while the twelve- to fourteen-year-old schoolchildren showed marked improvement on all dimensions. In general, the number of varying irrelevant dimensions did not affect the results graphed in Figure 5–6. Hence we can conclude that any difficulties experienced by our subjects in learning this kind of problem cannot be accounted for by the variability of alternative dimensions. On the other hand, the older children were learning to learn this problem fairly effectively, and in this case schooling seems to have increased the rate at which improvement occurred over problems.

A strong clue as to the reason for the lack of improvement across problems for the six to eight year olds and the improvement for the other groups was provided by an analysis of the performance of these groups up to the point where they reach the criterion of ten successive correct responses. Figure 5–7 shows a backward-learning curve for the third form problem for each of the groups. The right-hand end of the curves represents the median trial of the last error prior to criterion for

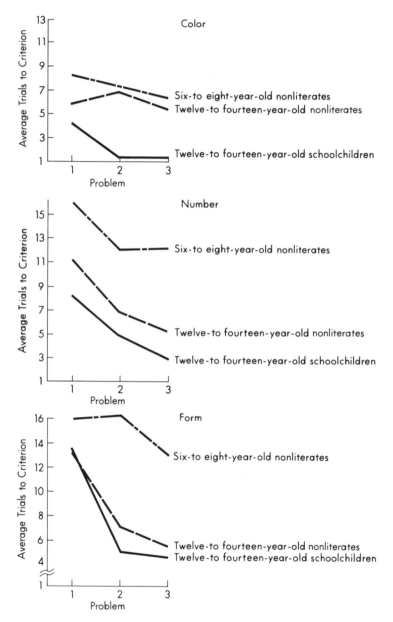

FIGURE 5–6 Learning-to-Learn as a Function of Dimension of Training for Each Group

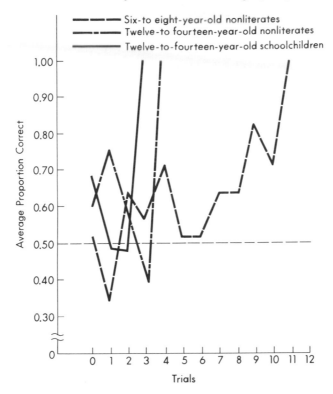

FIGURE 5–7 Performance Prior to the Last Error for a Form Problem. (The terminal point to the right of each curve presents the median trial of the last error for the designated group.)

the group in question (the technique for plotting the data is borrowed from Zeaman and House, 1963). The trials then extend backward from the criterion run to the beginning of the learning trials. As can be seen from Figure 5–7, not only did the six- to eight-year-old nonliterates require more trials to reach criterion, they showed a gradual improvement over the course of the precriterion learning period; the two older groups, on the other hand, showed no improvement prior to solution and chance performance on the trial just prior to beginning their criterion run.

In the light of recent analyses of concept and paired-associate learning (see, for example, Atkinson, Bower, and Crothers, 1964; Cole, Glick, Kessen, and Sharp, 1968) these data are consistent with the hypothesis that we are observing all-or-none concept learning in the older groups, and paired-associate learning in the younger group. Our reasoning runs as follows: the discrete jump from chance performance to 100 percent correct responding follows from the assumption that subjects learn the problem by considering various attributes until they find the correct one at which point the problem is solved in one trial; differences in rate of learning (such as the difference between color and form problems) reflect differences in the number of trials that it takes the subjects to hit upon the relevant attribute in the more difficult problem. Once the relevant attribute has been discovered, learning is virtually instantaneous in all problems. This all-or-none account describes the pattern of learning for the older educated children and to a large extent the behavior of the older noneducated children.

The younger children (and to a slight extent the older noneducated children) showed gradual improvement prior to the time they attained a criterion of 100 percent correct performance. We would expect this pattern of results if, instead of identifying relevant dimensions, these children were learning specific correct answers ("the three blue circles are correct"). When performance prior to criterion performance is measured, as in Figure 5–7, the improvement over the 50 percent level is interpreted as the learning of individual items; as the number of learned items increases, average performance improves. A very similar pattern of results has been observed by Suppes and Ginsburg (1963) and by Cole, Glick, Kessen, and Sharp (1968) in a verbal-discrimination learning context; in both cases a "mixed model" allowing for both item-based and concept-based learning has been proposed.

The most important fact about this analysis is that it provides a plausible explanation for the failure of young children to learn faster and faster with repeated exposure to the same kind of problem. We can expect to observe such learning to learn only when the basis for learning is conceptual, that is, when it is based on dimensions of the problem that go beyond specific instances. But our analysis of the learning pattern of the young children showed that just the opposite was true—they were learning specific correct answers. For them each new problem was just that—a new problem. For the older children, if the same dimension served as the basis of solution, the problem was not entirely new. It was "a problem like the last one" even though the specific correct answers were different. Learning occurred faster with each successive problem because the subjects continued to attend to the same dimension; so long as it was relevant, the "precriterion search" period was shortened and the problem was solved more quickly.

Additional groups in Sharp's experiment document the dimension-specific nature of the improvement from problem to problem for the older children. In groups for whom the correct dimension changed between problems (for example, a subject learned color-form-number or number-color-form), there was no improvement across problems for the twelve- to fourteen-year-old groups.

These results replicate our earlier findings, graphed in Figure 5–1, where there was no improvement from problem to problem if the dimensional basis of solution was changed. However, we can now identify with some confidence the learning mechanisms that underlie those earlier results. The improvement associated with a series of problems having a single principle of solution occurs only if subjects learn in what we have called a dimension-based manner. This dimension-based (concept-based would be an acceptable alternative term) learning, in turn, requires that the subject respond to subproblems as instances of a general problem, rather than learning each subproblem in isolation. These two ways of learning often occur together, but as our work with the pseudoreversal shift has shown, they need not, since subjects who show the concept-based learning pattern will do so even in the absence of a dimension common to all subproblems.

In identifying a pattern of learning that treats each subproblem as an isolated unit, we seem to have stumbled upon an example of what is ordinarily termed rote learning, although the context in this case is the domain of concept learning rather than memory.

Finally, the entire series of studies described in this chapter underlines the fact that it is very difficult to discuss "cognitive skills' in a context-free manner. In some of our experiments six to eight year olds were rote learners; in others they responded in terms of stimulus relations. Sometimes our twelve- to fourteen-year-old children responded differently from the younger children. But on other occasions, increases in age led to changes in the *way* in which learning occurred only if the child had attended school. We have identified patterns that we can call rote and concept-based learning, but we do not know the laws determining which situations will evoke which kind of learning. As was the case with our memory experiments from Chapter 4, we seem to be locating cultural differences in the occasion upon which a particular psychological process will be brought to bear on a problem, rather than in the existence or absence of the process itself.

SIX : Culture, Logic, and Thinking

> It begins to look as though formal logic, as we know it, is an attribute of the group of Indo-European languages with certain grammatical features.
>
> P. W. BRIDGMAN, 1958, p. 88

> The chief problem is ignorance of language on the part of all concerned.
>
> W. LABOV, 1970, p. 187

No aspect of the relation between culture and cognition has a longer history or has produced more controversy than the question of whether the logical processes of preliterate peoples differ from the logic of Western thought. It was primarily the controversy over logical processes that has served as a focus for arguments over "primitive thinking" discussed in Chapter 1. Typical of the views that "primitives think differently than we do" are the following two quotes, the first from an explorer, the second from a highly respected, early anthropologist:

The African Negro, or Bantu, does not think, reflect, or reason if he can help it. He has a wonderful memory, has great powers of observation and imitation, . . . and very many good qualities . . . but the reasoning and inventive faculties remain dormant. He readily grasps the present circumstances, adapts himself to them and provides for them; but a careful, thought out plan or a clever piece of induction is beyond him. [Bentley, p. 26]

. . . between our clearness of separation of what is in the mind from what is out of it, and the mental confusion of the lowest savage of our own day, there is a vast interval. [Tylor, 1965, p. 125]

As we pointed out in Chapter 1, to a very large extent such statements rest on two assumptions, both of which we rejected. First, it is assumed that we can directly infer individual thought processes from a society's belief systems. We found in Chapter 1 that Franz Boas

(1911) in particular had demonstrated the errors to which such an assumption leads. Second, it is assumed that individual thought processes must reflect the model of logic put forth by Aristotle and his successors.

The problem of concluding nonlogical thinking from a lack of a *formalized* Aristotelian logic in a particular language is clearly illustrated in the following discussion by A. F. C. Wallace (1962):

> There is, however, no real evidence that any primitive people characteristically and conventionally employs what Western logicians would define as a logical fallacy. And to suppose that the primitive is *unable* to think rationally, for instance, would lead to the expectation that the primitive hunter would perform the following feat of cerebration with suicidal consequences:
>
> > A rabbit has four legs
> > That animal has four legs
> > Therefore, the animal is a rabbit
> > [Wallace, 1962, p. 355]

Wallace's example is interesting for reasons he probably did not intend. In shifting to the use of the word *rationally,* he exposes a confusion in the use of the term *logic* as applied to cognitive processes. What he is really arguing is that to adapt, man must be "rational," but no inferences about the role of logic in cognition seem warranted.

Consider the following example which we touched on briefly in Chapter 1 (taken from Morgan, 1891): a man sees black clouds on the horizon and says it's going to rain. Did he make an inference, or did he simply remember the association, black clouds-rain? Complicate the example. Suppose that a man uses instruments to measure wind velocity and barometric pressure. A certain combination of wind velocity and barometric pressure is observed and he says it is going to rain. Did he make an inference? It would seem more likely than in the first case, but it is still possible that he simply remembered this case from an earlier experience. In fact, it is impossible to determine, without specific kinds of prior knowledge about the person and circumstances involved, whether a particular conclusion is a remembered instance from the past, or an example of inference based on present circumstances. Hence, evidence about the logic of the "inference" obtained from anecdotes or naturally occurring instances is always open to alternative interpretation.

This ambiguity is the target of the many contemporary definitions of thinking as a *new* combination of previously learned elements. As a consequence of this line of argument, problem-solving situations have come to be closely associated with the study of thinking. Another feature of contemporary thinking about thinking is that the notion of logic is not a part of the *definition*. Problems can be solved in ways that do not fit any known logical models. Whether or not the course of problem solving (thinking) is consistent with a particular logical model or not is a matter to be determined in the course of the experiment.

Chapter 2 provides ample justification for belief in the *rationality* of behavior in Kpelle society. However, we have rejected the idea that we can use group data to make inference about individual processes.

In this section we provide two examples where individual behavior seems to require analysis in terms of rational thought processes. These examples are instructive both because they seem to *require* the inference of rationality and higher thought processes and because they demonstrate the difficulties of making such inferences in a clear-cut, convincing manner.

Law Courts: A Sample Case

The use of judicial procedures to settle disputes is very widespread among the Kpelle. Because it is public, explicit, and relatively formal, and because debating is valued by the Kpelle, the law case offers one promising natural setting in which to observe individuals as they construct arguments and draw conclusions from data.

As an example of the kinds of arguments that are used in such cases, we will present in some detail an unpublished case collected by Professor Gibbs and graciously made available for analysis. The case was heard before Paramount Chief Wua of the Panta Chiefdom in Bong County, Liberia, on December 9, 1965. The entire case was recorded by Gibbs, transcribed by a Kpelle-speaking informant, and then translated by Gibbs and the informant.

There are four principals in the case, the paramount chief (PC); Tuang, the woman who is bringing suit for divorce; Baawei, her mother who received the bride price when she was married; and Baa, Tuang's husband. We will present a series of important excerpts from this case, with a summary of the intervening action.

The case opens with Tuang's request that she be granted a divorce from her husband, Baa. The paramount chief turns to the wife's mother, Baawei, whose responsibility it will be to return the bride wealth she received from the husband when the marriage was contracted. The mother agrees that she had arranged the marriage of the daughter, Tuang, to her father's sister's son, Baa. She does not want her daughter to leave the man, even though she agrees that she has the money available to refund the bride wealth. The mother then asks her daughter through the paramount chief why she is leaving her husband. This is an edited version of Gibbs' transcript, with comments by the editor in parentheses.

PC: (to Tuang): The old lady is questioning you. She said: "Are you leaving the man because of his ways?" That is an important question she is giving you. Don't think that she is playing.

UNIDENTIFIED VOICE: She does not want him. She does not want him. (There are also other voices speaking at the same time that are indistinguishable.)

PC: (to Tuang): Witchcraft cannot remain on "I don't know." (A proverb meaning that a witchcraft accusation cannot be sustained by saying "I don't know" when one is pushed for justifying evidence.)

TUANG: I said that I don't want him because of his ways.

PC: (to Tuang): You don't want him because of his ways. Isn't that so?

TUANG: Yes.

PC: (to Baawei): It reaches you. She said that she doesn't want your son-in-law anymore.

BAAWEI: (to Tuang): You should tell me: "I have left him because of his ways."

PC: (to Baawei): Yes, she said that. She said that she doesn't want him because of his ways. (He asks if Baawei can't accept her daughter's point unless she says "I have left him"? Isn't "I don't want him" the mother of "I am leaving him"? I don't want him!)

The paramount chief is irked at the excessive literalness of the mother and the obdurate "I don't want him" repeated regularly by the wife. He calls the husband and, in order to have him agree for the charges to be brought publicly before the court, asks if he will contest the divorce. The husband agrees to contest the case, whereupon the wife tells a *selective* tale of woe, although this selectivity is not apparent. She complains that her husband would not work for her or build her a farm, despite her help for him when he was sick, and despite the fact that she had had to visit her home when relatives died. She finally asserts that a child she bore when she was visiting her family died because of the enmity of her husband's family. In these assertions, she presents a picture of herself as meeting social obligations and of her husband as both socially irresponsible and possibly malevolent. The exchange continues:

TUANG: This person they gave me to—when I have a child, his mother eats it. (This is a witchcraft accusation).

PC: Who is that who eats human beings?

TUANG: (She points to her husband, Baa.) This person's mother. This is one of his mothers sitting here. When they are doing like that to you in a home, can you stay there?

PC: (to Tuang): Are you through?

TUANG: There (referring to what she has said) is why I say: "I don't want him." Because I took him from death and he overlooks me. He is just behaving like that to me.

PC: (to Baa): My brother-in-law, it reaches you. That is what the woman has said.

BAA: (to PC): Chief, I say, what really has she been saying?

PC: You heard what she was saying. If you want to question her, just question her.

BAA: (to Tuang): Are you saying that you are leaving the home because of the child's death? A palaver is just its head. (A proverb meaning that a dispute always has a single core.) I hear what you are telling me about the work. I say are you leaving because of the child's death?

TUANG: I am not leaving because of the child's death. But it is my keep that you are not taking care of properly. That is what hurt me enough to make me leave you. You are behaving like that to me.

BAA: (to PC): Oh, Chief! What for me. I am able to give a small explanation for what she has said.

PC: All right.

BAA: This is my wife standing so. This is my mother. It was my uncles who gave her to me.

PC: They didn't ask you about that. She said that you don't make a farm for her. (Several voices murmur approval.)

BAA: (to Tuang): You said that I have never made a farm for you ever since they gave you to me?

TUANG: When we were at Zowa you used to make farm for me.

BAA: Since we crossed the river?

TUANG: You have not made any farm for me.

BAA: Recently I made a farm for you. I can explain it.

PC: *Mama,* did you say this person has not made any farms for you?

TUANG: I said that he used to make farms for me. But since we crossed the river, he has not made farms for me nor built a house for me.

PC: And since you two came here?

TUANG: It was just recently that they told him that if he didn't come back across the river, his woman will no longer be his. This is why he came here.

PC: Since he came here, has he made any farm for you?

TUANG: I told you that I was at our home.

PC: Go and sit down. That is just what they said about you (implying that she is evasive).

CLERK: (to Tuang): The question self the old man (chief) gave you, you never talk it self (spoken in English).

At this point, the husband Baa is allowed to speak. He makes a long speech on his wife's sexual prowess and infidelity. In particular, she took many lovers when she went to her home in Guinea. And yet he denies ever insisting that her lovers pay adultery damages. He says he never beat her, but that she persisted in sleeping around, and that finally she disappeared, making it impossible for him to make a farm for her.

After this, standard procedure allows Tuang to cross-examine her husband. She does so ineffectually, to such an extent that the paramount chief feels forced to intervene. He says:

PC: Come now and do it. (Several voices groan.) Make (whatever) explanation you two are able to (the implication of the Kpelle is that neither one of them is able to explain well).

TUANG: I said that my father is not living. My father died in Zootaa. That was the reason why I went there.

PC: Ask him the question! (Several voices murmur approval.) How long has it been since you left your father's home? How many days?

TUANG: It has been a year and a half. (People murmur.)

PC: A year and a half?

TUANG: Yes. My father died and I went to greet the people. Not one of them (Baa's people) stopped there.

PC: Is that why you spent a year and a half there?

TUANG: Not one of them came and said that she and I were to go (back). (People murmur because she has evaded the question.)

PC: We are talking a palaver. (There is a dead silence and a pause.) Have you spent a year and a half there?

TUANG: Yes. Not one of them came to say that she and I were to go.

PC: Did you come from there to start (this) suit?

TUANG: Yes.

PC: (to Tuang): Woman, it is *you* who are wrong. This is what made your part (in it) wrong! You are a legally married woman. This is your husband. You said that you sued him because of his ways. But I didn't see any of the things you described here. As for him, bad ways or not, I didn't see him do it here today. It was only through our questioning and your (Tuang's) making it known to us that we saw one of the points that he tried to make. (It) was that you left this man and went to your home for a year and a half. If a woman spends a year and a half (away), can the man stay there and start a farm for her? Who will scratch it? And, in addition to that, who will he make the farm for? Now that farming season has come, just suppose you had remained with the man as a woman in her house who asks her husband for a farm. (If such a woman) says he (the husband) didn't make a farm for her, she has a power to sue her husband, saying, "I am with that man and he is not feeding me." But (when) you have left the man and gone to your father's home for two years, how can he feed you? You spent the two years with your father and you just left there to come and sue your husband. That's the thing that made your part (in it) wrong.

This presentation demonstrates both the strengths and weaknesses of using naturally occurring events as data about psychological processes.

The paramount chief's obvious disdain for the debating skill of Tuang and Baa indicates that this case is not a prime example of Kpelle argumentation. Even so, we can easily understand the lines of argument that developed. One important point is an analysis of how the wife selected the information she presented. The basis for her divorce action is a story of unmet social obligations combined with malevolence. What she seems to leave out of her account is her own socially unacceptable behavior.

Tuang was away from her husband for more than a year. Her justification for the long absence is that Kpelle custom requires that when a member of her family dies, a wife should go home until her husband sends for her. Judging from the behavior of the paramount chief and the spectators, the year and a half absence exceeded the "statute of limitations" on the custom Tuang had evoked. His summary emphasizes the *illogicality* of her argument (how can a man make a farm for a woman who is absent since her contribution is critical to "making a farm"?).

On the surface it seems that we have specific evidence of the way in which Tuang selects and uses information to further her argument. But this example contains many ambiguities. Gibbs notes that in the overwhelming majority of divorce cases, men are the victors. Perhaps Tuang is not selecting information, but the paramount chief is doing the selecting in order to justify a predetermined outcome. The existence of selectivity in either case would be interesting from our point of view, but we are left uncertain of who, if anyone, is doing the selecting and what is deliberately being left out.

In the light of data to be presented later, the explicit use of a hypothetical argument and juxtaposition of contradictory instances by the paramount chief should not be overlooked.

Malaŋ Game

Another context for the study of naturally occurring instances of problem solving is the malaŋ game, familiar under a variety of names in Africa and Southeast Asia. The game is played on a board with six holes on each of two sides. Initially, there are four seeds in each hole. Each player commands the seeds on his side of the board and must move on his turn all the seeds in any one hole. The object of the game is to capture all the seeds. A player moves seeds counterclockwise, dropping one seed in each successive hole or he can collect the seeds in his hand. He captures seeds by placing his last seed in a hole on his opponent's side that had either one or two seeds in it.

We studied this game closely by holding a tournament for sixteen players for the town of Sinyee. We recorded thirty sample games, which we then analyzed in detail in order to discover the strategy of successful play.

It became clear immediately that some persons played well and others played badly. Those who played well used a clear and consistent set of strategies. Those who lost games on the first round displayed no such care and precision and appeared to have no long-range strategies. Their style of play appeared inconsistent and careless and seemed to show no thought for future consequences of their moves. Not only can we isolate no patterned behavior from the games of these players, but also they lost their games decisively and quickly. First-round games in the tournament tended to be short and one-sided, whereas later games were progressively longer and were won by narrower margins. Moreover, the winning player in these later games often did not gain his initial advantage until after 150 to 200 moves, which can be characterized as probing combined with self-protection.

Our analysis of the malaŋ game showed that victory for good players eventually came because of careful counting of seeds and setting up of captures, controlled by a strategy. Hypothetical rules (if I play the seeds from this hole, and if he responds by playing the seeds from that hole, then I can play the seeds from that other hole on the next move and win five seeds) underlie all such captures.

The first strategy that appeared was waiting until the opponent had made the first capturing move. It is possible to avoid capturing by collecting seeds in one's hand. However, after the first capture this option is no longer open. In twenty-three out of thirty games, the person who captured first lost the game, although this was not inevitable. Even though it is not necessarily the theoretically best strategy, good Kpelle players attempted to outwait their opponents.

The second strategy is redistribution of forces. When a player was collecting seeds in his hand, hoping for the other player to move first and then to force a big victory, he sometimes found that he had not calculated correctly or that the opponent had outwitted him. In this case he redistributed his seeds and started again. In every game where two good players were matched, there were many such redistributions. As a result, games tended to be very long, one game having a total of nine redistributions and more than 300 moves.

A third common strategy is for a player to tempt the opponent to make a capture, which will prove in the long run unprofitable. He offers what seems a careless weak spot, but has projected his strategy into the future where he can take advantage of this weakness. In the games we recorded there were at least thirty such temptations offered and accepted, to the ultimate disadvantage of the immediate beneficiary.

A fourth strategy is for the player to keep large numbers of seeds in certain holes in the middle of his side of the board. This makes long strings of capture impossible and, in turn, poses a threat to the opponent. In every game such accumulations of seeds were made by the winning players. Such accumulations are part of a good defense. In the games we recorded, we noted thirty-one cases of poor defensive strategy by losing players, but only four cases by winning players.

In summary, victory in a malaŋ game depends on a set of strategies. The winning player makes sure he has solid defenses, that he catalogues the possibilities of every move, that he reserves time to himself, that he lures the opponent into making premature captures, that he moves for decisive rather than piecemeal victories, and that he is flexible in redistributing his forces in preparation for new assaults.

These two examples of traditional Kpelle problem-solving situations, the court case and the malaŋ game, are both analyzable in terms of psychological processes such as "selectivity in the use of information" and "strategies." However, the question remains: are these terms descriptions of the processes used by the participants, or descriptions of the outcomes imposed by us?

Attempting to overcome the ambiguities inherent in such naturalistic observations, we turn to the experimental method, cautioned by these observations not to accept evidence of mental confusion too quickly.

Verbal Logical Problems

In this section we describe our efforts to take a more direct approach to logical rules by posing logical problems in verbal form. The subject was asked to draw his own conclusion or to judge a conclusion we have suggested to him. By varying the structure and content of the logical problem, we obtained evidence on the relations between formal logical rules and logic-behavior.

The only research that we know of into the responses of preliterate people to verbal syllogisms was conducted more than thirty years ago by A. R. Luria (personal communication). Working in Central Asia with peasants who had not been incorporated into the large collective farms then being organized in the Soviet Union, as well as "progressive" peasants who had been collectivized, Luria found striking differences in the way these two populations responded to simple verbal syllogisms. For example, one noncollectivized (and presumably more traditional) peasant was posed the following problem:

In a certain town in Siberia all bears are white. Your neighbor went to that town and he saw a bear. What color was that bear?

The peasant responded that there was no way for him to know what color that bear was, since he had not been to the town. Why didn't Professor Luria go to his neighbor and ask him what color the bear was? Such responses were typical and seemed to be more or less independent of the particular content of the problem. More sophisticated subjects (those who had been living on a collective farm for some time and had been exposed to new farm practices and new cultural traditions) responded very much as we might respond. That is, they simply said something like, "Of course the bear must be white since you said only white bears live in that town."

Although anthropologists have occasionally reported anecdotes resembling Professor Luria's observations, his are the only data we know of that suggest some of the variables that might affect responses to such verbal problems. One such variable is degree of Westernization and another is literacy or education.

Group Discussions

As part of our general inquiry into Kpelle learning processes, particularly as they relate to logic, we began pilot work on the question of Kpelle responses to various logical problems and syllogisms. Our initial observations were made in the small town of Gbansu. Gbansu is a relatively isolated and traditional Kpelle town, approximately a five-hour walk from the nearest motor road. Although many of the young people in the town migrate to the road to join the wage economy, many traditional elders retain ties with the town. It was with these important individuals in the town that the pilot work was conducted. A number of village elders were gathered at one time to discuss the truth or falsity of several statements. The entire interview was tape-recorded and then transcribed. Presented below is a summary of the problems and typical responses.

Problem 1: Everybody who has a house must pay a house tax. I have a house. Therefore, I must pay the house tax.

Answer: It was unanimously agreed that the statement was true because it had been decreed by the government that we have house tax.

Problem 2: Some of the animals in the bush are black deer. I have seen an animal in the bush. Therefore, I saw a black deer.

Answer: No, you have to see that what you saw was a black deer because there are many other animals in the bush such as red deer and bush hogs.

Problem 3: Everyone in the town eats rice. The chief is in the town. Therefore, the chief eats rice.

Answer: Yes, it is true because it is already said that *everyone* in the town eats rice. The chief is included in that number.

Problem 4: Every Kpelle man makes rice farms. Some of the *kwii* people make rice farms. Therefore, some of the *kwii* people are Kpelle.

Answer: Some informants said: Yes, we know that all Kpelle men make rice farms. If anybody makes rice farms he will be included in the group. Some informants said: No, it is true that all Kpelle men make rice farms, but there are some *kwii* people who make rice farms and are not Kpelle men. Therefore, the statement is not true. Even this white man (John Gay) can make a rice farm, but he is not a Kpelle man.

It may be seen from these examples that in general, when engaged in group discussion, there was no difficulty in responding to such oral syllogisms. However, certain features of the responses ought to be noted. In Problem 1 the information that the government has passed a law making everyone pay a house tax is clearly extraneous. Problem 3 is interesting because it includes an explicit response to the relation stated in the premise. Problem 4 contains an example of an incorrect response which seems to occur because the respondents broadened the definition of "Kpelle" presented in the problem itself.

The group-discussion technique showed that verbal syllogisms were understandable and could be responded to appropriately. However, we also wanted to try to distinguish the conditions under which adequate and inadequate responses to such verbal problems were given.

Individual Testing

Our initial experiment used verbal problems, which were designed to parallel the problems presented above to groups. The logical relation depended upon the conjunction of statements, disjunction of statements, and the implication of one statement for another. The particular content of the problems was also varied. Some problems concerned animal folk characters, others concerned people, other cases involved institutions. The subjects were studied individually rather than in a group, and the problems were stated in a somewhat different fashion than in the pilot work just discussed. Instead of providing an entire syllogism and asking for the truth or falsity of the conclusion, the subject was asked to draw a conclusion from the premises. A few examples of these problems and typical responses to them will give an indication of the kinds of responses that were typical of traditional adults.

Problem 1

EXPERIMENTER: At one time spider went to a feast. He was told to answer this question before he could eat any of the food. The question is: Spider and black deer always eat together. Spider is eating. Is black deer eating?

SUBJECT: Were they in the bush?

EXPERIMENTER: Yes.

SUBJECT: They were eating together?

EXPERIMENTER: Spider and black deer always eat together. Spider is eating. Is black deer eating?

SUBJECT: But I was not there. How can I answer such a question?

EXPERIMENTER: Can't you answer it? Even if you were not there you can answer it.

SUBJECT: Ask the question again for me to hear.

EXPERIMENTER: (repeats the question)

SUBJECT: Oh, oh black deer was eating.

EXPERIMENTER: Black deer was eating?

SUBJECT: Yes.

EXPERIMENTER: What is your reason for saying that black deer was eating?

SUBJECT: The reason is that black deer always walks about all day eating green leaves in the bush. When it rests for a while it gets up again and goes to eat.

Problem 2

EXPERIMENTER: Flumo and Yakpalo always drink cane juice [rum] together. Flumo is drinking cane juice. Is Yakpalo drinking cane juice?

SUBJECT: Flumo and Yakpalo drink cane juice together, but the time Flumo was drinking the first one Yakpalo was not there on that day.

EXPERIMENTER: But I told you that Flumo and Yakpalo always drink cane juice together. One day Flumo was drinking cane juice. Was Yakpalo drinking cane juice that day?

SUBJECT: The day Flumo was drinking the cane juice Yakpalo was not there on that day.

EXPERIMENTER: What is the reason?

SUBJECT: The reason is that Yakpalo went to his farm on that day and Flumo remained in town on that day.

Each of these problems gives a good demonstration of the kind of result obtained by Luria in Central Asia many years ago. The subjects were not responding to the logical relations contained in the verbal problem. Rather they were (or seem to have been) responding to conventional situations in which their past experience dictated the answer. This is particularly clear in the last problem where the subject seemed to be thinking of a particular Flumo and Yakpalo. We have encountered other examples in which the subjects, when presented a problem such as the last, said something like "Yakpalo isn't here at the moment, why don't you go and ask him about the matter"? In short, it appears that the particular verbal context and content dictate the response rather than the arbitrarily imposed relations among the elements in the problem.

It seems reasonable that subjects have difficulty with problems in this second experiment, whereas problems in the initial experiment were considerably less difficult, because in the first experiment subjects were not asked to reach a conclusion, but had to evaluate the conclusion suggested by the experimenter. In the second set of problems and in the problems posed by Luria, subjects had to reach conclusions for themselves. Nevertheless, it was somewhat startling that our subjects had so much difficulty with problems that to us seemed so easy. Although we can understand how the nature of the task might be misperceived by the subject, our own intuition suggested that we would immediately respond to the formal structure of the problem. Hence we set out to investigate the conditions under which we would find Kpelle people responding in the manner just described and those under which people would respond to the logical relations within the problem itself.

In this third study we contrasted two groups who on a priori grounds might be expected to respond very differently to such problems. The first group consisted of nonliterate adults such as those who participated in the first two experiments. The second group consisted of high-school students from two high schools in the interior, the Lutheran Training

Institute and the Zorzor Training Institute. There were thirty subjects in each group. Each subject was asked to draw conclusions concerning three logical problems. The problems differed according to the logical connective that combined its separate elements and the particular content of the problem. Examples of the *structure* of the three different rules involved are the following:

Conjunction: Spider and black deer are in their house together. Spider is in the house. Where is black deer?

Disjunction: Flumo or Yakpalo is in the house. Flumo is not in the house. Where is Yakpalo?

Implication: If the superintendent is in the court, then the clerk is in the court. The superintendent is in the court. Where is the clerk?

Differences in the *content* of the problems can be understood from the following three examples (using conjunctive problems):

Story: Spider and black deer are in their house together. Spider is in the house. Where is black deer?

Story and example: Flumo (show a cola nut to the subject) and Yakpalo (show a palm kernel) are in their house together (point to an overturned cup in front of the subject). Flumo (cola nut) is in the house (point to the overturned cup). Where is Yakpalo (palm kernel)?

Example: A cola nut (show) and palm kernel (show) are in the cup (point to the overturned cup). The cola nut (show) is in the cup. Where is the palm kernel?

These three levels we conceived of as a traditional form of question (story), a traditional form in which the traditional elements were symbolized by a concrete object (story and example), and a nontraditional form involving concrete objects (example). We hypothesized that if subjects were being systematically ruled by the particular content of the logical problem, then these three levels ought to represent successive approximations to the ideal situation in which the content would play an important role and thus verbal deception would not occur. Hence, we thought that, in general, errors would be greater on the story problem than on the other two problems.

Unfortunately, there were absolutely no differences associated with the form of the problem. Nor were there any great differences associated with the rule involved except for a slight tendency for conjunctive problems to be more difficult than disjunctive or implicative problems. The number of correct responses for the nonliterate adult and high-school populations is shown for each of the rules in Table 6–1. It is obvious from Table 6–1 that although differences among the rules

TABLE 6-1

Percentage Correct Solutions for Logical Problems
Differing in Rule Structure—Study 3

RULE	NONLITERATE ADULTS	HIGH SCHOOL
Conjunction	27	73
Disjunction	37	100
Implication	40	97

(Based on *N* of 30)

were negligible, there was a very large and systematic difference among populations. The high-school students were correct in the overwhelming majority of cases, and the illiterate adults were incorrect in a majority of cases. These results confirmed our expectations that Westernized, literate Kpelle people would respond more or less like educated Americans to such verbal problems.

We were still interested in evidence of differential difficulty among conceptual rules in line with research on conjunctive and disjunctive problems to be presented later. Because these results suggested that the conjunctive rule is slightly more difficult than disjunction, we set out to replicate this third experiment with yet another experiment on verbal logical problems in which the primary interest was on differences among logical rules.

The use of nonliterate and high-school groups was maintained because, on the basis of some pilot work, we expected the particular logical relations embodied in the problem to affect nonliterate and educated subjects differently. This fourth experiment is so similar to the previous ones that only a few highlights of the procedure need to be reported. The general form of the problem was the folk story. Rather than three problems, each subject was now asked to respond to six different problems, presented (we thought) in a random fashion. The primary result of this experiment is presented in Table 6–2 for the two logical relations of primary interest, conjunction and disjunction.

From Table 6–2 it can be seen that the nonliterate subjects found the conjunctive and disjunctive verbal problems equally difficult and responded correctly only on about half of the problems. For the high-school subjects, there was a very large and significant difference between conjunctive and disjunctive problems, with response on the conjunctive problems being essentially perfect and response to the dis-

TABLE 6-2

*Percentage Correct Solutions for Logical Problems
Differing in Rule Structure—Study 4*

RULE	NONLITERATE ADULTS	HIGH SCHOOL
Conjunction	61	100
Disjunction	50	17

junctive problems being very poor indeed. Since the problems resembled closely certain of the problems in the previous experiment, at first we were unable to explain the difference in results.

However, an examination of the particular examples we used suggests an interesting interpretation. In this fourth experiment (as mentioned before) all of the examples were of the folk-story variety. By an oversight on the part of the experimenter setting up this problem, it turned out that all sequences of problems began with a conjunctive example followed by a disjunctive example. The juxtaposition of these two problems in this order created a complex situation exemplified by these two problems:

Problem 1: Spider and black deer always eat together. Spider is eating. What is black deer doing? (the proper answer is an affirmative answer— black deer is also eating.)

Problem 2: Flumo or Yakpalo is drinking cane juice. Flumo is not drinking cane juice. What is Yakpalo drinking? (The answer to this problem is also affirmative—Yakpalo is drinking cane juice.)

However, subjects in the high-school group overwhelmingly chose a negative answer to this problem. The most reasonable explanation seems to be that they were fooled by the contrast between the affirmative and negative wording of the two problems. Such an effect would be completely consistent with results obtained in a study of verbal syllogisms in the United States (Woodworth and Sells, 1935) where it has been found that American college students are susceptible to just such context effects. The interesting point is that the context in this case was not social, but has to do with logical relations in two successive problems.

If our analysis is correct, then high-school subjects not only responded to the verbal relations within a given problem, but also were sensitive to the relations between verbal relations on successive problems, which is indeed a sophisticated performance. However, this interpretation means that we cannot use these data to draw any strong conclusions concerning the relative difficulty of conjunctive and disjunctive problems. We can conclude only that high-school subjects responded strongly on the basis of the verbal relations in the problem, whereas nonliterate adults responded only weakly to verbal relations and were not correct much more than half of the time on any of the experiments.

This finding naturally raises the question of what degree of education is necessary in order to produce the level of sophistication displayed by the high-school students. In order to answer this question, we undertook a fifth study in this series. The only difference in form between the questions in this and the previous experiments was that now the question asked of the subject could be answered yes or no. For instance, a problem might be, "Spider and black deer always eat together. Spider is eating. Is black deer eating"? Once the subject had responded "yes" or "no," he was asked to give his reason for so responding and both his response and his reason for choosing that response were recorded. Thirty-six subjects participated in this experiment, nine subjects each from the following populations: nonliterate twenty-three- to forty-three-year-old adults, nonliterate ten- to twelve-year-old children, eleven- to fourteen-year-old second and third graders, and eleven- to fourteen-year-old sixth graders. Each subject was given nine problems, three problems for each of the logical rules conjunction, disjunction, and implication. The results of this fifth experiment are shown in Tables 6–3 and 6–4. Looking first at Table 6–3, we see that performance for the two nonliterate groups is only slightly above chance. The two school groups performed reliably better than the nonliterate groups, but the two school groups did not differ from each other. Turning to an analysis of difference in

TABLE 6-3

Proportion Correct Responses to Logical Problems

Adults	.65
Ten- to fourteen-year-old nonliterates	.64
Ten- to fourteen-year-old second and third graders	.82
Ten- to fourteen-year-old fourth to sixth graders	.89
Conjunction	.75
Disjunction	.61
Implication	.81

TABLE 6-4

Proportion Correct Verbalizations to Logical Problems

	CONJUNC-TION	DISJUNC-TION	IMPLICA-TION
Nonliterate adults	.58	.24	.29
Ten- to fourteen-year old nonliterates	.39	.36	.22
Ten- to fourteen-year-old second and third graders	.58	.17	.44
Ten- to fourteen-year-old fourth to sixth graders	.92	.60	.74

difficulty among concept types, we see that the disjunctive problem was the most difficult of all and that the conjunctive and implication problems were of roughly equal difficulty. All four populations showed the same differences among logical connectives.

Group differences did appear in the ability of subjects to explain their answer once they had given it. These data are presented in Table 6–4. The probability that a subject correctly verbalized the basis of a correct answer varied considerably among groups. Once again we find that the nonliterate groups were poorer in their performance than the educated groups. In this case, however, only the fourth to sixth graders showed any real proficiency in explaining their solutions.

We also find a sizable difference among concept types in the difficulty of verbalization. In this case conjunction was clearly the easiest kind of problem about which to talk for all except the younger nonliterate subjects. This latter finding is interesting in view of a continuing inquiry into the relative difficulty of conjunctive and disjunctive problem solving which we shall take up in the next section.

Looking back over the series of logical problems, we find that the ability of Kpelle people to make verbal logical judgments depends upon the subjects' education and on the way in which the problem is posed. For nonliterate people, to pass judgment on the conclusions reached by someone else presents no great difficulties. However, to reach a conclusion for oneself based upon premises handed down by others leads nonliterate Kpelle subjects to depend on the particular content of the problem in forming an answer. However, education shifts dramatically the mode of response to such verbal problems, so that the particular content no longer determines the answer. Rather, subjects begin to respond on the basis of the logical relations contained in the problems themselves. Under some circumstances there are differences between problems on the basis of the logical relation involved, but in general the problem type makes little difference.

The fact that content is of such great importance in the answers of the nonliterate subjects raises a further question. Is it possible to pose problems in such a way that the nonliterate subject will be led to respond appropriately to the conditions of the problem?

In a pilot study on this question each of several nonliterate adults was given three problems, in each of which he was to choose between two alternatives presented in the following story.

Flumo and Yakpalo set out one day to find beautiful girls to marry. They came to a man's house and found that he had a beautiful daughter. Each had brought gifts for the marriage, and in order to ensure that the man would give away his daughter, they told him they would kill him if he did not accept the gifts of one of them and marry his daughter to him in return. The point of the story was that the two men brought gifts which were slightly different, on the basis of which the householder could make up his mind. Each man presented his gift in one of the following three forms: "You must take _____ or _____"; "you must take _____ _____ and _____"; "if you take _____, you must take _____ _____"

On a given problem each of the two men used a different form to present his gift. There were three different combinations of money, sickness; money, a good name; a bad name, sickness. On a particular problem the two men had the same gifts, but different forms of presentation, and the subject had to decide which man presented a more advantageous package.

Each subject had one problem of each presentation form, and one problem for each pair of gifts. These were counterbalanced so that all combinations appeared an equal number of times in each position.

The results were helpful in understanding how the content influences the ability to solve the problem. When the gifts were money and sickness, there is a large distance between them as to their desirability. It proved relatively easy for the subjects to answer the questions in these cases, with eight persons answering correctly, two incorrectly. However, when both gifts were bad, namely, a bad name and sickness or when both gifts were good, namely money and a good name, subjects found the problem more difficult.

Some of the answers that skirt the question are of interest. In five of the cases, when both alternatives were bad, the person was willing to die rather than force such unpleasantness on his family. In a few cases, the subject referred the solution to his daughter, saying that she must make up her own mind. In one case, when both alternatives were bad, the subject accepted sickness since it is better than a bad name. Another more pragmatic subject accepted a bad name, since he said that he could still work and make a living.

These results suggest that it is possible to pose problems in a way that lead to responses in terms of the relations in the problem. What the set of these "ways" is, is a matter for future study.

Riddles

As we have mentioned before, a favorite Kpelle sport is for one person to pose a riddle for a group of people, who then debate the proper response. Our earlier observations (Gay and Cole, 1967) seemed to indicate that the way to win an argument concerning a riddle was to invoke a cultural rule. However, it is difficult to say by merely observing such debates what part of this is guided by some implicit tradition concerning the proper answer for the riddle. Consequently, we decided to separate these two aspects of responding to the riddles by posing an artificially constructed riddle with its own explicit rule for solution. Unfortunately, we were only able to conduct pilot work on this problem, but one or two of the results seemed reliable enough to warrant reporting. This investigation was carried out with nonliterate adults and with schoolchildren in first, third, fifth, and eighth grades by David Lancy. Three different riddles were investigated:

Problem 1
A. Any time a rice farmer sees something in the bush it is his to keep.
B. Sumo, the trapper, Flumo, the rice farmer, and Goma Togba, the hunter, are walking together in the bush behind Kayata. They have been walking for three hours and since the sun is very hot they are tired. As they pass a clearing, Flumo spots a very large leopard. Sumo quickly makes a trap and with it catches the leopard. But the leopard is very angry and dangerous still, so Goma Togba must take his gun and kill it.
C. Now, to which of these three people does the leopard belong?

Problem 2
A. A match and a cigarette packet always go together.
B. Do you see this matchbox and this cigarette packet? (The experimenter places these two objects on the table in front of the subject.) I can open

this matchbox and take out a match. (As the experimenter does this, he lays the match on the table next to the matchbox.) I can also open this cigarette packet and take out a cigarette. (The experimenter lays the cigarette next to the cigarette packet on the table.) I will light the cigarette with the match. (The experimenter does this, then lays the match and cigarette down on the table between the packet and the box.)

C. Which of these three things (he points to the cigarette, the matchbox, and the packet) does the match go with?

Problem 3

A. A match and a cigarette packet always go together.

B. I could have a matchbox and a packet of cigarettes. I could take the matchbox, open it, and take out one match. I could then take the cigarette packet, open it, and take out one cigarette. After doing this, I could strike the match on the side of the box, put the cigarette in my mouth and light it with the match.

C. Which of the three things I mentioned, the matchbox, the packet, and the cigarette, does the match go with?"

Each of these riddles has three parts, A, B, and C. Parts B and C are standard parts of the riddle, namely the riddle itself (Part B) and question at the end (Part C). Part A was introduced for purposes of this experiment. It contains the rule according to which the solution to the riddle can be found. Riddles 2 and 3 cannot be properly called Kpelle riddles. Rather they are artificial riddles each with its own purpose. Riddle 2 concretely exemplifies the relations contained in the riddle. Riddle 3 is the same as Riddle 2 except that it is purely verbal. Both Riddles 2 and 3 involve materials that are quite alien in terms of the material ordinarily contained in Kpelle riddles.

We computed the average percentage of correct responses to these riddles and found that only 10 percent of the nonliterate adult answers were correct, 50 percent of the third graders were correct, and 100 percent of the eighth graders were correct. Riddle 1 produced the largest proportion of correct responses (67 percent); Riddle 2 was next (25 percent), and Riddle 3 the least (17 percent).

Subjects were also rated for the degree to which their reason for responding corresponded to the rule given in Part A of each problem. Almost never did the nonliterate adults base their responses on the rule given in Part A, but all of the eighth graders responded in this way. The subjects in the lower grades responded in terms of the rule approximately half of the time.

The overall picture produced by this pilot study is that nonliterate adults, particularly when responding to the traditional riddle, base their responses on the content of the problem and their past experience with responding to riddles of this type. Their responses tend to be quite long and elaborate, and they tend to agree that the hunter in Riddle 1 should be the one to get the leopard. By contrast, the eighth graders always responded by saying something like, "You said that any time a rice farmer sees something, it's his to keep, therefore, Flumo, the rice farmer, should get to keep the leopard." Unfortunately, we do not have systematic enough data with respect to the responses of the nonliterate and educated subjects on the other two problems to allow us to make statements about how they rationalize their answers.

In the riddles experiment just as in the verbal logical-problems experiment, nonliterate subjects depended on the particular content of the problem, and responses were much more likely to be based on this content than on the particular logical relations inherent in the problem itself. We also found consistently that subjects at the junior high school or higher level responded on the basis of relations within the problem, a tendency that increases systematically with education.

A second issue raised by these experiments is the nature of the relation between problem structure (conjunction, exclusive disjunction, negation, and implication) and the adequacy of the subject's response. Both of these issues were the basis of further experiments.

Linguistic Connectives and Conceptual Rules: Conjunction and Disjunction

In our earlier work among the Kpelle (Cole, Gay, and Glick, 1968, pp. 176–178), we explored the ways in which various logical relations among phrase elements might help explain differences in problem-solving difficulty associated with the different logical relations. In some pilot studies we obtained evidence that the relation between natural-language rules for connecting elements of a sentence and the effect of these rules in concept-learning tasks was different for Kpelle and American subjects.

In particular, our early evidence indicated that Kpelle subjects found equally easy concept-learning problems based on conjunctive (red *and* triangle) and disjunctive (red *or* triangle) classifications. This is essentially the same finding that we have just reported for the verbal logical problems in the previous section, although in the case of the verbal problems, there was occasional evidence that conjunctions might be easier in some respects than disjunctions.

This result is curious because our own data collected with American subjects, as well as a vast array of other studies (Bruner, Goodnow, and Austin, 1956; King, 1966; and so forth), have shown conjunctive problems to be uniformly easier than disjunctive. Originally, we thought the difference in relative difficulty could be explained by a greater precision in the Kpelle language with respect to disjunction. Our initial linguistic analysis had suggested that the Kpelle distinguish clearly between inclusive disjunction (where "or" implies "red or triangle" or both "red and triangle") and exclusive disjunction ("red or triangle," but not "red and triangle together"). Unfortunately, later analysis has indicated that although Kpelle has two terms for disjunction, both are of the *exclusive* variety. This would imply a superiority for the Kpelle only in the sense of a lack of the disjunctive ambiguity found in English, but not in the sense of flexible linguistic usage.

Although there is some evidence that repeated practice can reduce the difference in difficulty between conjunctive and disjunctive problems for American adults, the pervasiveness of the difference has led to a great deal of speculation about universal conceptual tendencies. For example, J. S. Bruner, J. Goodnow, and G. A. Austin (1956) speak of an "abhorrence of disjunctiveness" and maintain that in English there is a tendency for disjunctive definitions to be modified over time into easily grasped conjunctive forms (p. 160). C. E. Snow and M. S. Rabinovitch (1969) offer a variety of explanations for the differences they observed in favor of conjunctive concepts, ranging from greater familiarity to the speculation that the brain works conjunctively (!).

All of this speculation, combined with the lack of difference between conjunction and disjunction in most of our previous work among the Kpelle (Gay and Cole, 1967, Chapter 10 and pp. 189–193 of this volume), led us to explore further the question of conceptual rules and learning.

We borrowed and adapted a special procedure from the work of L. E. Bourne (Haygood and Bourne, 1965; Bourne, 1967). The basic idea was to consider the usual concept-learning experiment as composed of two subprocesses: one process is the learning of the attributes relevant to solution; the second is the learning of the rule by which the attributes are joined. In a rather extensive series of studies (see Appendix I for details), we sought to simplify the usual concept-learning situation so that there would be a minimum of attribute learning and a maximum of rule learning.

The logic of our approach seemed quite straightforward—reduce the amount to be learned to include just the relevant aspect of the problem and thereby neutralize extraneous learning factors. The outcome was just the opposite of what we intended. Something about our "simplified procedure" made the problem difficult to solve. We are not at all sure what this "something" is, and can only make some possibly relevant observations.

Our pervasive impression while conducting our pilot work was that our subjects were involved in some "game" other than the one we had in mind. Often a subject who had difficulty with the problem (there are only four instances, a trivial task if one is simply observing the experimenter's behavior and remembering the instances identified as "correct") seemed to pay an extraordinary amount of attention to the experimenter's hands, as if their placement held the answer. Even if he solved one problem, the subject would persist in his attention to irrelevant details, apparently satisfied that he had "hit" upon the system last time and would be able to do so again.

When we questioned the Kpelle college students who acted as experimenters about this problem, they suggested that we might be inadvertently suggesting a game familiar to the Kpelle in which one member of a group is asked to leave. When he comes back, he must guess on the basis of observational clues which member of the group is holding a stone in his hand. These difficulties and the interaction between unknown aspects of the culture and experimental procedure serve as yet another reminder of the extreme caution required to infer the presence or absence of cognitive processes from cross-cultural data.

We had to admit failure in our attempt to study learning by specially devised techniques. We thus turned to a more standard psychological procedure which was slightly modified for our purposes.

Conjunction and Disjunction: Replicating American Procedures

This series of experiments (described in detail in Ciborowski, 1971) studied concepts built out of combinations of physical attributes. The stimuli were printed on cards and presented to the subject one at a time. The cards had pictures combining the following dimensions and values:

number (one, two, or three figures); size (small, medium, or large); color (red, white, or black); and form (circle, triangle, or square). Examples of conjunctive concepts might be *two red figures, black triangles,* and *small circles.* Examples of disjunctive concepts using these same attributes and values might be *two figures or red figures* and *small figures or triangles.*

Six problems involving six different concepts were presented to each subject. Half of the subjects learned conjunctive problems and the other half learned disjunctive problems. The six problems represented different combinations of relevant attributes so that each attribute was paired with each other attribute some time during the subject's six problems.

The decks of cards that made up each problem were constructed specifically for our purposes. For example, if the concept was green squares, there were nine cards with green squares, nine cards with green triangles or circles, nine cards with squares that were white or black, and nine cards with neither squares nor green figures on them. We did this in order to balance the type of instances to which the subject was exposed. We found later that this design had important consequences for our analysis of the relation between logical rules and concept learning.

To begin the experiment, the subject was shown the first and last cards of the deck, which had been previously randomized. One of these cards was placed on the subject's left, the other on his right. After he had a chance to examine them, the cards were placed back in the deck. Then the subject was told that the experimenter was thinking about certain cards in the deck. Each time a card was held up, the subject was asked whether the card was one of those that the experimenter was thinking about. All the "correct" cards were placed on the subject's right, all the "incorrect" cards were placed on his left.

This somewhat circuitous procedure, which in effect gets the subject to classify the cards into two groups, was arrived at after a great deal of pilot work. Of all the possibilities we tested, this procedure proved to be the easiest to administer.

Subjects were run to a criterion of ten successive correct responses on each problem or until they had gone twice through the deck of thirty-six cards. After a problem had been completed, the subject was asked to explain why he placed the cards as he did.

In addition to the comparison between conjunctive and disjunctive concepts, Ciborowski investigated the effects of age (twelve- to fourteen-year-old versus eighteen- to twenty-one-year-old subjects) and education (noneducated versus educated groups at each age level) on problem-solving performance, yielding a design with eight groups. The entire experiment was replicated three times with six subjects participating in each of the eight groups in each replication.

The subjects found the problems very difficult. About 40 percent of them were not solved, although even in these cases there seemed to be some learning. In order to study the process more closely, Ciborowski used as his measure the number of errors committed on each problem. It was assumed for purposes of analysis that a subject who had reached criterion committed no errors thereafter, even though the problem was terminated.

Although there were no large differences between groups, two differences were statistically reliable:

1. Conjunctive problems (14.1 errors per problem) were slightly easier than disjunctive problems (15.8).
2. Education enhanced the performance of the younger subjects (12.4 errors for the educated group, 17.4 errors for the nonliterate group) but there was no reliable difference between the older educated (14.6) and nonliterate (17.4) groups.

Overall, there was no significant variation attributable to age. Also important in view of the discussion in Chapter 5 was the fact that learning was more rapid on later problems than earlier ones, the error rate dropping from approximately nineteen per problem on the first problem to thirteen per problem on the last problem.

It appears that we have replicated the basic results of earlier experimenters (for example, King, 1966) in finding a difference, even though small, in favor of conjunction that is more or less constant across groups. We clearly did not replicate our own earlier finding of equal difficulty for conjunctive and disjunctive problems.

However, there are at least two puzzling features of these results. First, the difference between conjunction and disjunction was very small —much smaller than has usually been reported. Second, why should a difference between educated and nonliterate groups exist only at the lower age and education levels? Our previous experience had taught us to anticipate the opposite result.

While puzzling over these results, we noticed that our procedure had allowed correct responding on an unintended basis. In constructing our decks of cards we had inadvertently biased the number of times that a given card was placed on the subject's left or right side. Given an equal number of each kind of instance (for example, green and triangle or green but not triangle), nine cards were placed on one side of the table and twenty-seven on the other side in the course of running through any deck a single time. If a subject noted only this fact, and always responded to the more frequently correct *side,* he would be correct 75 percent of the time. This corresponds to only eighteen errors. Since our subjects averaged about fifteen errors a problem, they were doing little better than this pure position response.

Looking at the data from individual subjects, we found that pure position responding was very rare. However, we also found strong evidence that subjects were, to some extent, basing their responses on position information rather than stimulus information. In particular, we found that the probability of responding to the *side* correct on the previous trial was far higher than would have been the case if subjects had made their positional responses randomly.

In order to evaluate the relative degrees of sensitivity to positional information and sensitivity to the relevant stimulus information as factors controlling subjects' responses, Ciborowski constructed a simple mathematical model, which assumed that errors occurred only if the subject did not know the relevant stimulus information, in which case he responded to positional information and guessed incorrectly. In this model, correct responses occur either because the subject knew the response appropriate to the stimulus presented or because he guessed correctly on the basis of positional information. Although certainly an oversimplification of the underlying response process, this model yielded two very interesting results.

1. In terms of the stimulus-learning factor, conjunction (.35) was learned more rapidly than disjunction (.23). The ratio in this case is much larger than obtained for the error data. But in terms of positional responding, the disjunctive problems (.65) were more biased than the conjunctive problems (.52).

2. Younger educated children did better than their nonliterate counterparts solely because of increased *positional* responding. No difference in stimulus learning was obtained for these groups.

We were initially quite dismayed when we realized that subjects might be learning to solve the problem (in the sense of improving their performance) for reasons unrelated to logical rules and concept learning. However, the resultant pattern of behavior enriches our understanding of the way in which our subjects dealt with the problem. It appears that the conjunctive problem was considerably easier than the disjunctive problem in terms of stimulus learning, but that subjects compensated for the difficulty of the disjunctive problem by depending on position information, thus reducing the apparent differences between problems. The fact that the younger schoolchildren perform better by using positional information fits quite nicely with our earlier observations (Gay and Cole, 1967, Ch. 4) that there is a stronger dependence in the classroom on the teacher's concrete behavior rather than on the logic of the material being discussed.

At the time that these experiments were being conducted, we had not analyzed the data in terms of stimulus and positional information. We were concerned only to explain the slow learning that we had observed and the relatively small difference between groups. For example, we expected a much larger effect of education on the rate subjects learned this problem.

In an attempt to discover the subjects' difficulty, Ciborowski conducted a modified form of the experiment. In this case, when a card had been responded to, it was left out in view of the subject instead of being placed back in the deck. The major consequence of this procedure was to provide the subject with a continuously available memory aid during concept learning.

This memory-aid procedure made a major difference in learning for all groups. All but 4 percent of the problems were solved, and overall the average number of errors per problem was only 5.6. Conjunctive problems (4.2) were learned faster than disjunctive ones (6.9), but there were no reliable differences as a function of age or educational experience.

Ciborowski's results suggest some important points. First, he succeeded in identifying position cues as a mode of learning used by the subjects, a procedure we noted in other contexts, for example, the free-recall experiment. That position cues aided memory suggests one source of the overall difficulty of these problems, a difficulty that related directly back to our studies of attribute learning. Subjects did not make efficient use of information from past trials to arrive at a solution to the problem. Although the improvement over trials and the levels of performance indicate that there was cumulative learning, there was apparently less trial-to-trial comparison than efficient learning demands.

Second, Ciborowski showed that at least under some conditions conjunctive and disjunctive rules differ in difficulty for Kpelle people. The differences in rule difficulty are in the same direction as those found in similar studies in the United States, but are less in amount.

Inference

Our final study looks closely at the question we raised earlier of content and the application of logical rules because the dependence of traditional adults on the content of verbally presented problems may have implications for the application of reasoning to a variety of situations met daily in Kpelle country at the present time.

For example, an entirely new contextual problem faces Kpelle people when they are asked to reason about the unfamiliar contrivances that are introduced as part of the "progress" that accompanies the advent of Western-style schools, business enterprises, and the government tax collector. Flashlights, hurricane lamps, can openers, locks, sewing machines, and a myriad of imported goods are finding their way into even the most remote Liberian villages. Very often the tribal people are not adept at working with such devices, which the European claims "even a child can handle."

As part of our experimental program, we introduced a problem familiar in the United States and sufficiently "gadgety" to offer us some insights into the difficulties that a traditional tribal person encounters when working with such foreign mechanisms. In these experiments, the subject was *required* to combine separate subproblems in order to obtain a goal. One of the general questions of interest is whether Kpelle subjects experience more difficulty than Americans in making such integrative responses.

The experimental situation we used for this study was borrowed from the work of Kendler and Kendler (1967). In this article the Kendler's summarized a large series of experiments on what they term "inferential" behavior in children. They mean by inferential behavior the spontaneous integration of two separately learned behavior segments to obtain a goal. Thus, inference in this situation has a somewhat more specific meaning than it did when we spoke earlier of "inferring" the dimensional basis of solution, which in that case meant roughly, "using evidence to reach a conclusion." The Kendlers' research findings and theoretical position were summarized as follows (p. 186):

Inferential behavior can be analyzed into two components, an initiating response, and a response which integrates the two segments of the problem. Neither component is likely to occur in young children, but both become more likely in older children. It is assumed that integrating the two components requires that the subject recognize that the potential connector, the element common to the two segments, is the same thing, even though it is a part of different stimulus compounds in each segment. Young children do not integrate the two segments at the first opportunity because they treat the common element as separate *because* it appears in the different compounds. A necessary condition for integration is the abstraction of the relevant element.

It would appear from the Kendler's description that children improve in their ability to solve inference problems as they grow older. Moreover, the Kendlers believe that children learn to solve this problem along the same lines as in the discrimination learning task.

We have an interesting opportunity to test their theoretical position, as well as to gain information on inferential behavior among the Kpelle: young nonliterate children failed to use relevant dimensions to solve the discrimination-learning problem. Therefore, it might be expected, on the basis of the Kendlers' theory, that they would have trouble with this problem. If, as suggested by Kpelle performance in the complex reversal experiment, Kpelle children are capable of treating the subproblems as parts of a larger whole when the situation requires it, they should not have difficulty with the simple Kendler-type inference problem. We must also remember the fact that the Kendler apparatus is completely alien to Kpelle experience.

Replication of Basic Kendler and Kendler Procedures

As an initial experimental pilot study, we began by studying inferential behavior in five groups of rural Kpelle people from the Cuttington College area. Three of the groups were composed of nonliterate children aged five to six, ten to fourteen, and seventeen to twenty-two years. Two groups of educated subjects were run: ten to fourteen year olds (grades one to five) and seventeen to twenty-two year olds (grades four to nine). There were twenty subjects in each group. The groups were run in a mixed order so that we could eliminate systematic experimenter effects.

The apparatus for this study was borrowed from Professor T. S. Kendler. It had been used previously in one of Professor Kendler's experiments on inferential behavior in American children (T. S. Kendler, Kendler, and Carrick, 1966). The apparatus, as shown in Figure 6–1, was a metal box, the front of which was divided into three panels, each with its own door. The panel on the left is painted red. In the center of this panel is a button which the subject had to push in order to receive

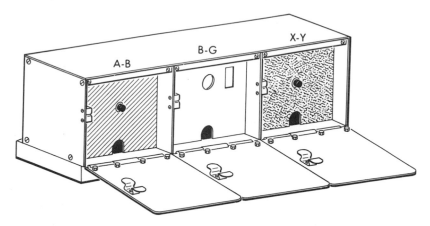

FIGURE 6–1 The Kendlers' Inference Apparatus. (Ball bearing and marble obtained from side panels; candy from the center panel.)

a ball bearing (or a marble, in half of the cases). On the right panel, which is painted blue, there is an identical button which yielded a marble (or a ball bearing) when pressed. The center panel was yellow; it had a small window through which the subject could see the reward, a metal charm. Just next to the window, through which the metal charm could be seen, was a hole into which the subject had to drop the correct object (either a marble or a ball bearing) in order to receive the final goal, the metal charm which dropped into a slot underneath the window. The subjects were paid ten to twenty cents for their participation in the experiment.

Our procedure in this initial experiment was modeled as closely as possible on that described in Kendler, Kendler, and Carrick (1966). We even used electricity to make the various parts of the apparatus work, which meant that we had to restrict our study to Kpelle towns that had electricity.

The general idea of the experiment is quite simple, although the details (given in Appendix J) can be quite complex. First, the subject was taught that he could get a marble from one of the side panels by pushing the button in the middle of the panel. Then he was taught that a ball bearing could be obtained from the opposite panel. Finally, he was taught how to obtain the metal charm by dropping one of these objects (say, the marble) into the hole in the center panel. We wished to know if the subject, seeing all three panels open for the first time, could combine the three separate learning sequences in order to choose the panel that contains the marble and place the marble in the center panel to obtain the charm.

We needed several items of information about the subject's performance in order to answer this question. First, how readily does the subject begin the task: does he have to be prompted to make his first choice? Second, how accurately can he choose the correct subgoal? Can he identify the object that can be obtained from one of the side panels and that will ultimately produce the charm for him? Third, how efficiently does he begin with the correct response and go on to complete the full sequence of choices? Such integrative responses, when no intervening responses occur, will be labeled direct-correct responses, following Kendler, Kendler, and Carrick (1966). The subject, however, may make a correct response initially, but then make some intervening response, perhaps pushing the button on the second side panel prior to making the goal response. In a great many cases, moreover, subjects pushed both buttons simultaneously, but went on to make the correct goal response. If the subject gave either of these response sequences, they were called indirect-correct solutions.

Fourth, how strong is the subject's tendency to make a goal-directed response, regardless of correctness? Does he realize that the two subproblems "go together"? We will term such behavior "integrative." Integrative behavior in practice may consist of either direct-correct solutions or indirect-correct solutions. However, we found in our experience with Kpelle subjects that several other patterns also were possible. For example, a subject who has to be prompted all along the way may make correct choices without showing integrative behavior. The results of our initial experiment are shown in Table 6–5.

The column labeled Spontaneous First Choice shows us that only educated subjects were initially inclined to start working with our strange apparatus. In many cases, especially among the nonliterate subjects, there were overt signs of fear. Very often subjects would sit quietly and wait for the experimenter to ask him additional questions. Others would play with extraneous features of the apparatus.

None of the groups showed any marked tendency to make direct-correct inferential sequences. In large measure this is because so many subjects make an initial choice by pressing both side-panel buttons.

The columns marked Indirect-Correct and Total-Correct show that the subjects, especially the older, educated subjects, were fairly good at obtaining the ultimate goal. But such a conclusion probably overestimates the extent of real integrative behavior. When subjects failed spon-

TABLE 6-5

Performance on Inference Experiment 1

GROUP	SPONTA- NEOUS FIRST CHOICE	DIRECT CORRECT	INDIRECT CORRECT	TOTAL CORRECT	INTEGRA- TIVE BEHAVIOR
Five- to six-year-old nonliterates	35%	30%	30%	60%	60%
Nine- to twelve-year- old nonliterates	45	20	45	65	45
Nine- to twelve-year- old schoolchildren	80	30	50	80	80
Seventeen- to nine- teen-year-old non- literates	65	15	60	75	55
Seventeen- to nine- teen-year-old students	90	30	50	80	75

taneously to put one of the subgoal objects into the goal to obtain the charm, they were asked, "Which ball should you use to get the charm"? Because of the strong initial tendency to push both side-panel buttons, the subject was likely to have both the marble and ball bearing in his hand. Consequently, a good deal of the indirect-correct responses were likely to be the result of chance selections.

The same negative conclusion emerges from the column marked Integrative Behavior. Here we have included only those instances where the subject, once he had either the marble or the ball bearing in hand, went on to make the goal response. Subjects who have attended school most frequently show this behavior.

On the whole we were impressed by the great reticence of our subjects in this experiment. Our strange apparatus, and perhaps our strange procedures, made subjects very unwilling, and we were not at all sure that our data were really comparable with American data such as that collected by the Kendlers. In America it had been found (see Kendler and Kendler, 1967, for a review of these data) that by third grade approximately 50 percent of the children studied made direct-correct inferences. Moreover, American college students almost always made such direct inferences.

Up to this point our work provides a model of how *not* to do a cross-cultural experiment because we really have no way to decide among various explanations for our findings. Is it fear of the electric apparatus that makes our subjects so slow to respond? Are the instructions unclear? Or is it some difficulty inherent in making arbitrary, although seemingly simple, inferences of the sort this experiment tries to elicit?

We leaned strongly toward the hypothesis that it was the way in which we had tried to study inference, not the inferential task itself, which had provided the difficulties. So, we set out to find a different task, embodying the same principles, which would permit us to make better judgments about inferential processes among the Kpelle.

An "Ethnic" Replication of Kendler and Kendler

In searching around for such a task, we finally selected the following problem, formally equivalent to the Kendler problem, but using materials familiar to the Kpelle. The subject was presented with two matchboxes, one of which was taped, the other of which was bare so that the boxes would be easily discriminable. A black key was placed in one of the matchboxes; a red key in the other. In the initial phase subjects learned, in a manner completely analogous to that in the experiment we just reported, to identify which box contained which of the keys. Once this had been learned, the matchboxes were put aside and a small box with a lock on it was brought out. The subject was told that one of the keys, red or black, would open the lock and that if he opened the box, he could have the piece of candy that he found inside. Subjects quickly learned that the red key (for example) opened the box. Then, the matchboxes were brought out again, so that both the matchboxes and the locked box were present together. The box was locked and the subject was told that if he did the right thing, he could get the candy. In this version of the problem, the matchboxes represented the side panels, the two different keys were the subgoals, and putting one of the keys in the lock solved the problem (just as putting the ball bearing or marble in the hole solved the problem in the previous experiment). Three groups of subjects were investigated using this procedure. The results are contained in Table 6-6. It is obvious from Table 6-6 that performance on the inference task is greatly enhanced by the use of the matchboxes and the locked box.

To begin with, there was a general and spontaneous willingness to engage in the task. First-choice probabilities were still at 50 percent for the youngest subjects, but performance for both the older school sub-

TABLE 6-6

Performance on Inference Experiment 2

GROUP	SPONTA-NEOUS FIRST CHOICE	CORRECT	DIRECT CORRECT	INDIRECT CORRECT	INTEGRA-TIVE BEHAVIOR
Seven- to twelve-year-old first graders	60%	80%	70%	20%	90%
Ten- to fourteen-year-old second to fourth graders	100	80	70	20	90
Nonliterate adults	70	90	80	10	90

jects and the older nonliterates was well above chance. Moreover, direct-correct solutions were now at a level superior to the performance of the American third graders reported in the earlier experiment. Similarly, the index of total integrated behavior indicates that virtually all of our Kpelle subjects showed integrated inferential behavior in this situation.

The problem now is to determine the critical difference between the two sets of experiments. One experiment suggests that the Kpelle had difficulty with inference problems of this kind. The other indicates that they did *not* experience such difficulties and in fact respond in a manner characteristic of American upper-grade schoolchildren.

In designing the matchbox–locked box procedure, our aim was anthropological. We were interested in devising a task that would be familiar and culturally appropriate to the Kpelle. However, it is quite possible that in our choice of components we stumbled upon a *genuinely* different way of doing the experiment, not just a difference in content. In particular, it could be argued that in the second experiment, the connection between the key and lock was highly overlearned prior to the time the subject began the experiment. All he really had to do was to learn which matchbox contained a key because he did not need to learn to open locks with keys. Everyone knows that keys open locks since such devices are quite common now in the Liberian interior. This interpretation would fit in quite well with the theoretical discussion offered by the Kendlers and presented above on pages 204–205.

Familiar and Unfamiliar Components

In order to determine which interpretation was correct (the familiarity hypothesis or the prelearned connection hypothesis), we constructed an experiment containing a series of conditions designed to separate the effects of different combinations of stages.

The general strategy in this experiment was quite simple. We wished to construct experimental conditions that represent all possible combinations of the features of the first two experiments in order to determine which features of the first two experiments are critical to good performance. We assumed that the first study consisted of unfamiliar components and that subjects had no knowledge of a link between subproblems. The second experiment represents familiar components and a prelearned link between subproblems. Among the experimental conditions we included problems with familiar first-phase components, combined with unfamiliar, unlearned second components (the Kendler box), and unfamiliar initial components, combined with a prelearned, familiar second phase (keys and the locked box). A number of conditions (seven in all), representing variations on this theme, were conducted with separate groups of twenty Kpelle schoolchildren aged ten to fourteen in grades one and two. Because the procedures we devised had not been used in America previously, groups of twenty first graders (aged approximately seven years) were run in America as well to give us a rough basis of comparison of the relative difficulty of the various conditions.

The results (shown in detail in Appendix K, Table K–1) rather convincingly demonstrate a cross-cultural *similarity* in the relation between problem structure and problem difficulty. Problems were easier if the initial link was familiar. However, a prelearned, familiar second stage seemed to have little effect on responding except to make the Kpelle respond a little more quickly overall. The fact that our American first graders showed general improvement when they began by dealing with matchboxes, instead of the specially built inference apparatus, suggests that their generally poor performance in the Kendlers' standard studies may be much less a matter of general deficits in "mediational" capacity than an ability to attend to relevant aspects of a problem involving a strange apparatus. Anthropological observation can be a two-way street. Our anthropological hypothesis appears to account for the results in *both* cultural groups!

Returning for a moment to one of the questions that motivated this set of studies, we can now conclude that where problem solution requires the subject to combine separately learned subproblems, neither Kpelle nor American subjects experience special difficulty in doing so, provided that the elements of the problem are not unfamiliar or do not induce fear. In situations where such combination is optional (the discrimination-learning studies in Chapter 5), concept-based learning may or may not occur, depending on factors that at present we cannot identify. Similarly, differences in the structure of logical rules (as in Ciborowski's work) may or may not influence learning (see Appendix I for details).

SEVEN : Conclusions

Custom for most men is a substitute for thought.

M. HODGEN, 1952, p. 73

In this last chapter we will first review the major issues raised in our discussion of the relation between culture and thought. We will then briefly survey our findings. Finally, we attempt to draw conclusions about the relation between culture and cognitive processes from the historical, observational, and experimental data we present in this book.

Two major points of controversy can be abstracted from our historical survey and discussion of methodology. First, is evidence from ethnographic analysis relevant to understanding individual psychological processes? Second, are observed differences in thinking to be interpreted as reflecting differing cognitive capabilities or differing applications of universal cognitive skills in specific contexts?

In the nineteenth and early twentieth centuries, the first question would have been answered in the affirmative. Traditional beliefs were the only source of evidence about "thinking," and the prevailing opinion was that "primitive beliefs imply primitive thinking." At issue was not the existence of different patterns of beliefs, such as those described so graphically by Levy-Bruhl (1910), but their interpretation. The first serious challenge to belief in the existence of a specifically primitive mentality came from Franz Boas (1911), who denied that everyday beliefs provide evidence about thought processes. Boas's position has, in the main, been supported by later generations of anthropologists, whose views are well summarized by M. Gluckman:

Very many scholars writing on social problems like to begin their analyses with a statement of what primitive man thought or did; they use the comparison to highlight their analyses of our own ideas. As anthropologists see it, what they do is to give the stereotyped presentation of what they would think were they, savants and scientists of our civilisation, presented with the social beliefs of primitive society. But I hope this analysis has brought out that the thinking processes of man in primitive society are more complex, and that neither his character nor the nature of his mind, nor his views of the universe can be simply derived from selected beliefs of his culture, particularly the myths and mystical beliefs. [1949, p. 87]

Although Gluckman's position is one to which most anthropologists and psychologists would subscribe, it has the unfortunate consequence of leaving classical anthropology without a theory of individual thinking. Recently, some anthropologists, notably Robin Horton (1967 a,b), have explored the functional similarities and differences that thinking fulfills in different societies. In so doing, Horton arrives at some predictions about individual psychological functioning which are empirically testable but which await confirmation.

Another approach to a theory of cognition in contemporary anthropology comes from the work of linguistically oriented anthropologists, who, in their desire to obtain unambiguous descriptions of native category systems, have left untested the relation between ways of classifying and ways of thinking. The relation between content and process has been assumed rather than demonstrated. Only in the speculative work of Claude Lévi-Strauss (1966) do we see an attempt to demonstrate that Western and primitive category systems lead to different ways for individuals to solve problems.

We have noted that their rejection of evidence from belief systems seems to leave anthropologists without a theory of the relation between culture and thought process. In fact, most anthropologists tacitly assume that *there are no fundamental differences in thought process among different human groups* whether these groups are differentiated along cultural or racial lines. This faith is summarized in the so-called doctrine of psychic unity (Boas, 1911), and reflected in current emphasis on category systems as alternative frameworks within which universal processes operate.

Twentieth-century psychologists have also rejected evidence from belief systems in testing theories of thinking. They claim not to be able to determine if differences in beliefs depend on different thought processes, or simply on different remembered responses to particular situations. For example, we no longer consider it logical to believe that the world is flat, but the process by which most of us come to believe that the earth is round is hardly scientific. Recognition of these difficulties has led to psychological definitions of cognition that emphasize the rearrangement of past experience or "going beyond the information given."

This is coupled with an insistence upon experimental methods that carefully control both "what is known" and "what must be found out."

The dominant method of contemporary psychologists is to use experiments and tests to yield information about the psychological processes of individuals and also, statistically, of groups. These processes are treated as individual properties that are "tapped" by the experimental or test procedure.

The stress of psychologists on thought as process provides one rationale for prior enthnographic study of the people with whom one wants to conduct psychological experiments. Certain kinds of differences among groups may "interfere" with the assessment of subjects' cognitive capacities. As an extreme example, it would be foolish to conduct one's experiments in English if the subject spoke only Kpelle, although in some places English IQ tests are still administered to Mexican-American children as they enter school.

By the same token, many investigators take great pains to make their instructions understood and to include culturally relevant materials, rather than materials manufactured ahead of time in the West. When adapting the test instrument leads to improved performance, the experimenter concludes that he has found a better measure of the underlying processes (Price-Williams et al, 1969). Thus, one object of prior ethnographic study has been to facilitate the adaptation of test instruments, which, in their modified form, can be treated as "culture-free" measures of psychological processes.

The almost universal outcome of the psychological study of culture and cognition has been the demonstration of large differences among cultural groups on a large variety of psychological tests and experiments. This has led to the widespread belief that different cultures produce different psychological (in the present case, cognitive) processes. Thus, we have cited several references to the concrete nature of traditional African thought (Cryns, 1962), to the inability of unschooled Africans to think abstractly (Greenfield and Bruner, 1966), and to cultural differences in psychological differentiation (Witkin, 1967).*

In the face of the experimental evidence of cultural differences offered by psychologists, how can the anthropologist maintain his belief in the psychic unity of all mankind? He does so by rejecting both the

---

* Since this book was completed, a rapprochement between the views put forth here and the approach adopted by Bruner has occurred (see Cole and Bruner, 1972).

psychologist's attitudes toward the people he studies and toward psychological tests.

We mentioned in Chapter 1 the linguist's caution that a person cannot be judged cognitively less competent than is necessary to master the complex rule system of his native language. In a like manner, the anthropologist *assumes* persons to be sufficiently competent to carry out the many complex functions required of them in even the most primitive societies. Societies, of course, vary in the kinds of tasks they pose for their members. Following the common-sense dictum that people will be skilled at tasks they have experienced often, cultural differences in the activities eliciting skilled performance are to be expected. But these are not "process" differences in the psychologist's sense, but are considered as specific adaptive skills that may or may not imply process differences. A fish seller will develop the mathematical techniques required for making a profit (H. Gladwin, 1970), a sailor will develop navigational skills (T. Gladwin, 1970), and the bard will master rules of story telling (Colby and Cole, 1972). Many such examples are familiar to the anthropologist.

Where a psychologist, on the basis of test results, concludes that the fish seller lacks the ability to think abstractly or the bard has a poor memory, the anthropologist is understandably skeptical of the psychologist's conclusion. Repeated examples of such clashing interpretations have left the anthropologist secure in his belief in psychic unity. The psychologist, convinced that tests (or experiments) measure process, and generally ignorant of the kinds of adaptive, intelligent performance cited by the anthropologist, remains confident in his own interpretation.

Our experience leads us to propose yet a third view of experiments, especially those involving cross-cultural cognitive comparisions. Instead of assuming a close relation between particular test situations and hypothetical cognitive processes or assuming that skills are only used in natural contexts, we view tests and experiments as specially contrived occasions for the manifestation of cognitive skills. It is true that we use the terms *process* and *skill* ambiguously in this context since we mean both underlying mental processes and specific material activities. We attempt, however, to make full use of this ambiguity by relating the outcome of experiments to relatively specific and identifiable ways of learning and solving problems. For example, we found that Kpelle people are skillful at measuring rice, but not at measuring distance. In like manner, expert navigators may use a complex natural compass, but fail to perform like American high-school students on a standard psychological test (T. Gladwin, 1970).

If experiments are occasions to demonstrate the use of skills, then failure to apply the skills that we assume are used in natural contexts becomes, not an illustration of cultural inferiority, but rather a fact to be explained through study and further experimentation. We assume that in these cases, skills are available but for some reason the context does not trigger their use. *We thus make ethnographic analysis prior to experimentation in order to identify the kinds of activities that people often engage in and hence ought to be skillful at dealing with.*

In effect, we maintain that neither ethnography nor an experimental approach alone is by itself sufficient. Ethnography is unable to separate the traditional from the "reasoned," suggesting that experimentation is needed to complement the implications of ethnographic analysis. Conversely, we have argued that if experimentation leads to results incompatible with ethnographic analysis, the experiment was probably culturally inappropriate, and needs an ethnographic base both as a guarantee for the meaningfulness of the experiment to the subject, and as a standard against which to interpret the adequacy of the experimental conclusion.

The ethnographic standard sets a goal for experimental work. If, after exhaustive experimentation that ethnographic goal is not achieved, we question both the form of the experiment and the ethnography itself. Similarly, the ethnography gives powerful suggestions about the form in which experiments should be run, and some of the major contextual variables that should guide the formulation of a series of experimental investigations. Experimental work and ethnography must interact, each approach setting standards for the other to maintain.

If we relate cognitive skills to specific activities, then we ought to be able to use cultural variations in order to evaluate their cognitive consequences in at least two ways. First, we ought to be able to look at variations in common activities *within* a given cultural setting and on this basis make statements about variations in cognitive activities. This enterprise is basically *ethnographic*. Second, we could extend this analysis to cross-cultural comparisons when we compare differences in the patterns of cognitive performance within each of two different cultures to differences in the patterns of activity between these same two cultures.

Ideally, we ought to be able to use specific cross-cultural comparisons to provide us with "natural experiments." For example, contrasts between schooled and nonschooled children are a natural arena for the study of differences in cognition. This enterprise we can call *comparative anthropology*, or in the terminology of Chapter 1, experimental anthropology.

In the remainder of this chapter we will consider our success and failures in the light of these issues and our own experience. We will then attempt to draw some general conclusions about the relation between culture and thought.

Ethnographic Concerns

We began the presentation of our research with a description of selected aspects of contemporary Kpelle culture. Originally, we justified this ethnographic concern on methodological grounds. Cultures are organized in complex ways, and in order to understand any given cultural feature, it is necessary to know the relation of that feature to the culture as a whole.

We were also motivated by the general hypothesis, which we have just discussed, that different cultures provide for different learning experiences. The tasks that a culture frequently poses for its members will be the ones with which they deal effectively. This is by no means a new idea. It is implicit in A. F. Chamberlain's remark (p. 14) that "it is not the minds so much as the schools of the two stages of human evolution that differ."

On both methodological and theoretical grounds, then, we sought to understand the characteristic activities of people that could be expected to influence the way in which they engage in such cognitive activities as problem solving, remembering, and rule learning. We then hoped to study these activities in specific experimental situations.

The gap between these goals and our specific achievements in this regard appears to us very large. With very few exceptions our search for general characteristics of Kpelle daily life as it is related to specific cognitive processes has produced guesses about differences in the activities and thought processes of different subgroups, rather than a detailed documentation of those differences. One reason for our failure to demonstrate detailed relationships is that no comprehensive theory of the relation between mundane activities and cognitive processes has proved acceptable, although there are many specific theories of the relation between particular activities and their cognitive consequences.

Some examples will clarify the problems we have in mind. The principle that says that people will be good at doing what is familiar to them led us to the study of measuring and estimating quantities of rice. In that case we seemed to describe a specific activity and its intellectual consequences. But what about rice farming? Farming is an activity that is technologically quite simple in the sense that only a few simple tools are required to grow upland rice. But a successful farmer has a great deal to learn. He must take into consideration many factors as he chooses his site and decides how big a farm to make, what additional crops to grow, when to plant them, and when to harvest them. To be sure, there are traditional prescriptions, but these do not specify most of the decisions which must be made. We understand only a few of the details of this decision-making process. Rice farming consumes a great deal of every Kpelle person's time. Yet we have almost no data on the intellectual components or consequences of rice farming.

Consider a second example. Time and again we have been impressed by the seeming subtlety of Kpelle social relations. We have provided data on the importance of speaking well, of debating, and of learning proper social roles. We have seen in the sample court case how people will try to use evidence and tradition to their advantage in arguments. We have followed in detail a complex intellectual game. Yet we have only the scantiest data relating these activities to the intellectual tasks that we experimentally set for our subjects.

A really major gap in our research involves the learning environment of the young child. Unfortunately, we have had to rely on rather superficial observation on our own part, as well as the scanty anthropological evidence provided by Sibley and Westermann and Gibbs. We have often relied on such anthropological observers as M. Fortes (1938) to inform us of the kinds of experiences met by children in other traditional African societies, and we have extrapolated to the comparison between the Kpelle and Western children.

The most important generalization on which we have failed to obtain concrete data is that children in nontechnological societies do a great deal of learning by observation and imitation. This failure was not from lack of interest on our part. Early in our work we began to collect data on children's activities, particularly when they were interacting with adults. But we were not satisfied with the data we obtained; it soon became clear that a really comprehensive field study using techniques such as those developed by J. W. M. Whiting and B. Whiting (B. Whiting, 1963) in anthropology and R. D. Hess and V. C. Shipman (1965) in psychology would be necessary. Lacking the resources and time for such an effort, we had to depend on asking hypothetically what the consequences would be if learning were generally imitative.

Such reasoning led us to note the difficulty subjects had in verbalizing the solutions to experimental problems and the comparable difficulties in explaining the principles of house building and rice farming. But the observation that learning seems to take place by observation and imitation does not allow us to predict specific cognitive difficulties. On this point we have virtually no data. Although we carried out some pilot studies of what we thought might produce imitative learning, none of these produced results systematic enough to warrant reporting.

Happily, cross-cultural research aimed directly at these questions is being undertaken by the Whitings and their colleagues (Whiting and Whiting, 1970). It remains, however, for us to apply this line of research among the Kpelle.

What is badly needed is a far-reaching extension of the thinking that motivated our ethnographic work. The literature on cognitive processes and cognitive development is filled with problem-solving and learning tasks. Many of these have analogues in everyday activity. These analogies must be systematically exploited in order to determine how the learning experiences provided by different cultures relate to the logical structure and content of specific cognitive problems.

For example, it is our impression that many social situations encountered by the Kpelle are analogous in form to various experimental situations. Examples of the learning of rules, as well as learning to use these rules in a contingent way, are suggested by much ethnographic data describing social situations. Yet we have no tools for distinguishing social and nonsocial problem-solving situations in an analytic fashion. In fact, almost all experimental situations are *nonsocial* in the sense that their successful solution requires manipulations of objects or words abstracted from context, rather than relations with people. Is it possible that were we to find the social analogues of these experimental situations, our informants would experience less difficulty and might even show themselves to be quite clever?

It seems suggestive to us in this regard that among the Kpelle the adjective *clever* does not apply to such technological operations as rice farming, house building, and car repairing. A farmer may be considered lazy or hard-working, but the term *clever* is restricted to the social sphere. A related fact is that the same kinds of people who found it difficult to explain the principles of good house building found it easy to tell us how their children should be raised.

Although it does not entirely fit our prescription of how things ought to be done, the data we gathered on the organization of Kpelle noun classes represents an extensive, if not exhaustive, description of one kind of Kpelle language behavior. Despite the serious problems that arose in classifying objects that could be fit into more than one taxonomic scheme, the organization of nouns represented by the *seŋ* chart (Table 3–1) was found to have implications beyond the rather structured situation in which it was elicited. We can have no doubt, based on the evidence from the sentence-substitution, free-association, and sorting studies, that the semantic groupings contained in the chart can serve to organize other linguistic as well as nonlinguistic classification. The relations of subordination and class inclusion we characterized as "horizontal" and "vertical" distance were reflected in the rate at which different categories were discriminated verbally. Having established that the relations among nouns described by the *seŋ* chart can describe the way the nouns are used in various verbal and nonverbal situations, we now want to ask, "what are the rules governing *when* they are used?" Here we can offer neither experimental nor ethnographic evidence.

In this, as in our other, work we believe our ethnographic concerns are justified. However, we must acknowledge that we have hardly begun to study the interrelation of cognitive and other activities within a particular cultural setting.

Experimental Anthropology

We not only searched for significant *intra*group variations in everyday activities that could be related to variations in cognitive activity. We also studied contrasts between significant subgroups of the Kpelle themselves as well as between the Kpelle and other cultural groups.

In Chapter 1 we discussed two drawbacks to a comparative experimental approach. First, it is considered dubious strategy to draw inferences from experiments that are alien to the culture concerned because it is believed that cultures are complex wholes, which cannot be picked apart in this manner. Second, the experiments confound a number of hopefully independent variables because the contrasts chosen are virtually certain to involve simultaneous changes in many aspects of the culture.

Nonetheless, comparative statements are commonly made, generally in terms of a theory of general cultural advancement as cultures become more Westernized. Rarely are the cultural institutions and cultures compared viewed as "different but equal." Schooling (Greenfield and Bruner, 1966), literacy (Goody and Watt, 1962), and acculturation (Doob, 1960) are all seen as providing people with new cognitive processes, new abilities, and new intellectual tools. The authorities claim that without extensive training, the mind is only capable of concrete thought; without writing, analytic thinking is not possible; without new technical challenges, culture and thought are stagnant.

One consequence of such a view is that the "deprived" groups (who lack formal schooling, who have not learned to write, and who lack Western technology), are seen as uniformly lacking in particular, "developed" skills. Another consequence is that the cultural transition to the educated, literate, technological world is often conceived of as causing a *transformation* in cognitive processes. According to this position, we can no more think like a savage than he can think like us.

It is possible that cultural changes lead in some ways to transformations in cognitive processes. However, we think that our data argue at least for a modification of the viewpoints expressed above. To begin with, let us consider how each of the major variables, age and education, affected the performance of Kpelle subjects. We will refer to some but not all of our experiments in so doing.

With respect to age we find, along with many other observers, little differences in the experimental performance of younger and older nonliterates. There is a slight improvement in the number of items recalled as a function of age in our early free-recall experiments, but no qualitative change in the structure of recall. There is also a slight tendency for older subjects (ten to fourteen years) to reverse a discrimination, or transfer a discrimination faster than six to eight years olds.

The really large differences, as in past research (Gay and Cole, 1967; Greenfield and Bruner, 1966), are produced by exposure to Western-style education. But the consequences of education are by no means uniform. Table 7–1 contains a rough schema of the various experiments involving educational contrasts and the degree of schooling at which differences in performances were observed. Table 7–1 makes it clear that we can make no simple generalization about which tasks (or processes) are affected by various degrees of education.

TABLE 7-1

Summary of Effects of Different Levels of Education on Performance

EDUCATIONAL LEVEL	TASK AFFECTED	HYPOTHETICAL MECHANISMS AFFECTED
2 to 6 years.	Pseudoreversal: spontaneous shifting (Ch. 5)	Combining instances
	Discrimination transfer (Ch. 5)	Combining instances: stimulus-specific versus dimensional learning
	Inference (Ch. 5)	Combining instances: initiating the problem
	Transposition (Ch. 5)	Dimensional control
	Verbal logical problems (Ch. 6)	Use of Hypothetical mode
	Concept discrimination	Combining instances via semantic class
	Color/form preferences (Appendix I)	Unknown
High School	Similarities mediation (Ch. 3)	Imposition of taxonomic grouping
	Free recall (Ch. 4)	Production of structure
Unaffected	Free association (Ch. 3)	Exclusive use of definitional mode
	Rule learning (Ch. 6)	Unknown

Certain tasks are performed better when the child has had a few years of schooling. With the exception of the verbal logical problems, all these tasks contain elements of a discrimination-learning procedure. Two sets of experiments are affected only if the subject has attended high school; namely, the constrained-classification task we called similarity mediation and the free-recall tasks. In the similarity-mediation study only the high-school students base their classifications on static, taxonomic categories. In free recall, although there was some indication of a change in the basic recall process for ten- to fourteen-year-old fourth to sixth graders (Appendix F), really striking effects are obtained only in the case of the high-school students who alone showed significant semantic clustering, pronounced serial-position effects, and clear-cut improvement over trials. Finally, the free-association study and the experiment on conjunctive and disjunctive problem solving revealed no striking differences in the performances of high-school students and their nonliterate age mates.

This patchwork of education-related changes in Kpelleland contrasts quite strongly with the results of comparable American studies for which data are available. In free association, free recall, the learning of conjunctive and disjunctive rules, inference problems, discrimination-transfer problems, and similarity mediation, performance improves from kindergarten on.

Using these facts as background, we will attempt to give a detailed answer to this basic question: what are the cognitive consequences of the cultural change induced by Western-style education in Kpelleland? We suggest that two closely related factors are affected by schooling. First, as many authors have suggested, the new cultural institution leads to the acquisition of new intellectual skills. This sounds like a recapitulation of the position we were criticizing earlier, but as we shall see, our view is more restricted. Second, the new cultural institution leads to a change in the situations to which skills are applied.

These two abstract propositions find support in many different aspects of our data. Let us begin by considering the discrimination-learning experiments discussed in Chapter 5. The major finding (summarized in Table 7–1) was that moderate levels of education led to performance that American research has found to be characteristic of a higher developmental level. For example, schoolchildren reverse faster in the pseudoreversal problems; they learn faster and acquire more skill at learning in the discrimination-transfer study.

If our analysis in Chapter 5 was correct, the education-related changes in discrimination learning occur for two reasons. First, educated subjects are more likely to treat the individual stimulus presentations as subproblems (or examples) from which the answer to *the* problem can be induced, while noneducated subjects are more likely to treat each presentation pair as a separate problem. Second, there is a greater tendency on the part of educated subjects to use a stimulus dimension such as color or size in solving the problem. In practice these two factors are closely related, because using a dimension-based method of solution requires that subproblems be seen as related. But the data from the pseudoreversal study indicated that the two processes are in fact at work separately. Even in the absence of a common dimension, older educated subjects treat the two problems as "instances" of a supposed general problem.

But we cannot conclude from these data that the observed differences in performance reflect differences in the cognitive skills possessed by the two groups. We cannot do this because our data also indicate that (1) under some conditions nonliterate subjects will combine subproblems, and (2) under some conditions nonliterate subjects use a common stimulus dimension to guide their responding.

Although the discrimination-transfer analysis strongly suggested that the nonliterate six to eight year old learned item by item, data from certain of the discrimination-reversal and transposition studies indicate that these children can use more generalized learning procedures. Dimension-based learning is seen most clearly in the transposition study. Children trained to choose the larger of two square blocks did not choose that block when given a choice between it and a still larger block; they chose the new larger one. The child who attends only to specific stimuli would choose the previously correct block.

Similarly, nonliterate children showed some tendency to use dimensional information in the discrimination-reversal studies, but only if they were required to make a reversal shift. They responded as if subproblems were independent if required to make a nonreversal shift. (Figure 5–3).

Finally, in a study on reversal learning conducted some years ago, we found that nonliterate Kpelle learned a reversal shift more rapidly than a nonreversal shift in a problem requiring the subject to sort sixteen stimuli (Cole, Gay, and Glick, 1968). Having shown that faster reversal learning requires something more than learning specific stimuli, the results of the latter study strongly suggest that under some conditions, ten to fourteen year olds will treat the discrimination-learning situation in a "conceptual" manner.

If we restrict our attention for the moment to these discrimination-learning tasks, what can we say about the cognitive differences that arise in conjunction with the cultural difference between educated and noneducated Kpelle children? We suggest that there is a different likelihood that a given situation will evoke a general, as opposed to a specific, mode of problem solving. It is *not* the case that the noneducated African is incapable of concept-based thinking nor that he never combines subinstances to obtain a general solution to a problem. Instead, we have to conclude that the situations in which he applies general, concept-based modes of solution are different and perhaps more restricted than the situations in which his educated age mate will apply such solutions.

It is common for psychologists to use discrimination tasks such as these to test hypotheses about mediating processes (Kendler and Kendler, 1968) or about the ability to switch the focus of attention (Zeaman and House, 1963). In particular, they infer the degree of use of general processes from discrimination-learning performance. Our data indicate that the relation between discrimination-learning performance and hypothetical underlying processes will be very difficult to establish, since our subjects sometimes seem to use the general process and sometimes do not.

At the very least, theories concerning any general process must contain statements that indicate when the process will be brought to bear on the problem and when it will not. This is the issue we were raising when we said that cultural differences in cognition may more nearly reflect changes in the situations to which various cognitive skills are applied, than they do general processes. According to the results summarized in Table 7-1, the noneducated Kpelle can use mediating processes: he can learn in a dimension-based fashion; he can combine subproblems. But the conditions under which he does so are different than the conditions that evoke such behavior in the educated Kpelle or Americans. The noneducated Kpelle subject more frequently learns in a stimulus-specific way on the experimental tasks we set him. The educated Kpelle, and particularly the older American child, only rarely learn in such a fashion.

The tendency for the American schoolchild to learn things according to some general scheme is very, very strong. In fact, in some cases the subject's assumption that he had to follow some particular unstated rule interfered with proper performance. For example, American children, more commonly than noneducated Kpelle children, used taxonomic categories as the basis for completing the similarities-mediation task (Chapter 3). The use of such categories is ordinarily considered by Western psychologists to represent a higher level of cognitive development than the use of functional categories. Yet so strong was this tendency that where the conditions of the problem made taxonomic classification difficult, or even impossible (as, for instance, when the child had to choose an item to place between a file and an orange), the American children would violate the instructions in order to maintain taxonomic classification. Instead of choosing an item that went with both of the constraint items, they would choose an item that was part of the same taxonomic class as *one* of the constraint items and ignore the other. The Kpelle subjects, even the high school subjects who used taxonomic classification widely, would not violate the conditions of the problem in this manner. Their performance indicated that they were capable of taxonomic classification, but they used the taxonomic mode under a narrower range of circumstances.

Another interesting difference between Kpelle and American use of general dimensions occurs in the concept-discrimination studies of Chapter 4. We found clear evidence that learning among the Kpelle was concept-based (because two semantic categories could be discriminated faster than two randomly formed classes). However, there was no transfer of training from one class to a closely related class. That is, the control of the concept was specific to the particular words being discriminated. It is truly unfortunate that our initial motivations for conducting those studies did not lead us to use educated comparison groups, because it is our strong impression that the educated groups would show not only a larger difference between rule and random classes, but positive transfer to closely related classes. That is, control of the rule should be stronger for educated subjects and should be applied more widely.

The pilot concept-discrimination data from American subjects reported in Chapter 4 indicate a reliance on concept-based learning so strong that it can actually interfere with learning if no obvious concept is involved. The American subjects are more likely to use class distinctions to guide learning, because the differences between rule and random classes are generally large, even for distinctions based on linguistic classes. But the evidence suggested that the greater difference between rule and random classes for the American subjects was largely the result of slow learning of the *random* classes, even though there were only eight pairs to learn. When these subjects were asked about their performance following the experiment, they indicated that they had gone to great lengths to discover a rule where in fact there was none. So intent were they on identifying the distinctive feature of each of the classes that they neglected, as it were, to learn what the class members were. Only after abandoning this strategy did they turn to simply recalling the correct instances, after which the criterion of learning was reached. Thus the relatively greater ease in discriminating semantic classes by these subjects seems to depend on a negative element. The greater difference between rule and random classes may have occurred because the subjects failed to treat the random classes in the way that would lead to most rapid learning.

In general, it appears that many of the experiments in which education affects performance or in which American subjects perform differently than their Kpelle counterparts are under the control of situational factors of which we had only a dim awareness at the start of our research and which we only poorly understand at present. It does not seem helpful to invoke a generalized change in cognitive processes to account for this pattern of results. At best we have identified specific ways of learning, which members of all groups we have studied *can* use under some circumstances, but which members of different groups use in different situations. This is not to deny the usefulness of general psychological constructs (mediating response, rote learning, attentional mechanism) for describing the results of many experimental situations. It simply does not seem appropriate to say that our groups differ because of the presence or absence of these processes.

Are there any results from our work that seem to *require* us to invoke differences in basic processes to explain group differences? This is a difficult question to answer as our discussion in this chapter has made clear. Failure to demonstrate identity of process between two groups may reflect either the absence of that process in one group, or our failure to determine the situations required to elicit it. For example, if we had relied on data from the discrimination-transfer studies to tell us about the way in which nonliterate Kpelle children learn discrimination problems, we might have concluded that they possess only "rote processes." However, we found concept-based learning in the transposition and reversal-shift studies. Similarly, the pseudoreversal studies suggested that nonliterate Kpelle fail to combine subproblems, but the inference data show this not to be generally true. Consequently, whenever we want to use an explanation that requires us to assume that one group "has a process" while another does not, our interpretation is open to question. It is always possible that further experimentation would turn up evidence of the hypothetical process under the proper circumstances.

With this caution in mind, we can consider the pattern of results produced by the series of studies on free recall. Our analysis of these data in Chapter 4 made use of the notions of storage and retrieval processes, two memory skills that appear to differ among high-school and noneducated Kpelle groups. At the end of Chapter 4 we offered a process interpretation of the effects of education. The nonliterate Kpelle have not learned to produce a structure for themselves that they can use for efficient storage and retrieval of information, while the high-school subjects routinely construct such structures. At this juncture, we would like to suggest the way in which this "production deficiency" (to use the term applied by Flavell, 1970) of the noneducated subjects is related to ob-

228

servations such as those made by Bartlett, Bowen, and many anthropologists about the keen memory capacities of nonliterate peoples.

In Bartlett's terms the to-be-recalled materials in our experiment are not reflective of a "persistent social tendency." Consequently, the subject cannot "fit" them into any pre-existing scheme of things. According to our present thinking, "persistent social tendencies" represent a ready-made organization that is habitually evoked by certain situations and used to structure recall. In the course of normal events, things are remembered because their natural contexts are organized in ways which are socially real for the individual. Presumably, our experiment in which to-be-recalled items were embedded in traditional-style folk stores provided the kind of structure that ordinarily serves to organize remembering, and in that situation we found the structure of recall matching the structure of the story.

But the more typical of our free-recall tasks failed to evoke any such natural structure. At least intuitively, one can see why this might be the case. Unlike most common memory situations, our experimental version of free recall uses grammatically disconnected material. The items named are familiar, but the motivation to remember them comes from an arbitrary source, such as the desire to earn money or appear clever. Recall is requested almost immediately.

In this sort of situation, there is good evidence that the typical American high-school student imposes his own structure on the to-be-remembered items. E. Tulving (1968) has shown that given sufficient practice, subjects will arrive at their own "subjective organizations," even when materials are explicitly designed to preclude obvious semantic connections. When semantic similarities are involved, they are quickly adopted, and significant semantic clustering is observed on the first trial of recall for children with five or six years of education (Cole, Frankel, and Sharp, 1971).

Nonliterate Kpelle, as well as elementary school children, show no evidence that they are imposing structure of the sort familiar among American schoolchildren. Over a wide variety of presentation conditions, the recall of our pre-high-school Kpelle subjects failed to improve markedly with practice or to show any marked organizational structure, despite a repeated search for organization in terms of order properties of the list or semantic categories. We even tried to apply measures that are sensitive to idiosyncratic organizations characteristic of individual subjects from one recall trial to the next, but had no success. Although we cannot logically *prove* the absence of some organizing principle, we have to conclude that there exists no organization that contemporary methods of analysis can detect.

Our interpretation of these results, as already stated, is that the nonliterate Kpelle do not respond to the request to remember our lists of words (or objects) by producing a structure that can organize the material for effective recall a few moments later. This negative conclusion is supported by the experiment on constrained recall. In that study subjects in one group were asked to recall the items category by category for four trials. On the very first trial, recall was far better than in control groups without these constraints. And when recall was no longer evoked in a constrained manner on Trial 5, performance was still excellent, and very marked semantic organization occurred. (The only comparable result came in studies that used external cues to recall [chairs], but in this latter instance, the facilitative effect was fleeting, coming and going for reasons that we very poorly understand, although the same principles are presumably involved.) The combination of good recall on Trial 1 and maintained recall on Trial 5 suggests two conclusions: First, difficulty in the typical free-recall task occurs because subjects do not retrieve material they have stored. Second, effective retrieval skills can be learned.

Clearly, a good deal of additional research is required to pinpoint the cultural differences in memory that underlie performance on our free-recall tasks. We need to determine in what cases persons will learn to retrieve as in this constrained-recall experiment. Will subjects who have learned to retrieve items from one list also be able to recall a new list, or is the effect list-specific? Are there situations, other than the story context, that will produce highly structured recall? Are those differences in recall skills associated with various traditional Kpelle specialties? For example, do renowned story tellers remember in measurably different ways than people who rarely tell stories? Recent evidence from B. N. Colby (Colby and Cole, 1971) suggests that Guatamalan Indian story tellers are accomplished at using structural features to organize story elements, while novices are not. Is this skill content-specific, or would the accomplished story teller be able to produce his own structure in situations such as those upon which we have concentrated?

Until future research uncovers the natural situations for the display of memory skills, we must conclude that the skills necessary for effective short-term recall differ among cultures. Specifically, it appears that people who attend Western-style schools learn to provide structures, which organize their recall of arbitrary material, while noneducated people do not.

In reviewing the remaining experimental results described in previous chapters, it appears that at least some suggest changes in basic cognitive processes for their explanation. For example, the responses to verbal syllogistic problems in Chapter 6 can be interpreted as reflecting "situation-bound" rather than hypothetical thinking. Possible support for this interpretation comes, for instance, from the experiment in Chapter 4 where subjects were asked to classify leaves using arbitrary group names (Sumo and Togba in place of tree leaves and vine leaves).

At present we are not willing to accept this inference. We prefer to pursue the hypothesis that members of the nonliterate groups studied in those experiments can reason hypothetically, but that they fail to see the applicability of such reasoning in our experimental tasks. Our preference in this case is based on ethonographic and experimental data, some of which are presented in earlier chapters of this book. For example, our discussion of secrecy in Chapter 2 (*ifa mo* "do not say it") and the paramount chief's summary of the court case in Chapter 6 both seem to require explanations in terms of an ability to entertain hypothetical states of affairs as preliminaries to action. In the case of the paramount chief, this process is made quite explicit. Similarly, our pilot work in which subjects were required to choose between two hypothetical offers of bride-wealth indicated that the premises of the problem could be made an important part of its solution.

There is no doubt, however, that in our experimental situation, such skills as the use of arbitrary labels to designate class membership or the use of hypothetical reasoning to solve a verbal puzzle are not manifested in ways we could consider obvious. Perhaps it is because the problems are in some sense counterfactual; perhaps it is because the experimental situation leads subjects to expect something different from the experimenters. Our task is to check alternative interpretations with a special eye toward the naturally occurring situations in which we think such reasoning is present. Is there an analogue in the use of the hypothetical mode to our recall study where the words were embedded in stories? If not, after we have exhaustively studied the use of arbitrary labels and hypothetical situations by the noneducated Kpelle and the changes in response that are caused by education, we may be in a position to specify the processes that underlie such performance and the factors that transform such processes. The pursuit of this question, and analogous questions having to do with other presumed cognitive processes, is not an empty chase after "proof" of a theory. It is experimental anthropology, the process by which we can come to understand the cultural determinants of cognition.

"Cultural Deprivation"— Culture and Cognition American Style

It should be clear from all that has gone before that the study of culture and cognition need not (and we believe should not) be relegated to the status of an esoteric inquiry, best carried out in exotic surroundings. On the contrary, we hope that the principles that have evolved in the course of our research will have direct implications for the study of cognitive processes in a wide variety of cultural settings, particularly the study of subcultural differences as they are manifested in the United States today.

As we noted above, in studying cultural change, the cultures being compared are rarely considered different but equal. Nowhere is this more clearly the case than in the theories of psychologists and educators on the cognitive development of minority groups in the United States.

In surveying the major summaries of research on the "culturally disadvantaged" (Deutsch, 1969; Hellmuth, 1967; and many others), it soon becomes clear that various minority groups (blacks, Latin Americans, Appalachians, Indians, and so forth) are viewed as "victims" in what S. S. Baratz and J. Baratz (1970) have termed a "social-pathology" model of cognitive development. On the basis of test results (heavy reliance has been placed on IQ testing, but data from discrimination-learning, memory, and problem-solving studies are also used), the conclusion is reached that minority-group membership results in stunted cognitive development. At present the social-pathology view of minority inadequacy is dominant in the United States; prominently featured in such explanations are the failure to use language as a tool of thought, inability to delay gratification or work for long-term rewards, lack of concentration, and a list of other "deficits."

As Baratz and Baratz (1970) point out, the logic of this position leads to emphasis on earlier and earlier intervention in the lives of minority-group children to make sure that the deficit never develops.

It is only a short step from the social-pathology point of view to the adoption of the hypothesis that the deficit is present at birth or even genetically based. The leading champion of this viewpoint at the present time is A. Jensen (1969), who began with the hypothesis that early environmental factors caused the inadequacies he measured in his experiments, but came later to believe that the difficulty was caused by inherited learning skills. Jensen's major thesis is that learning tasks can be categorized into two types on the basis of the kinds of skills required for their successful solution. Type 1 he calls "associative learning," a kind of learning that requires little transformation of the learning material. According to Jensen, groups do not differ with respect to their use of Type 1 learning. Type 2 learning, conceptual learning, requires transformation of the material for its successful completion. Jensen believes that whites possess this ability to a greater extent than blacks and thus show superior performance on certain tasks.

A third point of view, which is quite close to our own view, denies the existence of a general deficit, denies the existence of a social pathology (in the sense intended by psychologists and educators), and relies on observational and linguistic evidence to claim that the poor *performance* of minority groups on psychological tests is the result of various situational factors. A primary champion of this viewpoint is Labov (1970), who dramatically and effectively demonstrates the folly of concluding that substandard English implies substandard thinking and who goes on to demonstrate the existence of supposedly absent cognitive skills in naturally occurring situations.

We would like to suggest that the approach that we have used in this book can fruitfully be applied to the problem of subcultural differences in cognitive behavior in the United States. In particular, we want to emphasize our major conclusion that *cultural differences in cognition reside more in the situations to which particular cognitive processes are applied than in the existence of a process in one cultural group and its absence in another.* Assuming that our goal is to provide an effective education for everyone (and remembering that much of the trouble is caused by economic and political, not psychological, deprivation), our task must be to determine the conditions under which various processes are manifested and to develop techniques for seeing that these conditions occur in the appropriate educational setting. An important domestic step in this direction has recently been taken by Cazden (1970).

In reviewing contemporary thinking about minority-group deficits from this viewpoint, let us first consider Jensen's claim that non-whites inherit less Type 2 conceptual ability. Examples of situations said to reflect Type 2 learning which we have discussed in this book are transposition, discrimination reversal, and free recall. In each of these cases we found that all of our groups would, under some circumstances, show conceptual learning. Moreover, the rules describing the situations under which each kind of learning is evoked are by no means clear. Why should subjects use conceptual (relational) learning when transposing on the basis of size but not on the basis of brightness? Why should conceptual learning be manifested if the subject is given a reversal shift or many instances, but not if there is a nonreversal shift or only a few instances? Why should stories or chairs presented as part of a recall task produce conceptual-type learning, while presenting objects or telling people about the categories in the list fails to do so? How can brief training or exposure to the school experience so rapidly change the kind of process inherited by a person?

Although it is impossible to prove the absence of genetic influence on performance, what is required of a genetic theory is that it specify not only the processes, but the situations to which they will be applied. We find this prospect so unlikely that in the absence of some positive indication of its truth (and we have seen none so far), we suggest that it will be infinitely more fruitful to study the environmental-social factors that lead to changes in the application of skills that seem very widespread, if not universal, in their distribution across ethnic groups.

By this same token, we find ourselves very much in agreement with Labov and others who criticize the psychologist's and educator's view of cultural deprivation. However, we are also concerned with the fact that, for whatever cause, minority-group performance in a wide variety of educational settings is such as to insure their continued low position in American society. Assuming a willingness on the part of society as a whole to provide minority-group children with a first-class education (an assumption that is by no means clearly justified), we need to combine Labov's insights with a systematic study of why problem solving and learning skills are not applied in the classroom. Some of these causes, as Labov and others have suggested, are motivational. Since it does not pay off for a black child to work hard in school, he does not try. But as our data and common observation suggest, even when he tries, the member of the "minority" culture is likely to have trouble in school because he is learning in inappropriate ways. The problem of transferring skills applied on the streets to the classroom is not solved by demonstrating the existence of the skill on the streets. The child must be taught how to apply those skills in the classroom. But before we can do this, we must understand the nature of street and school activity. In short, we must combine ethnography and experimental psychology in the service of understanding the relation between culture and thinking.

APPENDIX A :
A Description of the Major
Subclasses of the Seŋ Chart

Consider things of the town as the first major subdivision of the *seŋ* chart. They are divided into four classes, namely, *people, playing things, structures,* and *town animals.*

The class of *people* is further subdivided in seven ways. These classes are not mutually exclusive, but cut across each other, depending on the basis of classification, as the labels in the subgroups indicate. *People* are classified into *children, adults, good persons, evil persons, workmen,* and *persons' appearance* and *status. Children* are subdivided in ways implying a theory of physical and social maturation. *Adults* are classed both according to age and increasing responsibility and according to wealth and power. *Good persons* are those who are respectful, helpful, clever, and capable of wise counsel, as well as those who are physically beautiful. *Evil persons,* on the other hand, are those who commit what the culture defines as a crime, or else those who are physically ugly. The tasks that define the class of *workmen* are first those that everyone in the society must be able to perform and, second, those performed only by skilled specialists. The final two subdivisions consider the ways in which a person can be beautiful or ugly, and a person's status, whether he is rich or poor, healthy or sick, tribesman or stranger. Shifting bases of classification within this domain are clearly indicated in this description.

Playing things are those that are used within the town for entertainment. They are in five groups: *masked dancers,* the *equipment* these dancers require, *musical instruments that are beaten, musical instruments that are blown,* and *games.* The first four classes have ties to the activities of the secret societies, but do not in fact include the important secret figures of those societies, which are classified as *forest things.*

Structures, literally called "town-works," are all those buildings in the town that are fixed in one place, as opposed to man-made objects that are movable. *Structures* are of five main types: *houses,* which have both roofs and walls; *sheds* (called in Liberia "kitchens"), which have roofs, but no walls; *fences,* which have walls but no roofs; *looms;* and *benches.*

Town animals are animals domesticated by man, which live in the town. The town is fenced in order to keep them in, since they can do great damage to farms and also can be caught and eaten by wild predators. *Town animals* are of two types: *birds,* including *chickens, guinea fowls,* and *pigeons;* and *walking animals,* including *sheep, goats, cows, dogs, cats, hogs, rabbits,* and *guinea pigs.*

Those things that are unambiguously identified as *forest things* are of four types. They include *trees, vines, shrubs,* and nonhuman spiritual beings called *evil things. Trees, vines,* and *shrubs* are classified according to their method of growth. *Trees* are plants (to use an English term in a non-Kpelle way, since for the Kpelle plants are specifically those things that are planted by man) that have a main stem and that are capable of standing by themselves. *Vines* are plants that have a main stem, but that cannot stand by themselves, requiring a host tree around which to wrap themselves. *Shrubs* are low leafy plants without a main stem. Each of these classes was subdivided by Kellemu's informants into *forest* and *planted* groups, but of those subdivisions only those that grow wild were strictly called *forest things.*

The class of *evil things* has seven subgroups. The first two are *namu* and *zele,* who are the supposedly supernatural leaders of the male and female secret societies, called *Poro* and *Sande.* These beings are not supposed to be human; they have the power to eat uninitiated boys and girls and then bring them back to life at the end of their training in bush school. The third class of *evil things* consists of *supernatural beings* that frighten persons at night by the roadside. The fourth class can be glossed as *witches,* usually people who transform themselves into animals in order to do evil deeds. Fifth are the *genii,* so called because they somewhat resemble the spirits of Muslim mythology. Sixth are *dwarfs* who inhabit the deep forest and can bring either evil or good fortune. And seventh are *spirits of the dead,* whose relation to the members of their family depends on the respect paid to them.

These two classes—*town things* and *forest things*—do not exhaust the universe of *seŋ*. There are objects that belong simultaneously to the town and the forest. Some things within the vine that marks the borders of the town belong to the world of growing plants, and some things within the forest are manufactured and controlled by man.

The first such shared subclass is the *earth*, which is the material substratum for both town and forest. The earth is of four types—*dirt, stone, sand* and *mud*.

Other classes that are found as subclasses of both *town* and *forest* are *planted trees, planted vines,* and *planted shrubs*. These are classed by the Kpelle with the *wild trees, vines,* and *shrubs,* but are also classed with *town things*. There was a substantial debate among the elders consulted by John Kellemu concerning the proper classification of these *planted things*. The conclusions reached by the debaters show clearly the shifting bases of classification. Some said that they are *forest things* both because they originated in the forest, and because they are only cultivated in the forest. Other elders said that *planted trees, vines,* and *shrubs* are town things since they are necessary to life and since they are taken from the town in seed form and planted in the forest. Moreover, some of these things are actually planted in gardens within the town boundaries.

The third shared class consists of *working things*, which form a kind of bridge between the things of the town and the things of the forest. Its members are in most cases made by man and in the remaining cases are things found by man in the forest and then put to use. *Working things* are subdivided into four major subgroups: *medicines, vehicles, traps,* and *household things*. Each of these subgroups consists of objects made by men from forest raw materials to achieve some specific goal. *Medicines* give man power over the life of the spirit and the afflictions that can come to man through uncontrolled spiritual activity. *Vehicles* are all objects that are hollow in form. Traps enable man to capture animals in the forest. And *household things* make possible the ordinary round of daily activity and life.

Medicines are divided into six subgroups. The first consists of *herbs* used for the prevention and cure of common diseases. The second consists of *charms* and *amulets,* which aid in such enterprises as hunting, traveling, gaining vines, raising good crops, identifying thieves, and exposing witches. The third category includes specialized *secret societies* (other than the principal tribal secret societies), which deal with witches, spirits, lightning, snakes, hunting, and water animals. The fourth group is *evil medicine,* including *poisoning* and *sorcery.* The fifth group consists of a series of *methods for divining reasons for events.* Finally, *western medicines* compose the sixth subgroup.

The translation *vehicle* is a lame approximation to the Kpelle concept. This class includes canoes, airplanes, and trucks. It also, however, includes the hollowed log in which palm oil is prepared as well as that in which raw rum is fermented. Finally, it includes drums used by certain secret societies as well as by cooperative work groups. The implication seems to be that these objects are all hollow, and all participate in an activity causing a change of state or position of some object or material.

The Kpelle are familiar with *traps* for animals ranging from mice to leopards to fish. The techniques of trapping are diverse and technically clever, including nooses that are sprung by the animal and enclosures to which access is easy but from which escape is almost impossible.

The fourth subgroup of *working things* consists of things useful to the daily life of the household. These are of four kinds, including *sleeping things, clothing, tools* and *things used for cooking (foods). Sleeping things* are of three kinds: *beds, mats,* and *sleeping clothes. Clothing* is divided into two basic groups, consisting of *men's clothes* and *women's clothes.* Both men and women's clothing include cloth, iron, wooden and leather items, while women's clothing includes also cosmetics and beads. A wide variety of *tools,* ranging from needles to spears, is used in Kpelle life. These tools are literally "iron things," since all are made by the blacksmith out of iron. Things used for cooking are of two types, *utensils* (literally "empty things") and *foods.* The *utensils* are all hollow objects used for preparing food, while the *foods* themselves are all the things the Kpelle eat.

Foods form a complex subclass of the Kpelle world. The basic division is into those foods that are clearly *town things,* kept in the house and used as needed, and those *foods* that are taken from the forest as needed. *Town foods* include condiments, such as oil, salt, and pepper, and prepared foods, such as greens, dried meat, and cleaned rice. *Forest foods* are divided into six groups, which overlap to some extent with the plants of the forest. They include *root crops, tree fruits, vine fruits, water foods, mushrooms,* and *meat.* The first three are divided into crops that are planted by man and those that grow wild. *Liquid foods* include *drinking water, oils,* and *honey.* The Kpelle name at least twenty-four different varieties of edible mushroom, in addition to many that are not edible.

The most complex subset of foods is that named by a term that can be translated either *animal* or *meat*. *Animals* of the forest are classified according to their foot structure. their mode of locomotion, and their habitat. These groups overlap considerably, so that the same animal may appear in two or three categories. *Animals* are classed according to whether they have two-part or four-part hoofs or claws; according to whether they drag themselves (for example snakes, fish, and worms), crawl, leap, fly, or burrow; and according to whether they live in trees or in the water. For instance, the tree squirrel is an animal with claws that lives in trees and that burrows to make its home. In the West we might prefer to make, for instance, the mode of locomotion the principal characteristic, and use the other classifications as subheadings, but the Kpelle informants do not choose to operate this way.

APPENDIX B :
The Application of the Similarity - Distribution Technique

The similarity-distribution procedure is applied as follows: a subject is verbally presented a set of items (in our case, nouns drawn from the *seŋ* chart) one at a time and asked to make up a sentence using each word. When each word in the set has been used in a sentence, the sentences become frames and the subject is asked to judge the appropriateness of using each word in each sentence according to a fixed criterion. The criterion that our subjects were asked to use was, does this sentence make good Kpelle sense?

A matrix with items (words) across the columns and sentences across the rows (see the example in Figure B–1) is made up, and the subject is interrogated concerning the entire set of sentences and words. Whenever a subject accepts a sentence using a particular word, a one is placed in the matrix at the intersect of the particular word-sentence combination. If the subject disagrees, a zero is entered in the intersect. Proceeding in such a manner, a symmetrical "frames-by-items" matrix is generated with each intersect containing either a one or a zero. The matrix is then subjected to computer analysis and the items rearranged such that items that show similar patterns of ones and zeros are placed next to each other, while those that show dissimilar patterns are placed further apart (Stefflre, 1963). For example, the informant might be given the following set of items: pot, orange, banana, hoe, hammer, pan, and cutlass. Figure B–1 represents the matrix elicited from an informant. When this matrix is subject to analysis, rearranging items according to similar pat-

Items	Pot	Orange	Banana	Hoe	Hammer	Pan	Cutlass
A ___ is used for cooking	1	0	0	0	0	1	0
An ___ is a fruit	0	1	1	0	0	0	0
I ate a ___	0	1	1	0	0	0	0
A ___ is used in farming	0	0	0	1	0	0	1
A ___ is used in building	0	0	0	0	1	0	1
There is milk in the ___	1	0	0	0	0	1	0
A ___ can be used for clearing	0	0	0	1	0	0	1

(Frames)

FIGURE B–1 Input Matrix for Hypothetical Distributional Similarity Data

terns of ones and zeros, a rearranged matrix is the result (see Figure B–2). As can be readily seen in Figure B–2, three groups, or clumps of items, appear to emerge according to the similarity of their patterns of ones and zeros. This technique is applicable either to matrices obtained from individual informants or to a group of matrices summed over individual informants. In our use of the procedure only the lexical items were common to informants, and rearranged orders of the columns were the data of primary interest.

The first study described in Chapter 3 employed the thirty-five major subheadings of the *seŋ* chart as presented in Table 3–1, while the later studies looked more closely at the relation between and within subordinate classes.

Two additional similarity-distribution studies were run to evaluate relations within the two major *seŋ* groups, *town* and *forest*. All proce-

Frames	Utensils		Tree Fruit		Tools		
	Pot	Pan	Orange	Banana	Cutlass	Hoe	Hammer
A pot is used for cooking	1	1	0	0	0	0	0
A pan can contain milk	1	1	0	0	0	0	0
An orange is a fruit	0	0	1	1	0	0	0
A banana is sweet	0	0	1	1	0	0	0
A cutlass can be used...	0	0	0	0	1	1	0
A hoe is used in farming	0	0	0	0	1	1	0
A hammer is used for building	0	0	0	0	1	0	1

FIGURE B–2 Rearranged Matrix for Hypothetical Distributional Similarity Data

dures were the same as those described in Chapter 3 except that (1) the terms used in one of the elicitations were all from the set of *town things,* while the other set was made up of *forest things;* and (2) the items used were all subordinate to the things named by the terms in the previous elicitation—in short, we selected more concrete items.

Once again we observed ordering of the stimulus terms that was consistent with the ordering in the *seŋ* chart (see Tables B–1 and B–2), although secondary inconsistencies again appear.

Some of these inconsistencies undoubtedly reflect ambiguities in the *seŋ* chart. Others probably reflect insensitivity of the similarity-distribution technique applied so that subjects choose their own sentence frames. Where subjects choose very general frames (as our subjects often did), lack of discrimination results.

TABLE B-1
Seŋ Chart Rearranged Town Items

ITEM	SUBHEADING	HEADING
hunting medicine farm and hunting charm hunting-society charm witch protection ⋯⋯⋯⋯⋯⋯⋯⋯⋯ .478 ⋯⋯⋯⋯⋯⋯⋯⋯⋯	medicine .629	work
water for drinking 1.00 ⋯⋯⋯⋯⋯⋯⋯⋯⋯ .412 ⋯⋯⋯⋯⋯⋯⋯⋯⋯	liquid foods	food
town birds (subheading) chicken with fuzzy feathers domesticated pigeon duck guinea fowl ⋯⋯⋯⋯⋯⋯⋯⋯⋯ .641 ⋯⋯⋯⋯⋯⋯⋯⋯⋯	town birds .715	
goat sheep cow walking animals (subheading) dog cat ⋯⋯⋯⋯⋯⋯⋯⋯⋯ .476 ⋯⋯⋯⋯⋯⋯⋯⋯⋯	walking animals .670	town animals .658
palm oil palm nut oil honey ⋯⋯⋯⋯⋯⋯⋯⋯⋯ .585 ⋯⋯⋯⋯⋯⋯⋯⋯⋯	liquid foods .792	foods
shirtlike dress dancing calabash dancing whip blacksmith charm hunting shells dancing bell ⋯⋯⋯⋯⋯⋯⋯⋯⋯ .544 ⋯⋯⋯⋯⋯⋯⋯⋯⋯	dancing equipment .644	
cow horn harmonica bugle military dance band wooden horn band ⋯⋯⋯⋯⋯⋯⋯⋯⋯ .264 ⋯⋯⋯⋯⋯⋯⋯⋯⋯	things that are blown .771	play .612

(continued)

ITEM	SUBHEADING	HEADING
body burier skilled worker farm worker	workers .842	
.881		
wise person shame person one who loves others	good way people .940	
.927		
lazy person 1.00	bad way people	
.926		
light-skinned person short person medium-skinned person dark-skinned person	people as made .949	
.931		
son of the soil 1.00	people's mode of being	
.908		
bad way person (subheading) liar	bad way people .939	people .902
.942		
adviser 1.00	good way people	
.960		
vagabond 1.00	bad way people	
.963		
story teller good way people (subheading)	good way people .955	
.905		
thief 1.00	bad way people	
.871		
medium-height person 1.00	people as made	
.888		
trader 1.00	workers	
.889		

(continued)

ITEM	SUBHEADING	HEADING
stranger westernized person	people's mode of being .846	people (continued)
. 659		
. . . . stupid person 1.00	bad way people	
. 457		
. . . . Gola masquerade Sande masquerade Gbande masquerade small boy's masquerade small girl's masquerade	things that dance .855	play
. 141		
. . . . night dew 1.00	liquid foods	foods
. . . .		

TABLE B-2

Seŋ Chart Rearranged Forest Items

ITEM	SUBHEADING	HEADING
large flat rock stone mud dirt sand		the Earth .407
. 245		
. . . . alligator 1.00	crawling animals	Forest animals 1 .466
. 282		
. . . . leech black swamp worm grey swamp worm large snakelike worm	worms .588	
. 285		
. . . . thorn-covered vine rubber vine medium-sized vine	wild vines .556	
. 232		
. . . .		

(continued)

ITEM	SUBHEADING	HEADING
sort tort wood pecker bamboo worm	crawling animals burrowing animals worms	Forest animals 2 .526
.531		
red and blue lizzard crocodile	crawling animals .559	
.666		
sky cassava snake Campbell's monkey red colombus monkey potto	tree animals .834	Forest Animals Total .719
.836		
bush tail porcupine armadillo	burrowing animals .879	
.875		
black deer grey deer red deer bush cow zebra antelope	hoofed animals .904	
.751		
horn bill tree squirrel crawling turtle	burrowing animals tree animals crawling animals	Forest animals 3 .737
.525		
pumpkin egg plant		foods 1 .710
.751		
beans water yam	vine fruits .794	Foods Total .669
.751		
corn air potato banana sugar cane oil palm		foods 2 .633
.498		
calambus palm .264 rattan palm	wild vines .820	
cocoa 1.00	cultivated tree	
.061		
scorpion	burrowing animal	

APPENDIX C :
Free Association

The free-association technique has had a long history in psychology. Originating in the association school of British philosophy, and later used as a psychoanalytic diagnostic technique, free association has recently become a major tool for the study of verbal behavior. The technique itself is quite simple. The informant is simply presented with a series of words and asked to respond to each word with the first word that comes to mind.

Experimental work over the past thirty years has led to several major propositions as to the nature of the relation between words and their associates. Early theorizing centered on the idea that words and their associates achieved their relation to each other simply because they occurred together previously in the person's experience. A second view, still within the behaviorist tradition, treats words and their associates as related through commonly conditioned mediators, that is, words and associates are similar to the degree that they are conditioned responses to common stimuli.

Until recently, most word-association studies required a subject to give a single response to a given stimulus word. Results from such studies with Americans generally yielded three or four responses of relatively high frequency common to the entire group of subjects, and a series of thirty or forty low-frequency or idiosyncratic responses. In more recent work the informant is required to give more than one response. The high-frequency responses still remain, but the relative frequency of the low-frequency responses increases drastically. These new findings have led H. Pollio (1966) to suggest that the associates to a given word represent members of the same semantic class as the stimulus word (words that have the same or very similar mediational elements to which they have been paired). The high-frequency responses (the so-called primary, secondary, and tertiary responses) are the responses that are, in general, those that are closest to the stimulus word in the hypothetical semantic space. The low-frequency associates, while still possessing mediational elements in common, are further away from the stimulus word in the semantic space.

Theoretical considerations such as these have led Deese (1962) and his associates to the position that stimulus words are similar to each other to the degree that they elicit common responses. This definition of similarity gives rise to the data-analysis techniques that underlie the discussion of free association in Chapter 3.

Once a subject's associations to a set of words have been collected, a matrix is constructed in which the columns represent the various stimulus words and the rows represent the response words given to each of the stimuli. In our work a great many different response words were given when an entire group of subjects was considered as a unit, so the resulting free-association matrices had a great many rows. Each time a new response word appeared, it was added to the row of response terms. Each time a response word that had already occurred was encountered again, its occurrence was marked in the appropriate cell of the matrix. For example, if "lemon" was first given as a response to the stimulus word "banana," it was listed as a response and a one was entered for the cell "banana-lemon." If "lemon" occurred as a response to other stimulus words, one was entered in the appropriate stimulus-response cell, and if other subjects gave "lemon" as a response, its frequency of occurrence in the appropriate stimulus-response cells was noted.

The result of this procedure was a matrix with the frequency counts for all stimulus-response entries, summed over a group of ten or more subjects (ten was the basic group size).

Then, following Deese (1962), we calculated a similarity score representing the extent to which each of the stimuli in the list in question tended to elicit the same response words. This score is defined as the number of times that two stimuli elicit common responses, divided by the total number of times that either stimulus word in the pair under consideration elicits those responses. For example, if banana and coconut each elicit twenty responses and in ten of these cases they are the same word, the similarity score would be .5 (technically, the formula for calculating similarity [S] is

$$S = \frac{2N\,(i \cdot i)}{N(i) + N(j)} \quad ,$$

where *i* is the number of responses to stimulus word *i* and *j* is the number of responses to stimulus word *j*. Note that *S* varies between zero and unity).

Once the similarity scores for a set of stimuli have been calculated, it is possible to treat them in various ways for purposes of analysis. Two analyses play a prominent role in the analysis of stimuli contained in Chapter 3. First, the average similarity between stimuli within hypothetical classes is compared with the similarity scores for stimuli that are hypothesized to come from different classes. If our assumptions about the nature of the classes are correct, within-class similarity scores should, on the average, be higher than between-class scores. Second, the similarity scores are treated as psychological "distances" between stimuli, and the data are analyzed in terms of Johnson's (1967) hierarchical clustering program to determine if not only classes, but hierarchical relations among items and classes, exist.

APPENDIX D :
Additional Data from
Similarity - Mediation Study

Table D–1 summarizes the object choices for the mixed-category pairs. As in the case of intracategorical relationships, the three non-high-school groups are similar in their choices of the objects to mediate the intercategorical pairs. The high-school group is also similar to the other groups except for the food-utensil pairing where the high-school students respond mainly with a food item, while the others usually name a tool.

In order to decide whether categorical membership was used as a basis to choose responses, we can calculate the proportion of choices that are within the categories defined by the two constraining objects. These percentages are presented in Table D–2.

Although there is considerable variation in the responses to different types of constraining objects, in two of the three types, the high-school students make intracategorical choices 85 percent of the time—a percentage significantly higher than the 58 percent expected by chance (there are eight possible categorical choices among the set of thirteen choice items). The other groups do not differ significantly from chance values. Finally, only the high-school group shows a predominance of static justifications of their choices (see Table D–3).

TABLE D-1

Category Membership of Mediating Object: Mixed Pairs

CONSTRAINING OBJECTS: FOOD-UTENSILS

MEDIATING OBJECT

	FOOD	TOOL	UTENSIL
NC[a]	0	24	8
A[b]	4	18	8
SC[c]	0	28	5
HS[d]	17	6	9

CONSTRAINING OBJECTS: FOOD-TOOLS

MEDIATING OBJECT

	FOOD	TOOL	UTENSIL
NC[a]	6	22	5
A[b]	2	23	3
SC[c]	0	28	4
HS[d]	8	22	1

CONSTRAINING OBJECTS: UTENSIL-TOOL

MEDIATING OBJECT

	FOOD	TOOL	UTENSIL
NC[a]	10	21	0
A[b]	5	18	4
SC[c]	10	18	1
HS[d]	7	19	5

[a]Ten- to fourteen-year-old nonliterate children.

[b]Nonliterate, traditional adults.

[c]Ten- to fourteen-year-old schoolchildren, grades two to five.

[d]High-school students, age sixteen to twenty.

TABLE D-2

Percentage of Responses within Either of the Constraining Categories

	FOOD-UTENSIL	FOOD-TOOL	UTENSIL-TOOL	AVERAGE
NC[a]	25	85	70	60
A[b]	40	90	81	70
SC[c]	15	88	66	57
HS[d]	81	97	77	85

[a]Ten- to fourteen-year-old nonliterate children.
[b]Nonliterate, traditional adults.
[c]Ten- to fourteen-year-old schoolchildren, grades two to five.
[d]High-school students, age sixteen to twenty.

TABLE D-3

*Justifications for
Intercategorical Pairs*

	STATIC	DYNAMIC
NC[a]	0%	100%
A[b]	2	98
SC[c]	3	97
HS[d]	74	26

[a]Ten- to fourteen-year-old nonliterate children.
[b]Nonliterate, traditional adults.
[c]Ten- to fourteen-year-old school-children, grades two to five.
[d]High-school students, age sixteen to twenty.

APPENDIX E :
Details of Free-Recall Experimental Procedures and Results of Standard Experiments

Instructions

Because they are an important part of the experimental procedure, and because a standard set of instructions evolved over a series of pilot studies, we will give a detailed account of the way in which these instructions developed.

We began with a simple set of English instructions, the sense of which was that the subject would be told a list of common things that might be found at the market of which he was to try to remember as many as he possibly could. These instructions were translated into Kpelle by one of our informants and tried out on a few subjects. They were then modified slightly and translated back into English by another informant who had not been present during the initial translation.

During a rather extensive series of pilot studies, the instructions were simplified until the final instructions came to read as follows in a literal translation:

You and I will do a play. The play which we will do will be about things we can do work with. I will call all the things' names first before you call their names. Listen to me carefully. (After the list had been presented) We are finished. You call the things' names now.

This rather sparse set of instructions yielded results comparable to our more elaborate initial instructions and met the criterion that our informants felt comfortable that their subjects understood the task.

Each experimenter was required to memorize the instructions, which were typed on a sheet of paper carried in each experimental notebook. In order to assure that experimenters followed a random order in running subjects from various groups and that they presented the lists in a proper manner, each recall experiment was laid out in advance with each data sheet labeled as to the condition required and each trial labeled with the list order to be used for that trial. The experimenters were allowed to violate the order when it was necessary because, for instance, a ten-year-old schoolboy was not to be found, but an illiterate adult was at hand. In certain cases there was reason to believe that list orders were not followed properly; in such cases, information about serial-order effects was lost.

Results of Experiment 2

The largest effect on the number of items recalled per trial was produced by the type of stimuli presented; objects (10.2) were better recalled than words (9.4). Presenting the stimuli in blocked order (10.1) also enhanced recall relative to random ordering (9.5). Although the educated groups (10.0) recalled slightly more than the nonliterate groups (9.6), the difference was not significant. However, the lack of an overall effect of education masks an interesting and unexpected difference in the way the educated and nonliterate populations were affected by the two kinds of stimulus materials (see Table E–1).

The following conclusions follow from the data in Table E–1: (1) when words were presented, the nonliterate subjects were slightly (but

TABLE E-1

Recall as a Function of Education and Stimulus Materials

	WORDS	OBJECTS
Educated	9.1	10.8
Nonliterate	9.6	9.6

reliably) superior to the educated subjects; (2) when objects were presented, the educated subjects were superior. This finding clearly clashes with the results of Experiment 1, where the educated subjects were superior when stimuli were presented orally. The contradiction may be real, but it is more likely that it is the result of a sampling error. When we compare the performance of the educated and noneducated ten to fourteen year olds in the first experiment for the clusterable lists, we find that the superiority of the educated subjects amounts to only .2 items per trial or one item over the course of the whole experiment. Consequently, it seems best to take a cautious attitude toward the relation between recall and education for orally presented material; there appears to be little difference between the two populations represented by our groups. Other data indicate superiority of groups with more education than that represented thus far, so the matter need not concern us unduly here.

Perhaps more interesting than differences in absolute levels of recall among the various groups is evidence that serial organization differs systematically among groups. An example of such a difference is shown in Figure E–1, which plots accuracy of recall as a function of education, the nature of the stimulus materials, and serial position.

Although Figure E–1 is a little difficult to interpret because of the irregularity of the curves, a careful examination will reveal that when objects are presented, a classical bowed serial-position curve is produced; however, when words are spoken, there is no relation between position and accuracy for the nonliterate subjects and only recency for literate ones.

These findings bear a rather close resemblance to the sequence of changes in serial-position responding that are posited by several contemporary theories of memory (Atkinson and Shiffrin, 1968; Bower, 1967; Waugh and Norman, 1965). According to these theories, a recency effect reflects the advantage of items presented just prior to recall because they are still in a readily available short-term memory state; primacy occurs because items occurring early on the list receive less interference from subsequent items and thus enter a long-term storage condition more easily.

Viewed in this context, Figure E–1 suggests that when objects are presented, both educated and nonliterate subjects manifest the use of both long-term and short-term retrieval strategies, but when words are spoken, the educated subjects take advantage only of the accessibility of items in short-term storage, while the nonliterate subjects show no dif-

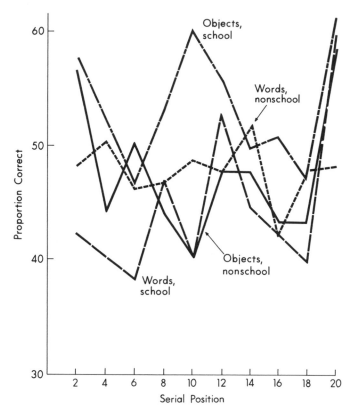

FIGURE E–1 Proportion of Items Recalled as a Function of Serial Position, Kind of Stimuli and Educational Status

ferential use of serial properties of item presentation. Because of their theoretical suggestiveness, we will pay close attention to serial-position phenomena in our cross-cultural comparisons.

One further aspect of the recall data in Experiment 2 should be mentioned before considering measures of semantic organization; recall improved much more markedly over successive trials than was the case for Experiment 1. On the average, Trial 5 produced approximately four more items than Trial 1. A significant interaction between the type of stimuli presented and the trials indicated that the improvement over trials was rapid only for the groups presented objects; little improvement occurred if words were used as stimuli.

The Effects of Age and List Organization
on Recall among Yucatec Mayans

The basic manipulations that were the focus of attention in our initial Kpelle experiments were included in the first study in Yucatan: clusterability of the list, list structure, and age (the next experiment discussed in this appendix considers education). These data were collected in December 1967 in Ticul, Yucatan, Mexico. (We are indebted to Professor Volney Stefflre and his associates in Ticul for their assistance in the conduct of this research.)

Subjects, Materials, and Experimental Design

There were ninety-six subjects, thirty-two each in the age groups six to eight years (average 7.9), eleven to fifteen years (average 12.9), and eighteen to sixty-six years (average 29.4). All of the subjects spoke both Yucatec Mayan and Spanish.

The stimulus words were chosen to be rough equivalents of those used in the American and Kpelle experiments described earlier. The clusterable list was made up of twenty nouns from the classes which may be translated as food, tools, clothing, and utensils. The nonclusterable list was made up of other nouns chosen to be familiar but not obviously clusterable.

The instructions and stimuli were read to the subject in Mayan. In all other respects, the procedure was designed to be as similar as possible to the standard procedure described at the beginning of this appendix.

Within each of the subject populations, four groups of eight subjects each were selected haphazardly to provide for the factorial combination of clusterable versus nonclusterable lists and blocked- or random-presentation orders (for the nonclusterable list, the blocking was done on arbitrary groups of five items, which were always presented adjacent to one another).

Results

As we have come to expect on the basis of our previous studies, recall increased with age for our Mayan subjects. However, the increase occurs between the six to eight year olds (8.6) and the eleven to fifteen year olds (10.2), who are slightly, but not reliably, superior to the adults (10.0). Neither clusterability of the list nor blocking of stimuli had any significant effect on recall, nor were there any significant interactions among these variables.

Like the American subjects, but unlike the Kpelle, there is a marked improvement across trials for all groups with oral presentation. The average number recalled increases from 6.9 on Trial 1 to 12.0 on Trial 5.

Both clusterability and blocking interact with serial position, but not the same way that we observed in our American studies. The main difference in the shapes of the curves is that the more easily organized list shows only recency (see Figure E–2).

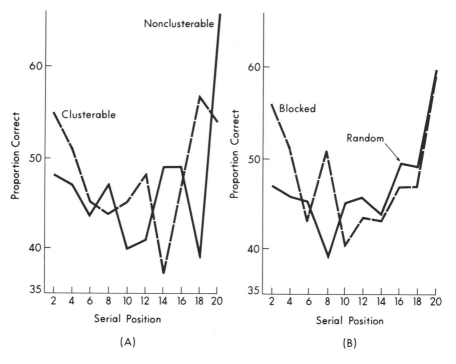

FIGURE E–2 Proportion of Items Recalled as a Function of Serial Position and (A) Clusterability of the Stimulus List; (B) Random or Blocked Ordering of Stimulus List

Looking next at semantic organization, we find that blocked groups show a significant, but very moderate, degree of clustering ($z = .61$), while clustering is not significant for the random lists ($z = .29$).

Overall, the Mayan groups show slight negative correlation between presentation and recall orders ($r = -.15$), which is consistent with the relatively large amount of recency observed in all groups (Figure E–2), and this negative tendency increases over trials in a manner similar to that which we observed in the American data.

The Effect of Education and List Structure on Recall among Yucatec Mayans

In Ticul, Mexico, as in Kpelleland, school attendance is far from universal and among the adult population in particular, there are many people who have never attended school. Consequently, it was decided to investigate the effect of school attendance on recall. In addition, blocked and random clusterable lists were presented.

Subjects, Materials, and Experimental Procedures

The ninety-two subjects were chosen haphazardly from the adult (average age = 33 years) population of Ticul, with the added requirement that the subject speak both Mayan and Spanish.

The forty-six subjects who had attended two or more years of school (average, 3.0) and those who had not attended school were divided into two groups. One was presented the random-list; the other, blocked-list orders.

Results

Consistent with the findings in the previous experiment, presentation of the list in blocked order did not generally enhance recall. School attendance also failed to affect overall performance. However, the educated and uneducated groups differed slightly in their responses on the blocked and random lists. The educated subjects recalled the blocked and random lists equally well, but the random list was significantly more difficult than the blocked list for the uneducated subjects. As with the Kpelle, there seems to be little overall effect of a few years of education on recall; however, in each case there are indications that where a superiority of the educated subjects does exist, it is in those conditions that are generally most favorable to recall (blocked presentation, objects).

In other respects the results of this experiment are essentially replications of those obtained in the previous Yucatec Mayan experiment. There is improved recall over trials, a moderate degree of clustering (average $z = .72$), and a slight overall negative correlation between presentation and recall orders. The correlation between presentation and recall is positive on Trial 1 and increasingly negative thereafter. There is also an interaction between list structure and serial position similar to that observed previously with these subjects; there is less primacy with the random than the blocked list.

The Properties of Recall
with Another Liberian Tribal Group, the Vai

To the west of the Kpelle, in the coastal area bordering on Sierra Leone, is the Vai tribe, numbering perhaps 25,000. The Vai represent an interesting contrast with the Kpelle in several respects, and hence the results of our experiment with them were thought worth presenting here. For one thing, the Vai have long been in contact with Western civilization, first as middlemen in the slave trade and later in other commercial and governmental capacities. In Liberian folklore about tribal characteristics, the Vai are considered a dominant, intelligent, and arrogant group used to being served by others, whereas the Kpelle are more often cast in the role of the slow-witted servant.

Of more immediate relevance than these tribal stereotypes is the fact that for the past 150 years, the Vai have had an indigenous form of writing, a syllabic system that was probably inspired by the widespread presence of the Koran among Moslem missionaries. (See Dalby, 1967, for an interesting account of the invention of Vai script and its early spread among the Vai. Dalby's article also contains descriptions of other indigenous scripts, some modeled on the Vai, but none are of so early an origin or so widespread in usage.)

The presence of a system of writing among a tribal people who are in many respects similar to the Kpelle seemed to afford an excellent opportunity to test hypotheses about the "consequences of literacy" (Goody and Watt, 1962), without confusing literacy with the difference between the rain forests of Liberia and the suburbs of southern California.

Subjects, Procedures, and Experimental Design

The subjects were sixty Vai adults ranging in age from eighteen to fifty with an average of thirty-five years. Half of the subjects were literate in Vai script, while the other half were not. None of the subjects was literate in English, although a few had attended school for one or two years. In general, this sample of Vai adults was more Westernized than the nonliterate Kpelle adults used in the experiments described earlier. Only twenty-three of the sixty were rice farmers; the remainder were tailors, carpenters, gasoline attendants, and other "specialists."

The thirty subjects literate in Vai script and the thirty not literate in Vai script were randomly assigned to two conditions: fifteen subjects in each group used clusterable lists, while fifteen used nonclusterable lists. These lists were composed of Vai translations of the lists used in our initial study among the Kpelle (Table 3–2). In all respects except the language used, procedures followed those of our initial Kpelle study. The experiment was conducted by Arnold Kandakai, a Vai student attending Cuttington College.

Results

The most interesting results of this experiment with the Vai were the following: (1) the two groups that were literate in Vai script recalled more (11.5 vs. 10.0) words than the nonliterate groups; (2) for the clusterable list there was a significant amount of clustering for the literate group ($z = .76$), but not for the nonliterate group.

There was no reliable difference in the number of items recalled between clusterable and nonclusterable lists for either group. In other respects, also, the performance of the nonliterate Vai was quite similar to that which we observed in Experiment 1 with the Kpelle. Recall was of the same order of magnitude, and improvement over trials was negligible, averaging only .6 items.

APPENDIX F :
Technical Aspects of the
Conduct of Cross-Cultural
Memory Research

When we first began to run pilot studies on the problem of free recall, we worked with an informant whose father was a well-known town chief, living in the administrative center of Gbarnga. One of the striking features of the recall protocols collected by this experimenter was a relatively large number of intrusions (items given as recall items by the subject that were not a part of the original list); moreover, in about 20 percent of the cases, the subject said "cow" as one of his words. Very rarely was "cow" given as a response in any of our other experiments, and as a rule, the number of intrusions was fairly low. We can only speculate, but it seems quite possible that the fact that our experimenter was the son of a chief (one of whose characteristics is the possession of a fine herd of cows, a rare attribute in Liberia) influenced the set of words used by subjects when asked to recall. Such idiosyncrasies clearly affect both intra- and cross-cultural comparisons.

One way to assess such difficulties, if not eliminate them, is to include evaluation of experimenter differences as a standard part of every research design. Another strategy is to use overlapping experiments in which at least one condition in each new experiment overlaps with (is identical to) a condition in an earlier experiment. In either case differences among experimenters or subject populations can be evaluated.

These precautions, which are summarized so easily, are very difficult to carry out systematically in practice. Wherever possible, we followed one or the other strategy, but in some cases it was not possible to do so.

264

The major difficulty with making the "experimenter effect" a part of every experimental design was the availability of only a limited number of experimenters, combined with the difficulty that experimenters often had in mastering one or two procedures, to say nothing of the ten or more different kinds of experiments that we conducted as a part of our research project. The difficulty with the overlapping-groups strategy involved not only the limitations on experimenter time, but limits on populations and money. The fact that we wanted to work with experimentally naive subjects meant that the experimenter was forced to move from town to town when the number of subjects he was required to run was very large. Although care was taken to randomize the order in which various treatment groups were run (in order to avoid confounding treatments and towns), the burden of partially replicating each experiment seemed too high a price to pay for purity. The time and money involved also represented a high price in more recognizable terms, so that all too often we skimped on replications. Unfortunately, we have paid the price of our decision in more than one instance in which we must remain ambiguous about the causes of our results. All we can do in such circumstances is to report the problems honestly for the reader's evaluation.

These remarks are immediately relevant to Experiments 1 and 2, which included the experimenter as a systematic part of the research design. Each of the groups of ten subjects in Experiments 1 and 2 was further subdivided into two groups of five, each run by a different experimenter (both of whom were native Kpelle speakers and students at Cuttington College). The performances reported earlier for these experiments were averages for experimenters Richard MacFarland and Paul Mulbah. In the first free-recall study, the overall performance of the two experimenters was the same for both number recalled and clustering scores; hence, one would assume a lack of experimenter effect. Unfortunately, the experimenter interacted significantly with a number of other effects. For MacFarland, the difference between subject populations was smaller than for Mulbah, while the difference among clusterable and nonclusterable lists was greater for MacFarland than Mulbah. Although there was no difference in clustering scores attributable to experimenters, Mulbah produced more pronounced recency and primacy than MacFarland.

Similar interactions were observed in the second free-recall study, where the differences among groups and serial position was generally smaller for MacFarland. Moreover, the difference in clustering and recall between objects and words was largely the contribution of experimenter Mulbah.

In none of these cases did one experimenter negate the result of the other, and the direction of the effects always remains the same. However, recognition of differences among experimenters has to temper our cross-cultural conclusions.

What keeps the situation from being hopeless is that we have conducted not one, but a large series of experiments. We have used not one, but several, experimenters, and in many cases we have been able to include overlapping groups so that *the pattern of the whole* yields a consistent picture in which the major fluctuations arising from theoretically uninteresting sources can be identified, isolated, and thus rendered less dangerous to our efforts at reaching valid generalizations.

APPENDIX G :
Recall of Items Presented
in a Story Context

The four basic stories, including instructions to the experimenter and the questions which the experimenter asked of the subject, were the following:

Story 1: A man was traveling in the forest and came to a town. In the town he met the chief who said to him, "I will show you all the things in this house. I will then close the door. You must tell me all the things in the house. If you succeed, I will let you marry my daughter. If you fail, I will kill you." The man agreed, and the chief showed him the following things in the room: (Name the objects on the list.) *What are the things the chief showed the man?*

Story 2: A chief had a beautiful daughter, and many young men wanted to marry her. Each of them brought many presents for the girl and left them with the chief. One brought (name the first group of objects). Another brought (name the second group of objects). Another brought (name third group of objects). And another brought (name fourth group of objects). *What things did the girl receive? Which young man should get the girl? Why?*

Story 3: A wealthy but foolish man came to a clever man because he was hungry. The clever man said he would help him, but must have many things. The foolish man agreed. The clever man asked for a hat to protect his head while he used the foolish man's hoe to dig up a potato from the man's farm and a pan to put it in, an onion and a pot to put it in, a pair of trousers so he could climb the man's tree and use the man's knife to cut his oranges, a file to use and singlet to wear while sharpening the man's cutlass in order to cut the man's bananas and a calabash to bring them in, a shirt to wear while he used the man's hammer to open the man's coconut and a cup to drink from it, and a headtie for his wife to wear while she served the things in the man's plate. The foolish man gave the clever man all these things. The clever man told him to wait until he came back. The foolish man is still waiting. *What were all the things which the foolish man gave the clever man? Tell the story over for me.*

Story 4: A very handsome man who happened to be a bogeyman came to town one day and met a beautiful girl. The girl did not know he was a bogeyman and agreed to marry him. On the night they married, she discovered he was a bogeyman. He told her she must come with him to his farm, but she said to wait a bit while she got her things together. She knew where the bogeyman's farm was, and so she put many things on the ground in her house to show her people the way to reach his farm. She put her plate first, since she always ate at home. Then she put the bogeyman's singlet to show that he took her away. Then she put a pot to show that he took her first in the direction of her family's kitchen behind the house. Then she put a knife to show that they went past the woodcarver's house. Next was a headtie showing they passed the store where she bought it. Next was an onion to show they passed the market, and a cup to show they passed the table where they sell palm wine. Next was a hammer to show they passed the house being built on that trail. She then put down a hat to show that the house belongs to the teacher. Next was a file to show they passed the blacksmith's kitchen. Then came a banana to show they took the road with the banana trees, a shirt to show they passed the place where they get drinking water. Then she put an orange to show that they took the trail with the orange tree, and a cutlass showed that the trail was newly cut. Then came the trousers to show they passed the weaver's farm, and a coconut to show they took the road with the coconut tree on it. Then came a hoe to show that she was on a farm, and a potato to show that it was a potato farm, and finally a pan to show she was at the kitchen on the farm. The girl's people saw all these things and understood where she had gone and came and rescued her. They caught the bogeyman and killed him. *Tell all the things she put on the ground and their meaning so that if you were the girl's family, you could find the girl.*

These stories were used as the basis for composing six groups with ten illiterate Kpelle adults in each. The groups were as follows:

Group 1: Basic oral presentation condition with randomized clusterable list.

Group 2: Story 1; the items presented were from the basic clusterable list with the order of items randomized.

Group 3: Story 2 with randomized, clusterable items; for example, each man brought a random selection of gifts.

Group 4: Story 2 with clusterable items presented in blocked order; for example, each man brought a particular category of gifts.

Group 5: Story 3.

Group 6: Story 4.

The stories were read by the experimenter, who wrote down the subject's responses in the standard manner. Then a tape recorder was turned on for Groups 3 to 6 in order to record the subject's version of the story.

The story was presented five times for each group. In conditions 1 to 4 the order of items was changed from trial to trial in the same fashion that such randomizing was done in earlier experiments. Since items were integral parts of Stories 3 and 4, no changes in order were made from trial to trial for Groups 5 and 6.

Results

The results of this experiment will be presented first in the standard form, and then the additional information provided in those instances where subjects recalled the entire story or interpreted parts of it will be discussed for the additional insight that it gives about the recall process. It should be clear that the conditions of recall are by no means equivalent for the different groups. For instance, a subject in Group 1 is asked to start recalling items approximately one minute after the first item is presented. By contrast, a subject in Group 5 has to listen to the entire story before he can begin to recall, a time of two or three minutes. Since these time factors may be operating in opposition to organizational factors, we must interpret evidence about the amounts recalled with some caution.

Groups 1, 2, and 6 were all roughly equivalent in terms of the number of items recalled (the average was approximately ten items per trial). This performance is in the order of magnitude that we have come to expect on the basis of the other experiments using oral presentation. The next easiest condition was for Group 5 (Story 3) (8.4 items per trial) followed by Groups 3 and 4 (only 5.8 and 4.8 items per trial, respectively). Thus it appears safe to conclude that embedding the to-be-remembered items within different contexts produces differences in the amount recalled. When combined with these overall differences, the differences in patterns of responding for the different groups are quite informative.

Stories 3 and 4, which present items in a meaningful, sequentially organized story, produce high correlations between the order in which the items are presented and the order in which they are recalled (r's = .56 and .51 respectively). These figures are far higher than we have seen under any other circumstances in any of our work. The correlations for the other story groups average about .15 and that for the control Group 1 was .21.

The measures of clustering are affected by the story context in much the same fashion, but a curious feature of the recall of Groups 3 and 4 makes clustering difficult to compare across groups, although the average was very low indeed. A close look at the data revealed that subjects in these two groups had a strong tendency to remember a particular category of items. This tendency was so strong in Group 4 that very often the subject named *only* the items that a particular man was said to have brought in order to obtain the girl. When this occurred, it was impossible to calculate a z score, but the "clustering" was perfect! Thus, one subject on every trial named items cutlass, hoe, and file in that order. For Group 3, where the semantic category and the person were in conflict, sometimes the person won out and sometimes the category. This same tendency helps to explain the poor recall performance of these groups.

For the remaining groups there was very little clustering. In the case of Groups 1 and 2, this means that we have essentially reproduced the standard findings of Experiment 1. For Groups 5 and 6, we know that serial organization, which works against clustering, is dominating recall.

APPENDIX H :
Stimulus Matching as a
Measure of Classification

In the stimulus-matching experiment, the subject is shown cards such as those shown in Figure H–1. Each time he is shown a card, he must indicate which *two* of the pictures on the card he thinks "go together." For the top card in Figure H–1 there are three ways that he can match stimulus pairs: by color, form, and size. For the bottom card he can match for form or color since all pictures are of the same size. In a similar manner we can make up cards that allow for comparisons of form and size and color and size.

Decks of cards were constructed to permit evaluation of preferences among color, form, and size in this way. Each subject was presented a set of cards allowing all three comparisons as well as decks permitting each of the pair-wise comparisons. After each deck was presented, the subject was asked to explain the basis of his choices.

The subjects in this experiment were Kpelle children and young adults from first grade (six to eight years old), fourth to fifth grades (twelve to fourteen years old), and seventh to ninth grades (eighteen to twenty-one years old) and their nonliterate age mates. There were ten subjects in each group.

The major results of this study are presented in Table H–1. The top section of the table gives the proportion of classifications based on color, form, and size when all three classifications were possible. It is clear from Table H–1 that *form* is the dominant classification dimension, with little to choose between color and size. The educational factor is not included in Table H–1 because there were essentially no differences among educated and noneducated subjects at each age level.

Except for a possible increase in the tendency to choose form when

FIGURE H–1 Examples of Stimulus Cards Used in Dimension-Preference Study. (The upper card permits grouping on the basis of size, form, or color, while the lower card permits grouping on the basis of form or color only.)

we move from the six to eight to the twelve to fourteen year olds, there is little in the way of group variation in the basis for classification, contrary both to the results of the sorting experiment reported in Chapter 3 and a good deal of research elsewhere in Africa.

One possible explanation for these discrepancies is suggested by the data in the bottom section of Table H–1. When only form and color are

TABLE H-1

*Proportions of Classifications Based on the
Color, Form, and Size Dimensions*

	ALL THREE DIMENSIONS VARYING		
AGE	COLOR	FORM	SIZE
Six to eight years old	14	52	34
Twelve to fourteen years old	23	62	15
Eighteen to twenty-one years old	17	66	17

	PAIRWISE COMPARISONS					
AGE	FORM (COLOR/FORM)		FORM (FORM/SIZE)		COLOR (COLOR/SIZE)	
	S[a]	N[b]	S	N	S	N
Six to eight years old	83	56	68	63	61	63
Twelve to fourteen years old	68	47	66	86	66	100
Eighteen to twenty-one years old	81	91	64	79	88	79

[a]School.
[b]Nonschool.

available choices, we obtain differences among groups as a function of both age and education. Among the schoolchildren, there is a preference for form classification at all age levels, but among those who have not attended school, there is no preference for form except in the oldest group. When form is pitted against size, all groups prefer it; when color is pitted against size, it is preferred to roughly the same degree.

APPENDIX I :
Rule Learning

A procedure that seemed to offer a good deal of promise for the study of conceptual rule learning was developed by Haygood and Bourne (1965). Haygood and Bourne were the first to emphasize that the problems that apply logical rules really consist of two aspects: learning what the relevant attributes of the situation are, and learning the rule that is used to combine attributes in order to determine which stimuli are examples of the class the experimenter has in mind. They conclude their study by stating that, "conceptual rules differ in difficulty initially regardless of whether or not the relevant attributes are known, but the differences decrease across successive problems. Further, it was found that knowledge of the rule represents valuable information . . . which improves performance significantly" (1965, p. 175). Their finding suggested that, if we could devise a situation in which attribute learning was reduced to a minimum, we ought to be able to get linguistically determined differences to manifest themselves with maximum clarity, since presumably the linguistic difference, mediated by differences in the way conjunction and disjunction are expressed should be localized more in rule learning than in attribute learning. Thus we began a search for what might be termed "attributeless" concept of learning. Unfortunately, we could not use the procedure developed by Haygood and Bourne because that required extremely elaborate instructions and relatively sophisticated subjects. We were working with people for whom pictorial symbols, in general, were relatively unfamiliar, and we did not want our procedure to introduce new and extraneous difficulties.

The procedure we finally hit upon is represented by the four examples in Table I–1. Table I–1 represents a standard "truth table," familiar to students of logic. But in this case the elements of the table represent possible positions of the experimenter's hands. The four possible

274

TABLE I-1

POSITION OF HAND		RULE				
LEFT	RIGHT	CONJUNC-TION	INCLU-SIVE DISJUNC-TION	EXCLU-SIVE DISJUNC-TION	EQUIVA-LENCE	IMPLICA-TION
1. O	O	+	+	−	+	+
2. O	C	−	+	+	−	−
3. C	O	−	+	+	−	+
4. C	C	−	−	−	+	+

O = Open
C = Closed

combinations are listed at the left of the table. At the right are listed the combinations which are "correct" according to each of five conceptual rules, conjunction, inclusive disjunction, exclusive disjunction, equivalence and implication. For example, if the rule is conjunction, then two open hands would be correct and all three other examples would be incorrect. If the rule is inclusive disjunction, then examples one, two, and three would be correct and only example four would be incorrect. We assumed that differences in the rate of learning using this procedure would imply difficulty in the learning of the combination rules, since there were essentially no attributes, or a minimum of attributes, to learn and only four exemplars in each case.

In our initial pilot work, we put this scheme to work in the following manner: A subject was seated opposite the experimenter, who gave the following instructions:

Do you see the pencil placed between us? Sometimes I will be thinking about the pencil and sometimes I won't. The idea of this game is to tell me when I am thinking of the pencil. Each time I will hold out my hands. Sometimes I will hold them out like this (shows both hands open), sometimes like this (left hand open, right hand closed), and so forth. Each time I hold out my hand, you must tell me whether or not I'm thinking of the pencil. After you tell me what you think, I will tell you whether you are right or wrong.

The four kinds of trials represented by the four combinations of open and closed hands in Table I-1 were given repeatedly in a random order. The rule designating when the experimenter was thinking of the pencil (the "correct" instances) were those shown on the right of Table I-1. Much to our surprise, we found that learning in this situation was extremely slow. Although some subjects learned rapidly, many, after as many as forty or fifty trials, still failed to correctly identify those occasions upon which the experimenter was thinking of the pencil. This difficulty was encountered regardless of the rule involved. How could this problem with only four instances be so difficult for our subjects when many, seemingly more complex problems had been handled with ease previously?

To determine the cause of the difficulty, we began to work with several variations on the procedure. In some of these variations we did not use hands but rather placed objects in cups; in others we elaborated the instructions, and in others we gave the subject a concrete reward of a penny for each correct response and took away a penny for each incorrect response. After several weeks of such pilot work, we had made very little progress. Finally, in the course of one of our studies, we decided to reverse the order in which the experiment began. Rather than the experimenter beginning by asking, "am I thinking of the pencil?" and holding out his hands, he began by having the subject ask, "are you thinking of the pencil?" In answer, the experimenter would then hold out his hands. Subject: "Yes, you are thinking of the pencil." Experimenter: "That's correct, I'm thinking of the pencil." This seemingly laborious, and minute, change in the procedure had a dramatic impact on how rapidly subjects learned.

A special experiment was conducted in order to compare the two procedures, and we found that in the experimenter-initiated version, it took an average of 13.4 trials to hit a criterion of nine in a row. In the subject-initiated version, the average number of trials to criterion was 5.9. This difference, which was statistically reliable, led us to adopt the subject-initiated trial procedure in all of our subsequent investigations.

Levels of Difficulty for Different Rules?

Having hit upon an acceptable procedure with our "attributeless" learning problem, we set out to investigate the rate of learning for different types of rules. Our first experiment of this sort involved five different rules, which are shown in the right-hand side of Table I–1, along with the stimulus displays that are correct for the particular concept. The five rules were conjunction (open and closed), inclusive disjunction (open or closed), exclusive disjunction (open or open, but not both open), equivalence (open and open or closed and closed), and implication (if open then open). As Table I–1 makes clear, each rule represents a different assignment of hand combinations (stimulus displays) to the categories "correct" and "incorrect," and we chose the rules in order to sample interesting combinations of correct and incorrect assignments. For instance, exclusive disjunction and equivalence both have two correct and two incorrect instances, but the instances that are correct are reversed in the two problems.

The acquisition of the concepts embodied in these five rules was studied with two groups of nonliterate Kpelle. The first group was composed of eight- to twelve-year-old nonliterate children; the second group of eighteen- to fifty-year-old nonliterate adults. A hundred subjects in all were sampled from each of these two populations. These one hundred subjects were in turn subdivided into groups of twenty, which learned each of the five concepts. The procedure was the version of the "hands procedure" in which the subject initiated the questioning. In all respects the procedure in this experiment was the same as that in the "hands procedure," except that the nature of the rule differed for different subjects as indicated in Table I–1. Subjects continued testing until they had completed forty-eight trials or until they had reached a criterion of nine successive correct responses.

The results of this larger experiment were consistent with those of the previous experiment in that learning was relatively rapid. Unfortunately for our interest in the relation between different logical rules and rate of concept attainment, there were no significant differences among any of our problems in this experiment. The groups that learned the fastest learned in approximately five trials; the groups that learned the slowest learned in approximately seven trials, and none of the group differences could be considered statistically reliable.

Two different interpretations of these results suggest themselves. First of all, it is possible that among the Kpelle concept learning of the type embodied here simply is not mediated by linguistically coded rules, such as conjunction and disjunction, which have been shown to affect the learning of a wide variety of American subjects. The other possibility is that we have so simplified the experiment in searching for an attributeless situation that learning no longer need depend upon any complicated linguistic mediation. It will be clear from Table I–1 that perhaps the easiest way to learn in this situation is simply to remember which response is correct for each of the four stimulus patterns taken as a unit. Viewed this way, there are four types of stimuli, and remembering four things is well within the immediate memory span of all the subjects. Consequently, we get the rapid learning, and we get the lack of differences among rules. Given the sweeping nature of the first possibility, it seemed necessary for us to thoroughly investigate the second possibility before we began to make any serious speculations about cross-cultural differences in the degree to which linguistic rules mediate concept formation.

Complicating the Problem

Our next experiment was a systematic attempt to complicate matters to the point where the solution of the problem would no longer be simple enough to allow direct and easy memorization. We also wanted to tie this work in with our earlier studies, so we began to use cardboard squares instead of hands as stimuli.

We attempted to manipulate problem difficulty by introducing three different levels of complexity into the experiment. Level 1 involved presenting one or two red cardboard squares on the table (the four exemplars were present-present, present-absent, absent-present, and absent-absent). Level 2 involved red and white squares, and, instead of the solution resting on the presence or absence of the square itself, it rested on the presence or absence of a particular color on the squares that were presented (red-red, red-white, white-red, white-white). Level 3 involved red and white squares and triangles; that is, the presence or absence of a particular value on each of two dimensions, color and shape. In Level 3 for the first time we introduced the presence of an irrelevant dimension, and we also shifted away from the question of presence and absence of a single attribute or object. Complicating the previous experiment by the introduction of the three different modes of presentation (presence or absence of an object, presence or absence of a particular attribute of two objects, presence or absence of particular attributes with an irrelevant dimension) meant that a very large number of subjects would have to be run if we were also to sample the basic kinds of rules contained in Table I–1. In this experiment, for each of the three levels of difficulty, we ran one hundred children so that there were three hundred children run in all. At each difficulty level there were five concepts (those contained in Table I–1). For each concept we collected data from ten schoolchildren and ten nonliterate children. All of the children in this experiment were in the age range nine to twelve years.

In spite of our rather elaborate preparations and justifications, and in spite of the rather large number of subjects participating in this experiment, the results from a theoretical point of view were extremely disappointing. For one thing, learning was very slow in *all* of the groups investigated. The average number of trials to the nine out of nine criterion was approximately twenty-two or twenty-three for all three hundred subjects taken together. Very much contrary to our expectation, there was no substantial difference between our three levels of difficulty. In fact, the problem that had the highest mean trial to the last error (twenty-five) was the condition that involved the presence or absence of a red square in each of the two positions. With respect to the various rules involved, again there were really no large differences but, if any rule gave evidence of being easier than the others, it was equivalence. There were no substantial differences between school children and nonliterate children. Thus, in terms of our initial effort, this experiment must be considered a failure, and in many ways a puzzling failure. First of all, there is the question of why learning, in general, was so slow. One possibility is that the experimenter was, in some way, misunderstanding the instructions himself, and, therefore, not explaining them properly to the subject. This hypothesis seems unlikely in view of the fact that the experimenter, when asked to do so, could give the proper explanation from memory and his procedures checked out exactly with those that we had used in our previous pilot work. Another possibility is that our earlier results were strictly the result of using hands rather than the presence or absence of a particular thing. Pilot data from our initial contrast of different ways to initiate the experiment indicated that subjects learned more slowly using objects than they did using the hands; that is probably a reasonable explanation for the slow learning in the presence-absence situation. However, it still does not explain why learning in the four-stimulus presence-absence problem was not easier than learning in the red-white/triangle-square condition where there were sixteen stimulus combinations in all. The sheer numbers of the situation would indicate that the red-white/triangle-square problem should be harder. And yet numerically (if not statistically) it was easier. A closely related question is why, when the problem is difficult, we failed to observe differences among the rules as we had originally hypothesized. Subjects were apparently not simply memorizing the instances, and thus it might be expected that their behavior would reflect the linguistic rules.

A more detailed examination of the individual learning patterns indi-

cated that far from trying to memorize individual patterns, many subjects seemed to be playing guessing games with the experimenter in
which the particular stimuli involved were not particularly important. A
few of the subjects went so far as to guess that the experimenter was
thinking of the pencil or guess that the experimenter was not thinking of
the pencil on all forty-eight of their trials. A more concrete measure
of the random nature of the response process is provided by an analysis
of the response patterns on trials prior to solution. Two aspects of these
presolution data stand out. First, responding was at chance level (50
percent correct) in all of the groups prior to solution. That is, we have a
random response process. Second, we found no differences among stimulus displays in the number of errors that were committed; whereas, we
might expect, if the subject was attending to the stimuli, that he would
notice differential frequencies of occurrence and base his responses accordingly. For instance, looking at the conjunctive rule in Table I–1, it
is clear that the stimulus display of red-red is the only one the subject
needs to learn in order to solve the problem. One would think that he
would tend to learn this most quickly and then eliminate errors on the
remaining problems, but this was not the case. The average number of
errors committed to red-red was equal to that committed to each of the
other stimulus pairs. The evidence that the subject was playing games
with the experimenter rather than attending to the stimuli was rein-
forced by the fact that, in this experiment, fully one-third of the subjects
failed to solve the problem at all; even though, as we indicated, there
were only four stimulus configurations to learn in two of the three conditions.

In this respect the present results contrast quite strongly with discrimination-reversal experiments where all of the evidence indicated
that subjects tended to remember particular stimuli and to learn extremely rapidly. The most reasonable source for this difference lies in
one important difference in the procedures of the two kinds of experiments. In the discrimination-reversal experiment the solution was, in
some sense, *in the stimuli;* that is, the subject either picked up or
pointed at the particular stimulus and was told whether he was right or
wrong. In the present experiments, regardless of who initiated the questioning and what particular stimuli were used, the solution was not in
the stimuli, but rather in the pencil that lay between the subject and the
experimenter. That is, the subject is asked to make use of information
from the stimulus display to make a decision about something that the
experimenter was thinking of which was external to those stimuli. In

such cases subjects had such a strong tendency to play guessing games that the actual stimuli used in the experiment had little control over how he responded. Although we could reduce this tendency to some extent by having the subject initiate the questions, it appears that even this manipulation was not as powerful as we would have desired because, when we went to a new experimenter and slightly different materials, the guessing behavior occurred once again. Consequently, in order to pursue the initial question that motivated this experiment, that is, the relation between particular linguistic forms and learning, we are going to have to come up with a procedure that is sufficiently complicated to require the use of those forms and yet one in which the way we present the material to the subject does not elicit inappropriate problem-solving procedure, for example, guessing. This is not to say that the guessing procedure would be inappropriate for all situations; rather, it is simply inappropriate from the subject's point of view in this situation because, in general, he will not respond well. It is inappropriate from our point of view because it precludes learning anything about linguistic mediation. Consequently, we sought yet another procedure allowing us to study learning that could, in principle at least, be mediated by some sort of linguistic rule. Since we had gotten into such deep water by going out on our own and inventing new procedures, we decided in this instance to retreat once again to a replication of a standard procedure in the hopes that some kind of orderly data could be obtained. Since we were no longer concerned simply with obtaining "attributeless" learning, the procedure introduced by Haygood and Bourne (1965) was settled on, despite our misgivings about its applicability.

APPENDIX J :
Procedural Details and
Instructions for Initial
Inference Experiment

At the beginning of each session, the doors to the apparatus were closed. The experimenter held the marble and the ball bearing, and the subject was told that he was going to play a game with two balls. The training began as the experimenter opened one of the side panels and said, "Do you see this button?" (He points to the button). "Push it and see what happens." After the subject obtained the ball, the experimenter said, "Now pick it up and look at it. Now give it back to me." The door was closed and the same procedure was repeated twice on the other panel. Then that door was closed and the instructions were repeated for the original panel. Both the doors were then opened and the experimenter held up one of the balls and said, "I want you to push the button that will get you a ball like this." This procedure was repeated until the subject could consistently choose the panel that would get the ball that the experimenter was holding up. The experimenter presented the balls in an order designed to counter balance position preferences. In the second segment of the experiment, which began when training on the side panels had been completed, the side doors were closed and the center door was opened. The experimenter said, "Do you see this window here? Do you see the toy? Soon you will be able to get the toy and play with it. Do you see this hole here? If you put the right ball in the hole, the toy will come out and you can have it." The subject was then handed a marble and a ball bearing, and the experimenter said, "If you can put the right ball in the hole, you can make the toy come out." The experimenter determined from a counterbalanced order whether the marble or the ball bearing was correct in a given session. After an incorrect response the subject was told, "No, that doesn't make the toy come out. Next time, drop in the ball that will make the toy come out." After a correct choice the subject was told, "Yes, that's the ball that makes the toy come out." After each trial the subject was given the marble and ball bearing and told, "Try again and see if you can put the right ball in the hole to make the toy come out." Training on this second segment continued until the subject made four consecutive correct responses.

After training on the center panel was completed, the experimenter opened all the doors and said, "Now I'm not going to give you anything, but all the doors are open. If you do what you are supposed to do, you can make the toy come out and you can have it. Go ahead and get the toy."

The subject was allowed sixty seconds to make a response after which, if he had not yet made any response, the experimenter said, "Which button must you press to help to get the toy? Go ahead." After the subject pressed either or both of the side-panel buttons, he was allowed another sixty seconds to put the ball in the hole. Sixty seconds after responding to the side panel, if he had not yet performed a response to the center panel, the experimenter said, "What must you do now to get the toy"? If the subject did not make the goal response after a total of three minutes, the experiment was terminated. The experimenter recorded the time it took to make the initial response to the first segment and the total time it took to solve the problem.

APPENDIX K :
Details of Final Inference
Experiment

In all, seven different conditions were presented in this experiment, which can be best understood by an examination of each of the conditions in some detail.

Condition 1: The procedure used is that from the first experiment with the Kendler apparatus with two small changes. First, no electricity was used; rather, the experimenter surreptitiously operated the relays so that the experiment was now somewhat less frightening and more mobile since it could be conducted in places where electricity was not available. Second, a piece of candy replaced the toy as the goal object.

Condition 2: This condition was identical to Condition 1 except for the following addition: at the beginning of the session the experimenter would hold up a piece of candy and say, "The idea of this game is to get a piece of candy. You will be learning things that will help you to get the candy."

Condition 3: This was the matchbox to locked-box condition used in the second experiment. It represented a condition with familiar elements and a prelearned connection between the first and second segments.

Condition 4: Condition 4 used the Kendler apparatus as the first segment of the experiment and the locked box as the second stage. A red and a black key were obtained from the side panels instead of a ball bearing and a marble; one or the other key then was made to go in a locked box, which was presented to the subject instead of the center panel.

Condition 5: Condition 5 used the matchbox as a first segment and the Kendler box as a second segment. The ball bearing was placed in one of the matchboxes and the marble in the other. Then, either the marble or the ball bearing had to be put into the center hole in the Kendler apparatus as the goal response.

Condition 6: Condition 6 used the same procedure as Condition 1; the Kendler apparatus was used throughout. The only change was that the subject was not required to make any manual responses. Rather, the instructions were modified to that when the experimenter held up the ball in segment one, for instance, he says, "Which button should I push to get you a ball like this?" In other words, the subject was simply asked to instruct the experimenter what to do.

Condition 7: Condition 7 used the matchboxes and keys, but there was no lock placed on the box, rather the box had a slot in it and the experimenter worked a device that opened the box whenever the subject put a key into a slot in that box.

Condition 1 was simply the standard procedure used by the Kendlers and by us in the first inference experiment. Both the initial and final segments were unfamiliar to the subject and he had to learn both. Condition 2 was the same as Condition 1 except that the experimenter emphasized the overall nature of the problem at the beginning of the experiment. This condition was included because it was felt that such emphasis might help the subject to organize his learning. Condition 3 was the matchbox and the locked-box condition that we used in our second experiment. In this case both the initial and final segments involved familiar objects, and the link between the goal objects of the first segment and the goal of the second was familiar and well-learned by the subject before he entered the experiment. Condition 4 gave us an opportunity to study a situation in which the apparatus used for the initial segment was unfamiliar (the Kendler box), but once the subgoal was obtained from the Kendler box, a familiar object (the locked box) was used in the final link, and the subject had the opportunity to use the prelearned key-lock connection. Condition 5 reversed the situation presented in Condition 4. The initial link involved a familiar object, the matchboxes, but the final link involved an unfamiliar object (the Kendler box) and the subgoal response had to be learned in the situation. Condition 6 was aimed at two questions. First of all, it was felt that subjects who simply had to tell the experimenter what to do rather than do it themselves would be less subject to problems of apparatus fear and, second, it was thought that perhaps the Kpelle subjects, who some say are good at imitation, would do exceptionally well on this particular version of the experiment. Condition 7 involved a familiar element in both initial and final links, but in this case the connection between the initial and final links could not have been learned before the experiment, since subjects presumably had little practice in putting keys in slots.

Results

Let us first consider the comparison between our Kpelle and American groups for each of the response indices in Table K–1. Looking first at the tendency to make correct first choices on the initial link, we find that on the average the Kpelle subject (81 percent) responded more accurately than the American subjects (56 percent). The figure for the American subjects is consistent with the data presented by Kendler, Kendler, and Carrick (1966). The Kpelle, on the other hand, respond far better than chance and better than the third graders run by Kendler et al.

We were able to calculate these results because our Kpelle subjects no longer tended to push both buttons at the same time (and showed less fear of the apparatus). It is also apparent that when there was a familiar initial link (Conditions 3, 5, and 7) choice probability is higher (93 percent) than when the first link was unfamiliar (Conditions 1, 2, and 4) (52 percent). Exactly the same relationship was found for the American subjects, who also showed higher probability for responding to Conditions 3, 5, and 7 (75 percent) than they do to Conditions 1, 2, and 4 (42 percent).

These same general trends reoccurred when we investigated total integrated behavior and time to solution. The Kpelle subjects responded somewhat better than the American subjects, and those conditions that had familiar initial links show better integrated behavior than those that had unfamiliar initial links. Only in the case of indirect-correct solutions did the Americans show generally larger scores than the Kpelle. This was presumably because they were making more incorrect initial choices and, consequently, could not make as many direct-correct solutions even though they were showing the same amount of integrated behavior.

Comparison of the performance on the fourth and fifth groups is particularly interesting because it gives a direct contrast of familiar and unfamiliar starting and final segments. It is clear that across the board performance was better on Condition 5, which began with a matchbox and the solution to which was to put a marble or ball bearing into the center hole in the Kendler box. This is directly contrary to the hypothesis that the easy solution in Experiment 2 occurred because subjects had

TABLE K-1

Performance on Final Inference Experiment

CONDITION	SOLVED SPONTANEOUSLY		CORRECT FIRST		DIRECT CORRECT		INDIRECT CORRECT		INTEGRATIVE BEHAVIOR		TIME TO SOLVE (SEC.)	
	Kpelle	American	Kpelle	American	Kpelle	American	Kpelle	American	Kpelle	American	Kpelle	American
1 (Kendler)	60%	40%	75%	35%	70%	30%	10%	20%	80	50	85	103
2 (Kendler goal)	35	60	75	45	75	40	10	45	85	85	82	56
3 (Matchbox to locked box)	90	95	90	70	90	70	05	25	95	95	37	19
4 (Kendler to locked box)	25	65	60	45	10	35	60	40	70	75	103	58
5 (Matchbox to Kendler)	70	95	95	70	80	70	0	25	80	95	71	22
6 (Observation)	25	25	80	40	80	30	10	20	90	50	80	113
7 (Matchbox to slot)	100	85	95	85	95	80	05	15	100	95	39	25
Average	58	66	81	56	71	51	14	27	86	77	71	57

prelearned the connection between the key and the lock. Rather, it appears to be the case that something having to do with the *initiation* of behavior was critical to the completion of the inference. The importance of the initial link is minimized in the theorizing of Kendler and Kendler (1967) whom we would expect would predict that performance would be better in Condition 4 than Condition 5.

A few other details of Table K–1 are worth pointing out. First of all, it appears that giving the American subjects an extra reminder of the final goal of the problem aided them, in that Condition 2 produced better performance for the American subjects. One of the characteristics of the Kpelle performance, which dominated our earlier observations, but which is not represented in Table K–1, is the extreme reticence of the Kpelle children to initiate responding. The measure of total time to solution indicated that the Kpelle subjects were generally slower to complete the problem than the American, but this gross measure failed to indicate wherein the difficulty lay.

Since our view of inferential behavior would indicate the subjects ought to do the entire problem spontaneously, we also calculated the results in column one of Table K–1, which shows for each group the proportion of subjects, American and Kpelle, who reached a spontaneous solution of the problem. This measure reflects the percentage of subjects who did not have to be prompted, although it might have been the case that they made an incorrect response at some point during the sequence. (If they made an incorrect response, however, they corrected themselves immediately and went on to the solution.)

From Table K–1 we can see a dramatic difference between those situations that began with the Kendler apparatus and those that began with the matchbox. In the former case the Kpelle average only 40 percent spontaneous solutions, whereas in the latter this average increased to 87 percent. Exactly the same trend can be found for the American subjects. For those situations that began with the Kendler box, spontaneous solution occurred on an average of 55 percent of the trials, whereas, for those situations beginning with the match box, the average was 92 percent. Once again, we are struck by the fact that the initial link in the problem-solving process seems to be of extraordinary importance.

Bibliography

Agency for International Development. The Department of Education, Elementary and Secondary Education, and Higher Education, Liberia: A Survey. Oregon State Department of Education, May 1967.

Atkinson, R. C., Bower, G. and Crothers, E. *Introduction to Mathematical Learning Theory.* New York: Wiley, 1964.

Atkinson, R. C. and Shiffrin, R. M. "Human Memory: A Proposed System and Its Control Processes." In J. T. Spence and G. Bower, eds. *The Psychology of Learning and Motivation.* Vol. 2, New York: Academic Press, 1968.

Baratz, S. S. and Baratz, J. "Early Childhood Interventions: The Social Science Base of Institutional Racism." *Harvard Educational Review* 40 (1970): 29–50.

Bartlett, F. C. *Remembering.* London: Cambridge University Press, 1932.

Bateson, G. *Naven.* 2nd ed. Stanford: Stanford University Press, 1958.

Bellman, B. L. "Some Constitutive Factors of Secrecy among the Fala Kpelle of Sucrumo, Liberia." Paper delivered at the meeting of the Liberian Research Association, Stanford, California, 1969.

Bellman, B. L. Field notes. January 10, 1968.

Bentley, W. H. *Pioneering on the Congo.* Quoted in R. Allier, *The Mind of the Savage.* New York: Harcourt Brace, 1929.

Bohannon, P. An Anthropologist's Description of a Culture Is Like a Myth in That It Is a Narrative That Organizes Data for Some Purpose. Quoted in J. Gibbs, ed. *Peoples of Africa.* New York: Holt, Rinehart & Winston, 1965.

Bousfield, W. A. "The Occurrence of Clustering in the Free Recall of Randomly Arranged Associates." *Journal of General Psychology* 49 (1953): 229–240.

Bowen, E. *Return To Laughter.* New York: Doubleday, 1954.

Bower, G. "A Multicomponent Theory of the Memory Trace." In K. W. Spence and J. T. Spence, eds. *The Psychology of Learning and Motivation.* Vol. 1, New York: Academic Press, 1967.

Bridgman, P. W. "Quo Vadis." *Daedalus* 87 (1958): 85–93.

Brown, R. "Discussion of Conference." In A. K. Romney and R. G. D'Andrade, eds. *Transcultural Studies in Cognition.* Washington, D.C.: American Anthropologist Association, June 1964, pp. 243–253.

Brown, R. W. and Lenneberg, E. H. "A Study in Language and Cognition." *Journal of Abnormal and Social Psychology* 49 (1964): 452–462.

Bruner, J. S. "Going Beyond the Information Given." In *Contemporary Approaches to Cognition: A Symposium Held at the University of Colorado.* Cambridge: Harvard University Press, 1957.

Bruner, J. S., Goodnow, J., and Austin, G. A. *A Study of Thinking.* New York: Wiley, 1956.

Bruner, J. S., Olver, R., and Greenfield, P. *Studies in Cognitive Growth.* New York: Wiley, 1966.

Burling, R. "Cognition and Componential Analysis: God's Truth or Hocus-Pocus?" *American Anthropologist* 66 (1964): 20–28.

Campbell, D. T. "The Mutual Methodological Relevance of Anthropology and Psychology." In F. L. K. Hsu, ed. *Psychological Anthropology.* Homewood, Ill.: Dorsey Press, 1961, pp. 333–352.

Bibliography

Carroll, J. B. and Cassagrande, J. B. "The Function of Language Classification in Behavior." In E. E. Maccoby, T. M. Newcomb, and E. L. Hartby, eds. *Readings in Social Psychology.* 3rd ed. N.Y.: Holt, Rinehart & Winston, 1958, pp. 18–31.

Cazden, C. "The Neglected Situation in Child Research and Education." In F. Williams, ed. *Language and Poverty.* Chicago: Markham Press, 1970, pp. 81–101.

Chamberlain, A. F. *The Child: A Study in the Evolution of Man.* London: Walter Scott, 1901.

Chomsky, N. *Cartesian Linguistics.* New York: Harper & Row, 1966.

Ciborowski, T. "Cultural Influences on the Development of Conceptual Rule Learning." Ph.D. diss., University of California, Irvine, 1971.

Clower, R. W., Dalton, G., Harwitz, M., and Walters, A. A. et al. *Growth without Development: An Economic Survey of Liberia.* Evanston: Northwestern University Press, 1966.

Cofer, C. "Does Conceptual Clustering Influence the Amount Retained in Immediate Free Recall?" In B. Klienmuntz, ed. *Concepts and the Structure of Memory.* New York: Wiley, 1967.

Cohen, B. H. "Recall of Categorized Word Lists." *Journal of Experimental Psychology* 66 (1963): 227–234.

Colby, B. N. and Cole, M. "A Cross-Cultural Analysis of Memory and Narrative." In R. Horton and R. Flannegan, eds. *Modes of Thought.* London: Faber, 1972.

Cole, M. "Culture and Cognition." In B. Maher, ed. *Introductory Psychology.* New York: Wiley, 1972.

Cole, M. and Bruner, J. S. "Some Preliminaries to Some Theories of Cultural Difference." Yearbook of the National Society of the Study of Education. University of Chicago, 1972.

Cole, M., Frankel, F., and Sharp, D. W. "The Development of Free Recall Learning in Children." *Developmental Psychology* 4 (1971): 109–123.

Cole, M., Gay, J., and Glick, J. "Some Studies in Kpelle Quantitative Behavior." *Psychonomic Monographs* 2 (1968): 173–190.

Cole, M., Gay, J., Glick, J., and Sharp, D. W. "Linguistic Structure and Transposition." *Science* 164 (1969): 90–91.

Cole, M., Glick, J., Kessen, W., and Sharp, W. W. "Conceptual and Mnemonic Factors in Children's Paired Associates Learning." *Journal of Experimental Child Psychology.* 6 (1968): 120–130.

Cryns, A. G. J. "African Intelligence: A Critical Survey of Cross-Cultural Intelligence Research in Africa South of the Sahara." *Journal of Social Psychology* 57 (1962): 283–301.

Dalby, D. "Indigenous Scripts of West Africa and Sierra Leone." *African Language Studies* 8 (1967): 1–51.

Dawson, J. L. M. "Cultural and Physiological Influences upon Spatial-Perceptual Processes in West Africa—Part I." *International Journal of Psychology* 2 (1967): 115–128.

Deese, J. "Serial Organization in the Recall of Disconnected Items." *Psychological Reports* 3 (1957) 577–582.

Deese, J. "On the Structure of Associative Meaning." *Psychological Review* 69 (1962): 161–175.

Deutsch, M. "Happenings on the Way Back to the Forum." *Harvard Educational Review* 39 (1969): 523–557.

Doob, L. *Becoming More Civilized.* New Haven: Yale University Press, 1960.

Doob, L. *Communication in Africa: A Search for Boundaries.* New Haven: Yale University Press, 1961.

Doob, L. "Exploring Eidetic Imagery among the Kamba of Central Kenya." *The Journal of Social Psychology* 67 (1965): 3–22.

Estes, W. K. "Reinforcement in Human Learning." In J. T. Tapp, ed., *Reinforcement and Behavior.* New York: Academic Press, 1969.

Fishman, J. A. "A Systemization of the Whorfian Hypothesis." *Behavioral Science* 5 (1960): 323–339.

Flavell, J. H. "Developmental Studies of Mediated Memory." In H. W. Reese and L. P. Lipsitt, eds. *Advances in Child Development and Behavior.* Vol. 5, New York: Academic Press, 1970.

Fortes, M. "Social and Psychological Aspects of Education in Taleland." *Africa* 11 (1938). Special Supplement.

Frake, C. O. "The Ethnographic Study of Cognitive Systems." In R. A. Manners and D. Kaplan, eds. *Theory in Anthropology.* Chicago: Aldine Publishing Co., 1968.

Frankel, F. and Cole, M. "Measures of Category Clustering in Free Recall." *Psychological Bulletin* 76 (1971): 39–44.

Gay, J. and Cole, M. *The New Mathematics and an Old Culture.* New York: Holt, Rinehart & Winston, 1967.

Gay, J. and Welmers, W. *Mathematics in the Kpelle Language.* Ibadan: University of Ibadan Press, 1970.

Gibbs, J. "The Kpelle of Liberia." In J. Gibbs, ed. *Peoples of Africa.* New York: Holt, Rinehart & Winston, 1965.

Gladwin, H. "Decision Making in the Cape Coast (Fante) Fishing and Fish Marketing Industry." Ph.D. diss., Stanford University, 1970.

Gladwin, T. *East Is a Big Bird.* Cambridge: Belknap Press, 1970.

Glick, J. "Cognitive Style among the Kpelle?" Paper read at annual meeting of the American Educational Research Association, Chicago, 1968.

Gluckman, M. "Social Beliefs and Individual Thinking in Tribal Society." *Memoirs of the Manchester Literary Society* 91 (1949–1950): 73–98.

Goodenough, W. "Componential Analysis and the Study of Meaning." *Language* 32 (1956): 195–216.

Goodnow, J. J. "Problems in Research on Culture and Thought." In D. Elkind and J. H. Flavell, eds. *Studies in Cognitive Development,* New York: Oxford University Press, 1969.

Goody, J. and Watt, I. "The Consequences of Literacy." *Comparative Studies in Sociology and History* 5 (1962): 304–345.

Greenfield, P. M. and Bruner, J. S. "Culture and Cognitive Growth." *International Journal of Psychology* 1 (1966): 89–107.

Hammer, M. "Some Comments on Formal Analysis of Grammatical and Semantic Systems." *American Anthropologist* 68 (1966): 362–373.

Harley, G. W. *Native African Medicine with Special Reference to Its Practice in the Mano Tribe of Liberia.* Cambridge: Harvard University Press, 1941.

Harris, M. *The Rise of Anthropological Theory.* New York: Crowell, 1968.

Havelock, E. A. *Preface to Plato.* Cambridge: Belknap Press, Harvard University Press, 1963.

Haygood, R. C. and Bourne, L. E., Jr. "Attribute and Rule Learning Aspects of Conceptual Behavior." *Psychological Review* 72 (1965): 175–195.

Hellmuth, J., ed. *The Disadvantaged Child.* Seattle: Special Child Publication of the Seattle Seguin School, Inc., 1967.

Herskovitz, M. J. *Cultural Anthropology.* New York: Knopf, 1962.

Hess, R. D. and Shipman, V. C. "Early Experience and the Socialization of Cognitive Modes in Children." *Child Development* 36 (1965): 369–386.

Hodgen, M. *Culture and History.* Viking Fund Publications in Anthropology, 1952, No. 18, p. 73.

Hoijer, H. "The Sapir-Whorf Hypothesis." In H. Hoijer, ed. *Language in Culture.* Chicago: University of Chicago Press, 1954.

Horton, R. "African Traditional Thought and Western Science: Part I: From Tradition to Science." *Africa* 37 (1967): 50–71, a.

Horton, R. "African Traditional Thought and Western Science: Part II: The Closed and Open Predicaments," *Africa* 37 (1967): 155–187, b.

Hsu, F. L. K., ed. *Psychological Anthropology.* Homewood, Ill.: The Dorsey Press, 1961.

Humphrey, G. *Thinking.* London: Methuen & Co., 1951.

Irwin, M. H. and McLaughlin, D. H. "Ability and Preference in Category Sorting by Mano Schoolchildren and Adults." *Journal of Social Psychology* 82 (1970): 15–24.

Jahoda, G. "Aspects of Westernization." *British Journal of Sociology* 12 (1961): 375–386.

Jensen, A. "How Much Can We Boost I.Q. and Scholastic Achievement?" *Harvard Educational Review* 39 (1969): 1–123.

Jesperson, O. *Language, Its Nature, Development, and Growth.* London: Allen and Unwin, 1921.

Johnson, S. C. "Hierarchical Clustering Schemes." *Psychometrika* 32 (1967): 241–254.

Kelleher, R. T. "Discrimination Learning as a Function of Reversal and Nonreversal Shifts." *Journal of Experimental Psychology* 51 (1955): 379–384.

Kendler, H. H. "The Concept of the Concept." In A. W. Melton, ed. *Categories of Human Learning.* New York: Academic Press, 1964.

Kendler, H. H. and Kendler, T. S. "Mediation and Conceptual Behavior." In J. T. Spence and G. Bower, eds. *The Psychology of Learning and Motivation* 2 (1968): New York: Academic Press.

Kendler, H. H. and Kendler, T. S. "Vertical and Horizontal Processes in Problem Solving." *Psychological Review* 69 (1962): 1–16.

Kendler, H. H. and Mayzner, M. S., Jr. "Reversal and Non-Reversal Shifts in Card-Sorting Tests with Two and Four Sorting Categories." *Journal of Experimental Psychology* 51 (1956): 244–248.

Kendler, T. S. and Kendler, H. H. "Experimental Analysis of Inferential Behavior in Children." In L. P. Lipsitt and C. C. Spiker, eds. *Advances in Child Development and Behavior,* Vol. 3. New York: Academic Press, 1967.

Kendler, T. S. and Kendler, H. H. "Reversal and Non-Reversal Shifts in Kindergarten Children." *Journal of Experimental Psychology* 58 (1959): 56–60.

Kendler, T. S., Kendler, H. H., and Carrick, M. "The Effect of Verbal Labels on Inferential Problem Solution." *Child Development* 37 (1966): 749–763.

Kendler, T. S., Kendler, H. H., and Wells, D. "Reversal and Non-Reversal Shifts in Nursery School Children." *Journal of Comparative and Physiological Psychology* 53 (1960): 83–87.

King, W. L. "Learning and Utilization of Conjunctive and Disjunctive Classification Rules: A Developmental Study." *Journal of Experimental Child Psychology* 4 (1966): 217–231.

Klineberg, O. "Negro-White Difference in Intelligence Test Performance: A New Look at an Old Problem." *American Psychologist* 18 (1963): 198–203.

Kluckhohn, C. *Mirror for Man.* New York: McGraw-Hill, 1949.

Labov, W. "The Logic of Non-Standard English." In *Language and Poetry,* F. Williams, ed. Chicago: Markham, 1970.

Labov, W. "Some Sources of Reading Problems for Negro Speakers of Non-Standard English." In J. C. Baratz and R. W. Shuy, eds. *Teaching Black Children to Read.* Washington, D.C.: Center for Applied Linguistics, 1969.

Liebenow, G. *Liberia: The Evolution of Privilege.* Ithaca, N.Y.: Cornell University Press, 1969.

LeVine, R. "Cross-Cultural Study in Child Psychology." In P. Mussen, ed. *Carmichael's Manual of Child Psychology,* New York: Wiley, 1970.

Lévi-Strauss, C. *The Savage Mind.* Chicago: University of Chicago Press, 1966.

Levy-Bruhl, C. *How Natives Think* (1910). New York: Washington Square Press, 1966.

Little, K. *West African Urbanization.* Cambridge: Cambridge University Press, 1965.

Luria, A. R. *The Role of Speech in the Development of Normal and Abnormal Behavior.* London: Pergamon, 1960.

McLuhan, M. *The Gutenberg Galaxy.* Toronto: University of Toronto Press, 1962.

Malinowski, B. *Argonauts of the South Pacific.* New York: Dutton, 1922.

Mandler, G. "Association and Organization: Facts, Fancies, and Theories." In T. R. Dixon and D. L. Horton, eds. *Verbal Behavior Theory.* Englewood Cliffs, N.J.: Prentice-Hall, 1968.

Mandler, G. "Organization and Memory." In K. W. Spence and J. T. Spence, eds. *The Psychology of Learning and Motivation.* Vol. 1. New York: Academic Press, 1966.

Mead, M. "An Investigation of the Thought of Primitive Children with Special Reference to Animism." *Journal of the Royal Anthropological Institute* 62 (1932): 173–190.

Metzger, D. and Williams, G. E. "Procedures and Results in the Study of Native Categories: Tzeltal Firewood." *American Anthropologist* 68 (1966): 389–407.

Miller. G. A. "The Magical Number Seven Plus or Minus Two: Some Limits on Our Capacity to Process Information." *Psychological Review* 63 (1956): 81–97.

Miller, G. A. "A Psychological Method to Investigate Verbal Concepts." *Journal of Mathematical Psychology* 6 (1969): 169–191.

Miller, G. A. and McNeil, D. "Psycholinguistics." In G. Lindzey and E. Aronson, eds. *The Handbook of Social Psychology,* Vol. 3. Reading, Mass.: Addison-Wesley, 1968.

Miller, N. *The Child in Primitive Society.* London: Kegan Paul, Trench, Trubner, 1928.

Moely, B. E., Olson, F. A., Halwes, T. G., and Flavell, J. H. "Production Deficiency in Young Children's Clustered Recall." *Developmental Psychology* 1 (1969): 26–34.

Morgan, C. L. *Mental Life and Intelligence.* Boston: Ginn & Co., 1891.

Murdock, B. B., Jr. "The Serial Position Effect of Free Recall." *Journal of Experimental Psychology* 64 (1962): 482–488.

Nadel, S. F. "Experiments in Culture Psychology." *Africa* 10 (1937): 421–435.

Neisser, U. *Cognitive Psychology.* New York: McGraw-Hill, 1968.

Nissen, H. W., Kinder, S., and Machover, F. E. "A Study of Performance Tests Given to a Group of Native African Negro Children." *British Journal of Psychology* 25 (1935): 308–355.

Orr, K. G. "Field Notes on Tribal Medical Practices in Central Liberia." *Liberian Studies Journal* 1 (1968): 20–41.

Osgood, C. E. and Sebeok, T. A. "Psycholinguistics: A Survey of Theory and Research Problems." *Indiana University Publications in Anthropology and Linguistics,* No. 10 (1954).

Paivio, A. "A Factor-Analytic Study of Word Attributes and Verbal Learning." *Journal of Verbal Learning and Verbal Behavior* 7 (1968): 41–49.

Piaget, J. *The Language and Thought of the Child.* N.Y.: Meridian Books, 1955.

Pollio, H. *The Structural Basis of Word Association Behavior.* The Hague: Mouton, 1966.

Price-Williams, D., Gordon, W., and Ramirez, M. "Skill and Conservation: A Study of Pottery-Making Children." *Developmental Psychology* 1 (1969): 769.

Raum, O. F. *Chaga Childhood: A Description of Indigenous Education in an East African Tribe.* London: Oxford University Press, 1940.

Riesman, D. *The Oral Tradition, the Written Word, and the Screen Image.* Yellow Springs: Antioch Press, 1956.

Rivers, W. H. R. *Psychology and Ethnology.* New York: Harcourt, Brace & Co., 1926.

Romney, A. K. and D'Andrade, R. G. "Cognitive Aspects of English Kin Terms." In A. K. Romney and R. G. D'Andrade. *Transcultural Studies in Cognition; American Anthropologist* 66 (3), Part 2, June 1964.

Sanders, B. "Pseudo-Reversal and Pseudo-Non-Reversal Shifts in Rats and Children." Doctoral diss., Yale University, 1968. *Journal of Comparative and Physiological Psychology* 74 (1971): 192–202.

Serpell, R. "Cultural Differences in Attention Preference for Color over Form." *International Journal of Psychology* 4 (1969): 1–8.

Sharp, D. W. "Discrimination Learning and Discrimination Transfer as Related to Dimension Dominance and Dimensional Variation among Kpelle Children." Doctoral diss., University of California, Irvine, 1971.

Sharp, D. W., Gay, J., Glick, J., and Cole, M. "The Reflection of Semantic Categories in Kpelle Verbal Behavior." Unpublished manuscript, 1970.

Sibley, J. L. and Westermann, D. H. *Liberia Old and New.* New York: Doubleday, 1928.

Snow, C. E. and Rabinovitch, M. S. "Conjunctive and Disjunctive Thinking in Children." *Journal of Experimental Child Psychology* 7 (1969): 1–9.

Spencer, H. "A Theory of Population, Deduced from the General Laws of Animal Fertility." *Westminster Review* 57 (1852): 468–501.

Spindler, G. D. *Education and Anthropology.* Stanford: Stanford University Press, 1955.

Steffire, V. *Some Aspects of Language and Behavior.* Paper presented at conference sponsored by the Social Science Research Council Committee on Intellective Processes Research, Merida, Yucatan, 1963.

Suppes, P. and Ginsberg, R. "A Fundamental Property of All-or-None Models: Binomial Distribution of Responses Prior to Conditioning with Application to Concept Formation in Children." *Psychological Review* 70 (1963): 139–161.

Thorndike, E. L. and Lorge, I. *The Teacher's Word Book of 30,000 Words.* New York: Bureau of Publications, Teachers College, Columbia University, 1944.

Tighe, T. J. and Tighe, L. S. "Discrimination Shift Performance of Children as a Function of Age and Shift Procedure." *Journal of Experimental Psychology* 74 (1967): 466–470.

Tulving, E. "Theoretical Issues in Free Recall." In T. R. Dixon and D. L. Horton, eds. *Verbal Behavior and General Behavior Theory.* Englewood Cliffs, N.J.: Prentice-Hall, 1968.

Tulving, E. and Osler, S. "Effectiveness of Retrieval Cues in Memory for Words." *Journal of Experimental Psychology* 77 (1968): 593–601.

Tulving, E. and Pearlstone, Z. "Availability versus Accessibility of Information in Memory for Words." *Journal of Verbal Learning and Verbal Behavior* 5 (1966): 381–391.

Tyler, S., ed. *Cognitive Anthropology*. New York: Holt, Rinehart & Winston, 1969.

Tylor, E. B. *Primitive Culture*. London: J. Murray, 1874. Reprinted New York: Harper Torchbooks, 1958.

Tylor, E. B. *Researches into the Early History of Mankind and the Development of Civilization*. London: J. Murray, 1865.

U.S. Army Area Handbook for Liberia. Superintendent of Documents, U.S. Government Printing Office, Washington, D.C., July, 1964.

Vernon, P. E. *Intelligence and Cultural Environment*. London: Methuen & Co., 1969.

Vygotskii, L. S. *Thought and Language*. Cambridge: MIT Press, 1962.

Wallace, A. F. C. "Culture and Cognition." *Science,* 135 (1962): 351–357.

Wallace, A. F. C. and Atkins, J. "The Meaning of Kinship Terms." *American Anthropologist* 62 (1960): 58–80.

Waugh, N. C. and Norman, D. A. "Primary Memory." *Psychological Review* 72 (1965): 80–104.

Welmers, W. E. *Spoken Kpelle*. Sanoyan: Liberia, 1948.

Werner, H. *Comparative Psychology of Mental Development*. New York: International Universities Press, 1948.

Werner, H. and Kaplan, B. "The Developmental Approach to Cognition." *American Anthropologist* 58 (1956): 866–881.

Whiting, B. B., ed. *Six Cultures: Studies on Child Rearing*. New York: Wiley, 1963.

Whiting, J. W. M. and Whiting, B. B. "Report of the Child Development Research Unit." Nairobi: University College, 1970.

Whorf, B. L. *Language, Thought and Reality*. Boston: MIT Press, New York: Wiley, 1956.

Witkin, H. A. "A Cognitive-Style Approach to Cross-Cultural Research." *International Journal of Psychology* 2 (1967): 233–250.

Woodworth, R. S. and Sells, S. B. "An Atmosphere Effect in Formal Syllogistic Reasoning." *Journal of Experimental Psychology* 18 (1935): 451–460.

Zeaman, D. and House, B. J. "The Role of Attention in Retardate Discrimination Learning." In N. R. Ellis, ed. *Handbook of Mental Deficiency*. New York: McGraw-Hill, 1963.

Index

The cultural context of learning
and thinking